To Gordon
who helped set the stage for a
memorable cruise on the
Maine Coast

Best

[signature]

BOOKS BY

MORRIS L ERNST

TOUCH WOOD *1960*

UTOPIA 1976   *1955*

SO FAR SO GOOD   *1948*

THE FIRST FREEDOM   *1946*

THE BEST IS YET   *1945*

TOO BIG   *1940*

THE ULTIMATE POWER   *1937*

AMERICA'S PRIMER   *1931*

WITH CO-AUTHORS:

FOR BETTER OR WORSE   *1952*

REPORT ON THE AMERICAN COMMUNIST   *1952*

AMERICAN SEXUAL BEHAVIOR AND

THE KINSEY REPORT   *1948*

THE PEOPLE KNOW BEST   *1949*

THE CENSOR MARCHES ON   *1939*

HOLD YOUR TONGUE   *1932*

TO THE PURE   *1928*

TOUCH WOOD

A YEAR'S DIARY

MORRIS L ERNST

TOUCH WOOD

A YEAR'S DIARY

—————◆—————

NEW YORK ATHENEUM PUBLISHERS

1960

TO MARGARET

———◆———

WITH WHOM I CAN AND DO COMMUNICATE
WITHOUT THE NEED OF AN ALPHABET OR WORDS

TOUCH WOOD

A YEAR'S DIARY

The diary of my complete year was, my editor told me, unpublishable—not because of obscenity or blasphemy, but because of sheer length. A man doesn't live his days and nights in brief paragraphs. TOUCH WOOD, uncut, would have made a volume of some six hundred pages, too heavy to read in bed. Now every phrase was precious to me, my own child. I could not be an Abraham poising the sacrificial knife over Isaac. So Dorothy Parker, Atheneum editor, and my wife, hereinafter referred to as Maggie, snipped away with the editorial shears. If any friend or foe is injured by being left out or included, the blame is theirs, not mine. I am threatening to take the deleted precious pages to another publisher to be brought out under my favorite title for most of life: LEFT OVERS.   M. L. E.

AUGUST

<hr/>

Saturday, August 23, 1958

This is the day when, according to the Bible, I am presumed to have licked the most evil myth of our culture. The greatest killer—greater than t.b. in my youth or cancer today—is that abominable shortener of life, the self-imposed idea that the ordained span of life is threescore and ten. No one knows precisely when this idea was first proposed. I must look up the reference to its origin in my Concordance. But no matter who originated the concept or what his motive, it's nothing but evil today. Thousands of years ago the life expectancy of the Jews was certainly no more than twenty or thirty years. *That,* in fact, is the life expectancy of most of the people on our planet today. Before Gandhi, it was twenty in India and although there are few—if any— reliable statistics in that country, we are told that the Gandhi-Nehru team has raised it to twenty-seven years. This increase arose mainly from reduction of infant mortality in a culture where only recently 17,000 female babies were left to die in the fields in one district alone.

But now we in our land have a life expectancy of about seventy years—a few years longer for women than for men, with a decreasing gap as men learn to use their leisure and women experience the tensions of jobs and responsibilities. Not too bad, when in 1787 the average age of delegates at our Constitutional Convention in Philadelphia was forty-one, with six under thirty. It challenges my ingenuity to name six men under thirty today fit to draw up a constitution, even for a golf club. Of course Ben Franklin was over eighty. If you lived past fifty then, you might easily hit eighty.

Nothing, but nothing, has reduced our capacity to survive so much as this concept imbedded in our culture: borrowed time after seventy. This Biblical limit— valid along the Nile now as then—must be abolished in our era. Let's start a new myth of greater validity— sevenscore and ten. One hundred and fifty is soon to be in reach. No longer do we make a fuss about the man who reaches ninety, as we did in my youth. To get a headline, you must hit the century mark.

Man lives, generally speaking, as long as he wants to live. Man dies when he is tired of living. My father at seventy-five kept saying he didn't want to live. But he was talking falsely to himself and to us, for he lived another decade. Ruth Hale,* a good friend, died because she no longer wanted to live; an autopsy could find no other cause for her death.

One sign of aging with me is that as I get older I want fewer possessions and clearly subscribe to the Holmesian gospel of the tyranny of things. Possessions are increasingly a nuisance, for our society has organized neither the values of the Chinese compound nor an emotional technique for reduction in living quarters, furniture and possessions. The toughest items for me to get rid of when necessity so demands are books. Moving

---

* *Heywood Broun's first wife, ardent feminist.*

from the big house on Eleventh Street in which our children grew up (with no other memory for thirty years except the Nantucket home for an equal period), we shifted to an apartment with the view of a tree—that rarity for Manhattan cliff dwellers. There was no space for our 4000 or more books. To give them away without a scar was impossible, even though, as Brandeis taught me, few books are worth reading more than once. No such attachment can develop between people and the radio or television set. Affection, I suggest, must stem from participation and not just from sitting as an audience.

A month ago my wife Maggie started scheming and contriving. Should there be a big party, or just the family, or some compromise? In the Eleventh Street house I enjoyed parties of fifty or sixty people on any excuse —Election Day, New Year's, Halloween or a natal day. During the past few decades the parties shrank, partly because I lost some of my hearing until Dr. Samuel Rosen performed one of his now routine miracles, and partly because I became less interested in the What, When, How and Where than in the really significant Why.

The party here in Nantucket was fun. Fog, quite exaggerated this summer, did not delay Roger and Jean* in their special week-end trip from Washington. All six children and three of the five grandchildren were around, and the festivities for which I had been tagged commenced at five P.M. for the grandchildren and ran until about midnight when the real kids, Sarah and Sidney Fay,† deep in their eighties, went home.

---

* *My son and his wife.*
† *Former Harvard professor, historian.*

We solved the world's problems sitting at separate tables in small groups; then, as so often happens, we all gravitated to one spot, a transit for which I can seldom dope out the Why.

Sunday, August 24

A letter on my birthday from Harry S. Truman surprised and delighted me. I really suspect he would run for the Senate if the occasion could be developed short of the murder of one of his competitors. He was always an admirer of John Quincy Adams, our vague president who later sat in the House for seventeen years, rendering more service there than during his term in the White House. Maybe Truman admires him because Adams was so violent against the gag rule.

My main delight, or vanity, came from a resolution voted by the Selectmen of Nantucket. I don't recall such an official birthday pronouncement by the City Fathers since old Mr. Woods—whose great-great-grandchildren are driving taxis instead of his surrey—celebrated his eighty-fifth or ninetieth birthday back in the 1920's. There was also a card from the Rotary, which must have been suggested by some kind friend. I'm not a Rotarian, and in Nantucket no lawyers belong; but the signatures of forty or fifty leading citizens of this community were appended.

These two communications pointed to the joys of intimacy impossible in overbig cities like New York. Thank God most of the people in our republic use big cities only to visit on rare occasions. I am always amused by the answer New York residents give when asked, "Why do you live here?" They reply, "Here we have opera and the Philharmonic." Then I ask, "When did you last go to the opera?" And the rationalizer runs off in shame.

The big surprise was a telephone call from Marie* in London. She has been my great needler and invigorator for the past few years and now, damn it, she goes off to England to get married. To hear her voice again choked me more than a little.

The weather was good for reading but, given Roger and Jean's passion for picnics, we cooked in the garden, taking the food to the indoor table to eat.

Tuesday, August 26

Summer is my fiction-reading-escape-catch-up period. Today I had rich pleasure reading Silone's new book, *The Secret of Luca,* an entertaining tale of heartbreaking dedication to love. Although the court conviction may seem to the layman to be a miscarriage of justice, the verdict of the jury was always under the control of Luca, who had a choice during most of his life, but put devotion to his lady love ahead of freedom.

For lunch, that engaging team of free-lance writers, Jhan and June Robbins. Jhan helped me on the Brandeis piece for *The Reader's Digest,* an article that subsequently brought me more unexpected fan mail than anyone could have anticipated except maybe Hobe Lewis,† who commissioned the piece. Several bankers' associations wanted hundreds of copies of the piece just because I clarified L. D. B.'s objection to bigness, which

---

* *Dr. Marie Jahoda, formerly of New York University, social psychologist, now Mrs. Austen Albu.*

† *Editor,* The Reader's Digest.

included branch banking. But the banks will continue to merge and help push our republic into statism. I rather think that the Bank of America and the Chase are a greater peril to our economic and spiritual freedom than all the parties of the left, from socialist to communist. Surely we would be better off as a people if our banking services were more expensive but did not reduce branch managers to robots. Why has not the example of our greatest bank produced a rash of copy cats? I refer to the House of Morgan with no branches and a policy of selecting depositors, which features point toward quality rather than quantity and are unique, considering our national zeal for the Gargantuan.

Wednesday, August 27

Must leave for New York and a breakfast date with the counsel of a Senate committee concerned with the fast march toward Communism in South America. Recently I suggested to a high CIA official that Russia will have a beachhead government in South America within five years. His reply: "Why so optimistic? It will take less than three years."

Our trouble is subtle but clear. Our national heritage is rooted in our revolution from England; we are emotionally conditioned to the "outs," the opposition, the guerillas. And still we have no skill or equipment with which to capitalize on a government upset in any nation on the planet. We don't even know if the opposition, for which we automatically root, is Communist-infiltrated or not; but as adolescents in liberalism we have a basic belief that the "outs" are to be preferred to the "ins." It's high time someone explored and exploded the dangerous content of words like democracy and dictatorship as we use them. I hold that there can be no election of rulers by any people without literacy and communication. Word of mouth is too slow—see India, where Russia took over the State of Kerala (population of fourteen million) without firing a shot. To be sure, literacy and communication do not guarantee democracy—they did not in Russia or Hitler's Germany—but without these tools it's silly to talk of democracy. One of our national problems stems from an inability to advise and help people who live on mud floors, have no concept of literacy and have been told by church and dictators for centuries that there is no hope in this life. What a comforting but evil gospel it is to preach that the only decent life is in Heaven, and to use the fires of Hell as a corrective!

Got a hitch from Woods Hole to Boston in Ed Manville's sweet Mercedes. He was a delightful companion on the wet and miserable two-hour trip. Then by plane to New York—in bed by two A.M. at Two Fifth Avenue. Little sleep is needed for the excited. How close boredom is to the need of sleep—note certain music, hum of a motor: boredom, monotony, sleep.

Thursday, August 28

Busy day at the office, followed by delightful dinner with representatives of Protestant Council, discussing techniques for resolving the New York City Hospital birth-control dilemma. I think we may have an answer, through Syd Baron's* good offices. Namely, protecting the Catholic physician's complete right to refrain

* *Sydney Baron, public-relations expert.*

from giving contraceptive advice, but at the same time giving non-Catholics that medical aid long held by most medicos as vital to one's physical health and mental well-being. All it will take is diplomacy—a nearly lost art. The myth that the press is entitled to *all* facts comes near at times to destroying social advances. What is more absurd than open covenants *openly* arrived at! Even the Founding Fathers passed an early resolution that all debates at the Convention of 1787 in Philadelphia should be secret so that the delegates could more readily change their minds. I have met few people who dared admit publicly a change of opinion on a matter previously openly expressed. (I am truly grateful that my mother taught me that only cowards and the insecure are afraid to admit error.) How can agreements be made in a gold-fish bowl—even if we had a responsible press?

Friday, August 29

Back in Monomoy. Hurricane signals. It's exhilarating. For many it's part of the pleasure of bad news. Someone soon must show up the National Safety Council whose announcements, by the time I hear them, sound like, "We predict 423 deaths this week end—goody, goody!" It's one more example of persuasion by repetition or by glands rather than by thoughtfulness. What is 423 compared to total passenger miles that week end? No one says.

The blow subsided. The island is safe from the attack of the sky. In the evening, good talk at Roger's tenants, the Blums, where the three offspring seem not only to be thoughtful but truly fond of one another.

Saturday, August 30

The weather was fit for reading and I had a rather common experience—little fun until the end of the book. It was *Gallery of Women* by Bernard Glemser. At the end I cried, something I don't normally do unless alone; one of those damnable shames produced in youth when show of emotion was considered soft and sissy. But that girl's approach toward death was so adult, so desirable and so unusual that it got me in my insides. I usually read two books at a time; the other was *The Journals of Arnold Bennett,* with the perfect introduction by Frank Swinnerton. Bennett was a bookkeeper at heart; he lists the number of words he writes each year.

I like diaries—although they represent less than the truth, of course. In fact, they invite falsity. But surely, conceal as we will, when we write or talk we give away more than we think. The best examples of such self-revelation I know are in the autobiography of Eleanor Roosevelt and John Gunther's story of the death of his boy. In the law office, the most significant help is to watch what clients do *not* say, or their slips of the tongue or the artificial laugh of embarrassment. Counseling in divorce cases depends peculiarly on these clues. Since the human life is led to a large extent in the mind, there is no reality derived from such a conference except through what the client really thinks rather than through what he or she says. What is actually in the other person's mind is more important than the true facts—if man can ever get at truth. Maybe what one dreams or thinks or wants has more significance than reality. This shows up in law offices especially because there we learn that few people live fully and that misery flows mainly from acts of omission.

Sunday, August 31

It's fall. The town is empty and we can park on Main Street. Now we revisit our island friends. A real zip in the air. The morning dip off the pier before breakfast really wakes me up, although, except for two separate months in the past forty years, I have always waked up with excitement. I suggest that only those who are bored at their jobs use alarm clocks. Others—and I'm one—have an inner clock. I can wake up within five or ten minutes of the time I set when going to sleep. What evidence of the power of the unconscious! To be able to keep pace with a clock, man's mechanical invention, while asleep is a feat I can perform, but not while awake. I wonder if the clockless peasant can awake himself by thinking? Does he get up when the sun comes over the hill or past the branch of the tree under which he rests? And what happens when the days get longer or shorter? Does the internal timekeeper adjust to the equinox?

Sailing was good and I taught Ellen Gleitzman,* who had never been in a boat, to sail alone in one hour. It's easy as long as teachers don't overlay education by special vernaculars—for example, halliards, topp'nlift, etc. —to befuddle the pupil.

In the evening had a chance to sit with General James M. Gavin at Connie and Mike's.† The General

---

* *Monomoy neighbor.*
† *My daughter and her husband, Michael Bessie.*

is a paradox to me. Our republic lost his services, I believe, because in our too-big government only the employee who has ideas and takes responsibility gets in
Dutch. You can't get in trouble by doing nothing. If I'm
right, it's a disaster for our nation and explains why we
are becoming a second-class power (as Drew Pearson's
forthcoming book will show). Gavin is soft-spoken, a man
of moderate understatements, but, whether right or
wrong, he took positions. This the administration could
not stand. Rather a thousand silent nitwits than one explorative, eager mind. An idea is more dangerous than
a bomb. This mood is the mood of big business. Vice-
presidents are notoriously the carriers of ulcers, are inclined to support the orthodoxies of Senator McCarthy
and are frightened of responsibilities. I never deal with
vice-presidents if I can help it, although after one of
them becomes president he changes—he raises his stature and fits into the great list of presidents of U.S. big
corporations—a truly magnificent elite. The best proof
of this theory is clear if one compares officials at J. P.
Morgan with the vice-presidents at Manufacturers Trust
Company.

I cut the grass with the new, gas-engine lawn mower
—too fast but easy and fun. And still no machine can
do the edges or go close to the root of the crab-apple
tree. Machines carry their own blessed limit, thank God.
An auto with a power plant equal to 150 live horses gets
stuck in the snow and it needs me and my shovel to give
it mobility. So at times I am equal to the power of 150
horses!
Boats magazine, in which I'm still interested, arrived.
Al Stanford's editorials are the only cultured, subtle
writing in this leisure field—he's a sailor and not the

owner of a motor boat. I missed him this summer. For years I chartered back *Episode,* the sloop we loved and sold to Al. After a few years, however, I wouldn't go aboard my old vessel because Al added an improved radio direction finder and dozens of other doubtlessly wise betterments. But I was attached to my old boat. It's like picking up again with an old love who has been reconditioned and bettered by some other man. The bloom was off the peach.

SEPTEMBER

Monday, September 1

Busy around the place—fixing the irons on the float, repairing the ladder battered by the storm, sailing, swimming, cutting fire wood. Having built much of the furniture in our house, I'm now at the end of an era. We don't want more things, so Maggie breaks things on purpose, I suspect, to give me work to do in the shop. I'm probably finished with this chapter of my life since Joan,* Connie and Roger are building their own furniture. Though the four houses are close to one another on the shore, the passing generation should not butt into the next one, not even with offers to build bookcases, desks, outside staircases, etc. We parents dominate in too many ways without knowing it. Of course our motives are always good, we believe.

I recall *Look Homeward, Angel,* where a well-meaning mother perpetrates vast cruelties. In fact, at one great talk with Wolfe at the Eleventh Street house, this was all too clear. He wanted to hate his mother for what she did to him. But it's not easy to despise a person of good wishes and high motives.

* *My daughter, Joan Goldstein.*

In the evening, to the Gallery on Main Street to see Walter Pollak's collection of pictures painted on Nantucket. That's my idea of a valid collection without the indecencies of ordinary collector motivations. No regard for market values; pictures bought for use and enjoyment in his home on the Island.

Tuesday, September 2

No one can enjoy repairing a fence or painting the trim on a rented house; the sense of ownership is missing. Of course, the fun of performance is the same and the difference is not a lack of altruism in wanting to deprive a landlord. Rather, it's of the essence of freedom that one own, if possible, a plot of land and a home. Everyone should live *in* his investment rather than on it, and Congress wisely gives one of its few spiritual tax benefits to home owners.

Mike, Connie and I started to fix up their shower-bath entrance during the week end. The shower is outside, on a side of the house, next to the laundry-drying yard. Connie bought from Sears Roebuck a pair of swinging doors, the old-fashioned barroom type. Nick,* aged six, immediately translated this double-swinging instrument of privacy into the distortion of television. "Yes," he said, holding his hands at his hips as if he toted guns, "Open up!" And he pushed through. Thus do TV and tabloids—the creators of our national images—take a young mind and turn double-hinged doors into barricades for murder. In my youth such doors evoked only ideas of beer and the poor man's club.

In the morning we put up the doors. The double-

* *Nicholas Bessie, grandson.*

action hinges stumped us for a time, so we turned to the printed instructions. As I might have expected, the instructions were written by an expert who knew so much that he was unable to communicate to our ignorance. I'd like a job at Sears going over all their instruction slips, increasingly necessary when many mass-produced items come knocked down into pieces. One would imagine that shippers would have learned that no expert can popularize knowledge. Dave Loth, my friend and collaborator, once told me after he wrote two books on medical subjects that he could not write a third. As he said, "I'm disqualified; I know the vocabulary." This explains why no lawyer has written the essence of the high drama of law and jurisprudence except in fiction format like *Tutt and Mr. Tutt.* Some day the great foundations, which have been responsible for the discovery of much estimable knowledge, will turn their attentions and fortunes to the problem of popularization. Our world suffers from a deluge of knowledge. Man can no longer be cultured and rounded. We are a nation of specialists. Far worse, we fail to let the expert explain his ideas to an uninformed popularizer who, in turn, could translate these for our enjoyment.

In the evening to the Dick Lees', down the lane. Good talk on education with a schoolmaster. How do we create symbols of prestige for our teachers, without which prestige our people will not vote the money needed to educate our children? I thought I would get up a list of what we prefer for our dollars. Last year, for instance, we spent over fifty million dollars on stomach sweeteners and a hundred and twenty million on shampoos. Do we really prefer these things to the education of our children?

Wednesday, September 3

The grandchildren came back from the farm with some sweet corn, which we ate in the garden—the place to eat anything. Jo and Ellen* have turned these trips into a regular ritual—and what an education for city kids, two to six years of age, those unfortunates who never see nature at work or animals outside a zoo or feel the process of ripening food.

Called the Fays for lunch. We need them. The people of our generation are dying off and we find a decreasing number who aren't bores in the sense of leading nonobservant, narrative lives. The gap between the young and us is great and although in the office I want, as Cass Canfield† once wrote, an office boy to the left of me, it's not easy to live with the next generation— at least not easy for them. That damnable element of respect for old age intervenes. One more Biblical burden: "Honor thy father and thy mother." As Maggie wrote in the *New Masses* thirty years ago, the fifth commandment should be set on end. Parents should take the burden off their children and behave so that they deserve and truly earn affection and support. To hell with that naked honor stuff anyway.

In today's papers (or rather Tuesday's, because the papers arrive a day late, which makes little difference) I read that church membership has climbed in absolute figures but declined in proportion to population. What invalid figures! What is membership? Adherence? Going to church once or twice a year? Born to a church and

* *Josephine Houlihan, our maid of more than thirty years, and Ellen McDonagh, our summertime cook.*

† *Chairman of Executive Committee and editor, Harper & Brothers.*

deserted thereafter but for formal purposes? Above all, who invents the figure? Where is the central register? The Jews have no organization authorized even to guess at the figure of five and a half million I see on the list. Have not the Greek Orthodox joined the stream of counting only heads of families? Have their two and a half million been raised by the multiple of five? Why did all the churches beg to abolish the religious questions in the census? Afraid of real figures? My guess is that many of our people may lead deep and significant religious lives, but far less than a majority of our population belongs—in any real sense of the word—to any church. I'm glad to note that the Buddhists have admitted that their drop from sixty-three thousand in 1956 to ten thousand in 1957 doesn't imply a Buddhist exodus but rather a "more realistic estimate." And where do the ten million Catholics—to take Bishop Pike's estimate—who sidled over to Protestant groups show up?

Saw the northern lights—always exciting because unpredictable and as yet to me unexplained. Also saw one of the Sputniks. At the airport the taxi drivers were congregated, saying, "There she is—she's gone—there she is," as clouds or something intervened. I enjoyed detecting it—a little spot of light—but for the life of me can't figure out why I experienced this passing pleasure.

Thursday, September 4

Barometer high, tide low when we went for a prebreakfast dip. Temperature scant 70 degrees, low humidity. What a day! It validates Sidney Fay's theory that each summer on Nantucket adds a month to life. He's lived in the same house for over eighty years. It is a home his father moved from town about a mile to the cliff, at a time when moving houses in slabs and with horses and a dray seemed natural and easy. No wonder Nantucket homes were knocked into bits and pieces and put on boats, so that we now find them up the Hudson; at Dunkirk, France; in Milford Haven, England; in California; and in many other places to which these migratory whalers hiked their families and houses.

The shrinkage of population in Nantucket, after whale oil was replaced by Pennsylvania oil finds, left the town without slums and ready to supply good housing for every regular islander or summer visitor. I have a thing for islands anyway—they help you draw a circle around your living domain—a kind of psychological security lost in Manhattan's crowds, or even on Martha's Vineyard because that island feels like a big piece of the mainland or what Nantucketers call the United States. This is exemplified by Bob Mooney's tale. Bob is the representative at Boston elected from Nantucket—the first Democrat ever elected. His grandparents came from Ireland about a century ago. Their ship was wrecked at Tom Never's Head off the south shore of our island. They were saved, came to Nantucket, vowed never to go on a boat again and, in fact, never went to the United States, thirty-five miles to the northwest by sail.

In the past fortnight I've had a dose of adolescent-girl-seduction tales: *Lolita,* Vladimir Nabokov's pathological case history with a sales boost by its suppression in France; the Françoise Sagan line of unadult female adventures; and now *The Red Room* by Françoise Mallet-Joris, about a purposeful eighteen-year-old who gets her fish—which doesn't taste or smell good. My trouble with all such synthetic characters is that I can read them only as case histories. Seldom are they real people to the extent that I care what happens or doesn't happen to them. Maybe adults need this type of material to take the place of Davy Crockett. We have never had female symbols other than such masculine ladies as Annie Oakley, Florence Nightingale, Joan of Arc— all with oversupplies of masculine hormones. It's high time a female equivalent of Davy Crockett is invented, even though for centuries our girls have grown up with some relation to an adult female. Mothers taught young girls a little about housekeeping, cooking and taking care of the baby. Boys, except on farms during the period of industrialization since 1850, saw little of their fathers who worked eighty-hour weeks—then off to the saloon, club or bed. But now, with the forty-hour week —soon to shrink to thirty hours—fathers and sons are meeting each other again in the boat with an outboard motor, in the shop where one quarter of all our homes have some sort of jigsaw or other power tool. And now we should either reduce the spread and potency of the Crockett symbols for adolescent males or develop new ones for our young girls and particularly for the girl who is no good at tossing a ball or wrestling with the boys. This *tomboy* type has no difficulty adjusting while young. It's the others who need a symbol to counteract the movie-television false myth that moves them without effort or education from glamorous youth into the role of housekeeper, mother and matrix of a family. Likewise, the boys who are sensitive and like music, painting or poetry are pushed around by the Crockett symbols. Even though our State Department released most of its social scientists, this should not prevent NBC or CBS from tapping this comparatively new skill that is concerned with the ways and whyfores of men and women.

Friday, September 5

This is the last week when the clan—minus the little Ernies,* already returned to Washington—will be in Nantucket. Next week end I go to Hartford to speak at the Second Judicial Conference. The values of these conferences do not lie in the speeches or in the development of vigorous, new ideas, but rather in the opportunity given to a hundred or so lawyers to meet the federal judges of New York, Connecticut and Vermont —and the judges are ordered to attend. This year Justice Warren and our own Justice Harlan will be sitting in Washington on the eleventh on the Little Rock case. I have a hunch Judge Warren will have regrets. I have seen the pleasure he gets from informal meetings of the bar. His simplicity of language gives him untold power; in fact, a more scholarly and less secure jurist could not have written the opinion in the original desegregation case in 1954—an opinion so simply expressed that any high-school boy or girl can comprehend it.

While waiting for Irving† and Mike I kept on doing

* The Roger Ernst family.
† Our son-in-law, Irving Goldstein.

chores—fixing the gate, getting the rowboat ready for a paint job, cleaning up the shop. No similar chores can be enjoyed in an apartment house in Manhattan. Maybe every apartment house will soon have a hobby room available to tenants for carpentry, painting, photography work, pottery and the like.

Drove out to Squam and Quidnet. Penelope* suggests that this wet summer which has made the island so lush may leave it with fewer colors on the moors in October. She believes that Old Lady Chlorophyll may carry on with her green banners into the snowless winter.

Saturday, September 6

Irving's birthday. A party—that is, a cake with candles—is called for. For many decades I have been unmindful of anniversaries. So much of our American tradition of celebration is artificial. We trump up parades to increase or demonstrate our national spirit. We give dinners to celebrate the induction into office of thousands of minor officials; ditto on departure. I'm convinced that much of this is a racket generated in New York by the promotion departments of hotels. Surely most people attend out of compulsion—a kind of evil societal pressure. Much like funerals, which I don't attend; I think I have been to fewer than half a dozen in the past twenty years. Thankfully, my immediate family does not set any value on death ceremonies and won't carry on with such forms that compel people to attend for fear that their absence might be noted.

But the party this evening was fun. Nick played his

* *Who must remain unidentified.*

harmonica with gusto and Steffie* danced her favorite twirling-skirt number. And so to bed after doing a doublecrostic. In looking over an old file of 1945 I ran across a doublecrostic that Mrs. Elizabeth Kingsley, the laureate of the field, invented and sent to Maggie and me on the occasion of the publication of *The Best is Yet.* I like it when people—so often strangers—take out a few minutes to send on unsolicited and hence unexpected extensions of their warm feelings. How much more friendly are Americans than they dare express. Who doesn't enjoy being picked up on a bus, train or, if alone, in a restaurant?

Sunday, September 7

Temperature 70 degrees outside, 70 degrees inside; barometer 29.9, slightly falling; humidity 60; tide high at 7:17 A.M.; anemometer 17; wind from southwest; small-craft warning up at coastguard station across the harbor, a mile away.

Such are the automatically observed readings recorded every morning in Nantucket. Weather is significant for all people who can see the sky, particularly if they must deal with the sea. In those canyons of Manhattan, especially on the stylish avenues such as Park Avenue (so falsely named), few people see the clouds and the sky or feel the wind or the sun. When we first realized this gap between city life and real life, we installed an inside-outside thermometer plus Edna Ferber's gift barometer for rare occasions. The rest of the time we read the line at the head of the paper—primarily as a guide to taking an umbrella to the office.

* *Stephanie Goldstein, granddaughter.*

Off to New York early tomorrow with Hartford, Connecticut, as my objective for a few days. Thence to talk with Fowler Harper about tactics in the new birth-control cases that are starting in the Connecticut courts. One of the minor difficulties stands out with peculiar clarity at this moment of judicial history. The women plaintiffs in Connecticut who sue because they have been denied important accepted and medically indicated contraceptive advice are reluctant to have their intimate emotional, sexual and biological histories spread on the public records. Privacy is a valid desire, which courts should and at times do respect. On the other hand, society wants no star chamber—what goes on in the courts must be subjected to public criticism, since criticism is the only corrective of institutions as well as of people. So, risk for risk, we must appraise values. We can't have both privacy of the individual and publicity of court processes. Increasingly I bend toward the protection of privacy. Because the search for truth is at best so difficult, I favor the reduction of publicity, the abridgment of what might seem like the rights of a free press, in order not to disturb what lawyers call due process—in other words, a fair trial. Hence I'm opposed to the use of television in courtrooms and legislative hearings and wherever truth can flow only from a matching of wits—an adversary relationship.

Monday, September 8

The worlds of the law office and of a big city differ greatly from that of Nantucket. I'm reminded that when I was very young—say eight or ten—and the family came back to town after a Long Island or Catskill summer, I would look out of the elevated train and see a strange world. Each fall the city looked old and unfamiliar, not too different from my first views (later in life) of Casablanca, Beirut or Bangkok.

It is lucky that I have lived in two very separate compartments, geographically speaking. The shift in what the eye can see is the token of so many other changes. The family takes on a different mien. The family of the law firm—subjected to constant effort, bustle and frayed nerves—requires interludes. Surely when Judge Brandeis wrote his economic brief in favor of the power of the state to limit man's working hours he was directing attention to man's decreasing capacity for concentrated work after long hours of labor, varying in relation to emotional, mental and physical strains. (A good example is the decrease of accidents on Monday after a relaxing week end.) Of course, at this time practically no one had a vacation. A few of the office help received one week off each summer with pay. Now we are at the two-to-three week vacation level, soon to reach the full month. This has inevitably created a vast new industry of vacations and travel. Nor could this aspect of leisure operate without the induction of thousands of college girls and boys into what was formerly called "menial" work— waiting on table, washing dishes, making beds and mixing salads. We are, I suggest, close to getting a redefinition of that word "work." Is what one enjoys work? Do the boss, the manager, the professional man, the self-employed want vacations as do the drones—the millions transferred from the pleasure of skills to the boredom of the belt?

A call from Cass Canfield for lunch. Cass is one of the most cultured of our publishers. Literate, subtle, delicate—his depths only apparent after a drink or two. And even then he holds tight to his real, secret self. Few know about his sophisticated youth.

Pleasant conversation with Cass and Mike at the Century Club. We explored the danger of Russia joining the Universal Copyright Convention—a move, I think, that the Soviet will make in order to prevent the translation in the United States of their technical material that has been developed in book form. The entire Convention needs a fundamental revision at this point because the copyright law is little more than a bonanza to the lawyers engaged in copyright problems. The thinking has been far too much concerned with minor technical details. When I was in Russia and sat with Pavel Chuvikov, Director of Publishers of Foreign Literature, I mentioned the fact that American publishers do not plagiarize as was their habit before the turn of the century when we stole from England before we had our own literary culture. I even mentioned that publishing clients and friends of mine had thousands of dollars due Russian authors or publishing trusts. I must say I was surprised that no one at the conference asked, "Where is the money?" The absence of such a normal query was surely due to the fact that they knew my next question would be, "Why do you keep on stealing from American authors?"

If Russia now joins the Copyright Convention, it is

with the hope that no American publisher will be allowed for a period of seven years to translate a Russian work into English for use in the U.S. I think I have prepared a technique that will defeat this evil approach of the Soviet. I doubt if any court in our land would enjoin the publication of a translation from Russia, on the theory that injunctions are not lightly given and are a special form of benefaction that theoretically flow only to a petitioner with clean hands. I cannot imagine anyone with dirtier hands than those of an author or publisher who has been offered a good, clean market at the highest conceivable compensation but denies the publishing rights to prevent knowledge going to a sector of the human race.

I was in touch with Adlai Stevenson and his staff before he went to Russia, and I am most anxious to see him now that he has returned and confirm whether he found, as I did, that the Soviet wants to force our authors and publishers to deal through our government. This would be an additional symptom of statism. I also sensed in Russia that they would prefer dealing with tens of thousands of authors rather than a handful of publishers because they could then drive their literary tanks among our unbusinesslike authors and bargain on the basis of kudos or money. Under our law, however, the publishers could band together without violating our antimonopoly laws.

Tuesday, September 9

For some years we have had occasional luncheon meetings of the lawyers in the office. We are not a big shop. Once when we had twice as many lawyers, I touched the lamp Judge Brandeis gave me from his Supreme Court Bench and, relying on a kind of osmosis, suggested to Eddie, Herb and Laurie* that we were making no more money after taxes and turning out no better craftsmanship and were no happier than when we were half the size. With great effort we reduced the size of the office and, I trust, have improved the quality of the work.

Since law, like any other profession, operates in a field where clients require ingenuity and invention above all, I have become increasingly convinced (despite Dr. Paul Dudley White's plea for "stress") that lawyers should always operate in a relaxed climate—I don't mean temperature, but rather an office climate. This takes a lot of doing and many varied techniques.

In the corporate field the position of chairman of the board is necessary not only to provide a promotion but also to assure that there is at least one person without a function in the operational end of the business, whose sole duty is to dream and dream. Some years ago I heard that a meeting of all officials was called at the Guarantee Trust Co. Very few present knew the names or the faces of the others. The story goes that a top official presided and did not recognize half of the people in the room— a situation similar to the old days when the big banks

---

* *My partners, Edward S. Greenbaum, Herbert A. Wolff and the late Laurence S. Greenbaum.*

had boards of directors running to thirty or forty men. The meeting of such a group is more of a convention than a thoughtful exchange of ideas between men of good will.

Today we have invited all of the lawyers for one of our regular luncheons at the Overseas Press Club. This is a good but feeble move in the direction of picking brains, not on specific matters but on trends in the law. Law trends are particularly important because the law schools, in the main, still teach law with too much respect for *res adjudicata* and *stare decisis*. In fact, the reason lawyers have lost their leadership in our communities may be that we represent the only profession that has the duty of slowing up society. Every other skill is praised if it upsets our economy. The chemist invents a new drug and puts fifty drug companies into bankruptcy; such suffering is accepted as a payment for progress. But with lawyers a client wants to know whether the contract is good today and then asks, "Will it be good in twenty years?" In a slow-moving society such as existed until 1900 lawyers could lead because they were not singled out as the sole profession dedicated to preventing progress, which so often, of necessity, must result in discomfort. Today the leadership of the bar is at a low point, particularly in big cities. Since the leaders—a synonym for the financially lucky—seldom deal in matters of social principle, the function of an office lawyer is to negotiate and compromise, and his main function consists of pushing a little money across the desk or getting a little money pushed his way on behalf of his client. Seldom does he fight on matters of societal interest. This—coupled with the fact that the leaders of the bar seldom get into courtrooms and, above all, find no financial wealth in defending liberty—results in the criticism, often exaggerated, of the role of a lawyer in our society.

These lawyers around the table are good and will remain so as long as we have no agenda. An agenda is an instrument often used to prevent man from roaming freely, or what in Nantucket we call "rantumscooting." This word merely means that you drive your buggy on a rutted road over the moors while you don't quite know, and certainly don't care, where you will end up.

Dinner with the genius of the American Institute of Graphic Arts, Joyce Morrow—intelligent, thoughtful and, although competing in a man's world, not predatory. Ran into the improbable Marlene* who scarcely fits into our tense, fast-paced culture.

Wednesday, September 10

On Tuesday midnight I appeared on Barry Gray's radio program for about an hour. This is one of the few platforms in our land from which I can reach a million people without censorship and no controls other than taste, and from which unpopular causes can be discussed with good will. Barry asked me about the crime-sex reporting that dominates our media of communication. He was exercised about the front-page devotion to the Eddie Fisher-Debbie Reynolds-Elizabeth Taylor Todd story while our republic is in trouble with China, the Near East and South America.

The tawdry tabloids are a real problem, but the *New York Post,* the paper for which Barry wrote, wins the prize for intellectual corruption. With an orgy on the

* *Dietrich, of course.*

front page one day and a girl's cut throat featured on the next, this paper no doubt gets many kids to believe that mayhem is a normal daily occurrence. The pretense of the paper makes the *Post* more objectionable than the run-of-the-mill tabloids. It professes to use the gutter to get people to read Max Lerner *et al.* I wonder if the same people read both. Like the owners of the television networks, the paper in effect says, "We must follow the mob because we lead it." I object particularly because this paper at times takes the best liberal positions of the day.

Thursday, September 11

Drove to Hartford yesterday, a delightful city. Since it is the home of so many insurance companies, its people are more white-collar than in any other city. I miss my old friend Morgan Brainard,* a typical liberal in everything but politics. He was a saucy Peck's Bad Boy. I'm reminded (not by M. B.) that our first notable pornography appeared in Hartford. Mark Twain, between the writing of *Tom Sawyer* and *Huckleberry Finn,* wrote a brochure addressed to his clergyman. This was seized on by a literate public servant, John Hay, who had it privately printed at the West Point army presses. This, plus the Ben Franklin pornography published later, always reminds me of the gap in our culture between public professions and actual mores.

At the Second Circuit Judicial Conference, good discussion about the need of the indigent to get counsel. I think we are on the wrong track. The Legal Aid Societies must be reappraised in historic terms; for a few

* *Former head of Aetna Life.*

dollars they allow the bar to absolve lawyers from their shame at not taking on one or two additional "indigent" cases a year. To be sure, most of today's leading lawyers are unskilled at court appearances and in matters of criminal law—that is, the defense of liberty. Still, the leaders could lend their names and their young lawyers. Thus prestige would accrue to help the indigent, and the lesser legal luminaries might follow suit.

On the other hand, some of us favor Public Defenders. This has its humorous side, inferring that the States will finance both sides of the legal gaming table—a promotion of the idea that law is only a game. We might try the British system of turning over to the defendant all information of innocence that comes to the prosecutor's attention. "The crown can't win. The crown can't lose." Let's see if one district attorney would pursue justice on the British principle instead of victory for just one year. Then let's review the present popular escapes from guilt used by the bar—Legal Aid and Public Defender.

All day tidbit talks with lawyers and judges. Maybe these opportunities form the most important part of the conferences. Lawyers, one at a time, can be delightful, but in mass are hard to distinguish from Legion, Rotary or taxpayer groups.

Friday, September 12

The panel discussion Harold Gardiner* and I had on censorship probably added little to the bar's chaotic thinking on the problem. Harold startled the audience when he pointed out the infirmities of the Catholic Index and the absence of any American novel

* *Harold Gardiner, S.J., literary editor of* America.

on it. His speech made clear that the Roman Catholic Church is not of one mind in regard to censorship.

On the same morning there was a discussion of passport controls. O'Connor of the State Department was bombarded with questions that showed how the bar has gone to hell—more interested in communism than in sex! Charlie Tuttle, feeling sorry for Harold and me, then asked one question on the censorship problem. Next year we ought to speak on "The Sexual Motive for Joining the Communist Party"—then some of the questions will be directed at us.

Professor Kalvin of Chicago Law School and an overly large panel discussed his survey of what goes on in jury rooms and jurors' minds. I have one real caveat as to the findings: we have two different jury systems in our land. In New York City a juror who has read about a case is usually excused from duty, whereas in Nantucket you can't impanel a jury without at least one juror being intimate—via marriage or business—with one or more of the witnesses, parties or lawyers. This was the original basis of the jury—a judgment by people from the vicinity. I suggested to Professor Kalvin at dinner that if his statistics tried to merge the practices of metropolitan centers and the rest of our republic, I would be reminded of the time I was in a hospital when the average fever was 101.5 degrees for all patients but I knew mine was about 104. The concept of average is so evil—maybe we must abandon it for median.

Sunday, September 14

Drove with Alan* to New Haven to meet Fowler Harper and Miss Rorabach, the lawyers who are retesting the Connecticut bootleg-contraceptives situation. Harriet† met us for a brief lunch. The most heartening talk I have heard on the problems of legal tactics vis-à-vis our only antagonist, the Roman Catholic Church. We discussed selling a book, preferably the great volume on contraceptives of Dr. Rock (a Catholic communicant); the talk also revolved around the constitutional rights of an Episcopal divine to follow the precepts of the recent pronouncements at Lambeth Palace. I wrote to my friend Fisher, the Archbishop of Canterbury, for copies of the report. We reviewed the publicizing of the approved Catholic rhythm method and the possible dangers of deception that the spread of such calendars carries to married and unmarried women. I wonder why papers like the *Times* and the *Tribune,* which ordinarily report fully, have failed to mention the orders issued on several occasions against fraudulent representations accompanying the Roman Catholic rhythm calendars?

Plane to New York and then to Maggie waiting at Nantucket. Caught a glimpse of Bob Mooney, who captured both the Democratic and the Republican nominations for legislative representative—this on an island that never had elected a Democrat to office until last year! I wish more Mooneys would go into active party politics. I wish I had.

* *Alan U. Schwartz, law associate.*
† *Harriet Pilpel, partner.*

Monday, September 15

Indian summer weather—clear, warm when out of the wind. I understand why the trees grow only as tall as their protection from the wind.

The kids went home. Only Mittens the cat is left—could not be found to catch the airplane on time.

Up the hill Bob Congdon is building a new home and every day we will be sidewalk superintendents. Too bad the kids have left the island. What better education than seeing life in operation—the matrix must ever be the building of a home.

When telling Maggie about our drive to Hartford, I brought up the inadequacy of our travel facilities. Our maps are shamefully limited compared to the French Guide Michelin; not only the maps but the guide with its pictograms of forks and knives, etc., to show hotel and restaurant standards. Why doesn't one of our gasoline companies invest a little of its money now devoted to television shows to produce and give away a good map? Also we remembered the wise Swiss policy of putting mirrors at road intersections. In the States, however, the builders of our big concrete highways, who are familiar with distances, fail to realize how distance-milage information would comfort travelers. It needn't be in tenths of a mile, as in India where people travel by camel or other animal or on foot and one-tenth of a mile is a meaningful figure, but between towns or exits where long-distance markers would cost little and would be appreciated.

In 1787 it took six weeks to get from Salem, Massachusetts, to Richmond, Virginia, and mail in the winter was often sent from Boston by boat to England and then back to Georgia rather than being subjected to the road gullies on an overland trip. How easily man gets soft and forgets the past! Before and maybe after the federal government made a monopoly of the mails, postage was seldom affixed. Rather, letters were sent C.O.D.— to reduce the cost in case of the prevalent hijacking of mail pouches.

We have just had a great scar inflicted on us. The road builders on the island, corrupted by so-called free money from the Commonwealth of Massachusetts, have changed our adequate, narrow, rolling, dirt lane into a macadam road, leveled like a thruway. All over our nation roads are the great means of boondoggling, and here the road gangs envy the concrete city streets and are so stupid as to think that city folks want concrete roads while on vacation. How foolish can our two folkways be in misunderstanding each other!

Took in the kids' clothespoles, and otherwise messed around closing their houses. Messing is fun even if, or particularly if, with no high purpose. Each little chore is an accomplishment and carries the satisfaction of finality, without loose edges or further demands. Moreover, such chores carry within themselves no depressive symbols such as par in golf. There is little, if any, ingredient of the competitive life in them.

Just read that Bob Fowler's* report on the Royal Commission on Television and Radio for Canada has been put into partial effect. I do hope Canada preserves its own culture over the air and does not allow us to submerge it by the extension of our ether programs, even though we can export our gangsterisms cheaper than they can create their own indigenous array of taw-

* *Canadian friend, attorney, leading spirit for newsprint industry.*

driness. Maybe the fortuitous fact that Canada has dual cultures—French and English—will save it from being taken over by us, and surely we will be benefited by having a different folkway to the north. I never did value the pressure for Americanization, which suppressed the cultural values of immigrants who came to our shores. Variety is the spice of a nation even though orthodoxy may seem to save time and money and promote other elements that overshadow the value of eccentricity—which is needed in every family and every nation.

Another gift from one nation to another is reported in the press—England gave Christmas Island to Australia. Is the giving away of possessions a new national trait, a forerunner of change from the historic pattern of wanting more lands?

For a couple of days now my mind has gone back to a five-inch story that appeared in some London paper, telling how one nation gave up a piece of territory to another nation. What a paradox in these times when the Communists are grabbing all the land they can! I think I saw a map showing the location of Gwadar. It is a little enclave on the Gulf of Oman shore of Pakistan. Oman has ceded this—its sole overseas colony—to Pakistan. I gathered that England was the intermediary that got one nation to transfer land to another. I must look up and check how many people were transferred with the land.

I remember in the 1930's I went down to the Virgin Islands for F.D.R. when we had purchased these islands from Denmark for about twenty-five million dollars, bought not only the land but also the people who went with the land. Ironically, these twenty thousand Virgin Islanders had made a substantial part of their living out

of rum, and our purchase coincided with the Eighteenth
Amendment. This enactment of prohibition was a dis-
astrous experiment that was not noble, as President
Hoover declared it to be, but ignoble, particularly for
the Virgin Islanders.

Why didn't the press carry as a big front-page story
this gift of a harbor and land from one nation to another? I believe the owners of the press are misguided
in their belief that nobody enjoys good news, but I don't
know how we can prove it to them unless at least one
radio station or one newspaper gives good news its fair
chance of headlines day by day.

Tuesday, September 16

Congressmen, senators and other persons concerned with the Jesus de Galindez million-dollar mystery have been communicating with me about a statement carried in *The New York Times* of September 11.
It purported to be a quotation of a charge by Congressman Charles O. Porter that Franco was responsible for
the kidnaping of Galindez in the Jerry Murphy plane.
No one of objective good will who has looked at the
facts still holds to the *Life-New York Times* theory that
Galindez collected his million dollars from Basque people. The Galindez ledger kept in his own handwriting
gives the lie to such a statement. That Galindez was an
agent—and probably a double agent—was made clear
by the 171 letters he had written of which copies were
turned over by me to my government for translation.
These letters, as our report showed, revealed the code
he used.

So now the papers that praised the Congressman as

a great detective merely report his accusation against Spain—which should, but probably won't, be the turning point in the education of our public on this odd episode. Perhaps there will now be a demand for the facts on the basis of which he accuses Spain of kidnaping.

Good zip in the air continues. Too windy for a picnic sail to Coatue, so we went to Quidnet, a wind-protected beach. Had a swim and lunch. I also swam after lunch, since Penelope has taught me to listen with doubt to all general caveats such as "Don't bathe after a meal, no matter how light."

For dinner to Joe and Connie's.* They really deserve a Pulitzer prize for their decade of competitive journalism on Nantucket, if for no other reason than to dramatize the fallacy of the big lie spread in all fields of journalism that the evaporation of a competitive press is necessary because towns can't economically support competing papers. Here, with a winter population of about 3500, two weeklies do their jobs with no visibly intolerable burden on the merchants and readers. And what competition does to enrich both papers is so startling that the areas with only one paper should take a look at Nantucket!

The reviews of Thor Heyerdahl's book on Easter Island fascinate me. I must read it, particularly because the carbon tests for age seem to be bettered of late, and nothing may be as old as we think, just as we now believe the last ice age was not so long ago. Penelope suggests that evidence points to the next one arriving from the Arctic in about ten thousand years, give or take about two hundred years.

* *Joe Indio, owner and editor of the Nantucket* Town Crier, *and wife.*

Wednesday, September 17

I read that monkeys develop ulcers when they take part in executive-type experiments. Penelope, with her gracious, inquiring approach, asked if this applies to female as well as male monkeys, since, in our culture, ulcers in women are different from masculine ones in quality and frequency of occurrence.

Low tide when we woke up. Bad swimming at low tide. I must ask Penelope to check the new theory, confirming Lord Kelvin's idea of eighty years ago, that the circular wobble of the earth's poles carries small ocean tides. Jealous moon, beware!

Learned only today that Mr. Richter, a lawyer on the staff investigating the Galindez million-dollar mystery, has sued CBS for libel. I haven't seen the complaint but assume that Roger Hunting, a delightful barrister, is representing Richter as he did at the CBS hearing when their publicized complaint against Richter in defense of their own reporting brought up charges that might have led to Richter's disbarment. I wonder if CBS gave publicity to the complete vindication of Richter by the Government? But when does a retraction or apology ever catch up with a libel or slander?

Years ago, I addressed the Society of Newspaper Editors and urged a law that would relieve newspapers of all libel suits (save only if malice could be proven) if the paper gave fair space to a prompt retraction. As I expected, the press prefers the expense of defending libel actions to the horrors of exposing their many previously published mistakes. And why not, since a virtual cartel exists: never refer to a libel suit even if your competitor is involved! And what delicious and intriguing subject matter is found in the scores of libel suits brought to New York courts every year!

Brought in the little catboat to take off the mast and rigging. Putting boats and possessions to bed has a peaceful connotation even though always a trifle on the sad side.

After a busy day between light rains and overcast skies we drove up to see the new MacAusland house up harbor. From the water it looks like four or five seperate houses. Everything about this home has a touch of simple elegance. And why not? He is Mr. Gourmet—without the ostentation that accompanies lesser *Gutschmeckers.* I always like to see a sensitive, soft-spoken man at the head of a successful, competitive enterprise. Not only the rough-and-tumble operators get on top in our marketplace of money making.

Thursday, September 18

Blustery weather, last swim, breakfast snugly close up to oil heater. Maggie goes through the ritual of closing the house. Much of it part of tradition handed down from Danny,* and probably no longer meaningful. I remember that when we left the city for the summer in my youth, pictures were all covered with cheesecloth! Sheets also over chairs. In Nantucket, I recall, we used to pull down shades—until we thought it through and realized sunlight was good for a closed house.

Up the hill, on the telephone wires in front of the home of our bookstore friend Adelaide Russell, there are hundreds if not thousands of birds resting (for how

* *Margaret's mother, Helen Samuels.*

long I don't know) on their way south. No one has really
solved the mystery of bird migration. How do they set
their internal compasses? What drives them to fly thousands of miles at times, past rich feeding land to a spot
of meager bird resources? The eels in the Sargossa Sea,
the salmon of the Columbia—it's all a good puzzle for a
thoughtful child of the future.

Word just arrived that the New York City Hospital
Board has ruled in favor of protecting Catholic doctors
from the compulsion of giving contraceptive advice
against their religious principles, but that patients are
entitled to such advice in city hospitals. There is a
further issue unresolved. Suppose a non-Catholic goes to
a Catholic doctor; contraceptives are indicated as result
of diagnosis—what does the Catholic doctor do? Surely
he cannot allow the patient to be deprived because of the
doctor's dogma. One man's dogma may be another man's
death. Should he not refer the patient to a doctor not so
embarrassed? Do the Catholic doctors then lose all their
patients who are not Catholic and, in view of the equiv-
ocal position of the Catholic Church on rhythm (a new
doctrine dating from 1930), run the danger of losing
Catholic patients? Is referral a violation of religious
principles? The tactic I used in the City Hospital case
allowed the solution of the issue to rest on the law of
malpractice. It's clear that malpractice results not only
from acts of commission but also from acts of omission.
Failing to prescribe or recommend a doctor not hindered
by religious limitations will bring the Catholic doctors
into serious lawsuits.

Letter from Marie in London, full of her expected
wisdom. Mixed cultures, housing shortages, discrimination on jobs and too few West Indian women all add up
to the Notting Hill troubles. I wonder why, if there

must be quotas for immigration, man did not first think in terms of enough women for men, rather than only of some senseless national-origin quotas. Man might have learned by looking at birches or holly, which will not grow unless planted with male and female close to each other.

If the immigration is solely masculine there must be trouble—look at the Puritan sexual perversities subdued only by the need of survival in a new land. If there were sufficient women immigrants, much of the restless dissatisfaction would be drained off in family living or at least in acceptable sexual outlets. How can it be otherwise when, in Delhi, advertisements appear in the dailies stating that males want wives, ask for color of skin, caste and size of waist? Why are the white people so insecure that they seldom report bigotries among nonwhites? In Harlem we have gone to dance halls and restaurants that cater only to light-skinned people—high yellows—and exclude people of black-hued skin if possible

The U.S. will lick this problem during the next century and lead the people of the planet to a red-chocolate tint. I wonder how many one-hundred-per-cent black people there are in our land. I should think our southern whites have broken through this color barrier with their dark-skinned mistresses. Moreover, the myth that Negroes are better lovers than whites will soon be exposed to the test of our mass media. Kinsey and others indicate that sexual attitudes do not follow racial lines but do accord to general cultural patterns of wealth and educational backgrounds.

Today I turned pedagogue. It's really Maggie's forte, but she does not particularly enjoy addressing groups, small or big—although she is very good at it if she once accepts. But for any request on Nantucket I'm a pushover. So at noon I addressed the high-school assembly. I tried out a hunch that I have long urged teachers to experiment with and that I had used at Exeter in the 1930's.

I took the pupils on a trip around our planet, showing that no one can travel far without running into a large or small bigotry. For instance, the Catholic-Protestant clash of cultures in Montreal, Negro-white in our south, Arab-Jew in the Near East, etc. And then I traveled with them to victims of minor bigotries: the Ainus in Japan who are still only meat handlers, although they were the original inhabitants, but who are unfortunately easily identifiable because they have hair in their armpits; and then those Jews in Majorca who became Catholic converts during the Inquisition, adopting established Spanish manners, but who still worship separately from other Catholics after five hundred years.

What lazy people we are if we ape insecure people who push down others by words such as *mick, kike, wop* and *nigger*. Bigotry is a crutch. I suggested a game of swapping stories about our first remembrances of bigotry—a lazy mind's acceptance of seeming superiority. When did the pupil first hear a bigotry? Who used it— and above all, why?

Friday, September 19

Off in a small Piper Pageant plane—thirty minutes to Newport to see the first Lipton Cup race tomorrow, on the Lipton boat with Bob Smallwood.

In the lobby of The Viking, the congregation of sailors looks quite different from a Legion, Rotary or lawyers' convention. There is a special camaraderie because sails

are their only hobby—a total accent. There is a buzz in
the air and a degree of politeness that does not emanate
from skippers who use powerboats. Artificial decorum
needed for safety provides a good residue of ordinary
consideration of one's fellow men. I imagine the powerboat fold could not be distinguished from hot-rod
fiends. There is little art and no real need for deftness
at the wheel of a powerboat. Powerboat sailors represent
a cross section of mankind that worships competition
and speed, two attributes of a rat-race life that does not
appeal to the family looking for gunk holes on the Maine
Coast, always seeking the peaceful harbor that appears at
first glance to be closed to the sea and inside feels en-
cased, secured and remote from mankind.

I do hope that *Sceptre* wins. Man always has two reasons for anything—the real one and the one he mentions
publicly. I think my real one in this case is an unthink-
ing emotional support of the underdog. Where this
comes from I don't know, unless it's because my father
was, in a sense, pushed out of Czechoslovakia. My ration-
alized reason is that it would be good for racing if England won. But this is less than valid, because I'm not
much for racing. If there are to be races, maybe they
should be open to all boats used for a period of years in
normal fashion, with two classes—day sailors and cruising boats. This might develop a real art of design rather
than producing the freaks compounded for special occasions. No race, I note, on Sunday—a heritage passed
down from the time when churchgoing was the vogue,
and no gentleman would compete on the Sabbath. In
my youth golf on Sunday was controversial.

Before lunch we strolled along the wharves. It's the
first time in about twenty-five years that we maneuvered
Newport. The walk was one of "serendipity" (I shall

always thank Walpole for fabricating one of the best invented words). We saw *Sceptre* on the way and *Maid of Honor,* a doll of a tug. I wonder if all the big handlebar-mustached, elderly men are British.

We ran into Olin S.* In England he would have been knighted years ago. Too bad the Founding Fathers in their symbolic withdrawal from Mother England had to reject titles—a means of giving prestige symbols to the deserving.

Saw *Cat On A Hot Tin Roof.* It's a good example of the indecencies of Hollywood. What is tawdrier than to let the public believe that a homosexual can become what we call normal just because of a brief series of family events? The movies are bound to suffer because they are so profuse, need not be as subtle as the stage, and above all cater to quantity instead of quality.

This is an interesting city. I feel a kind of affection for history. The Viking Tower in Newport can, I assume, now be tested for age as we are testing the diggings in Greece. I rather hope the story of Celtic origin antedating the Viking period—about 1000 A.D., I think it was—proves true.

Saturday, September 20

Slept well at The Viking which should send someone over to Scandinavia for lessons from Vikings on how to run hotels—with more taste and less expense.

Not much wind—not a close race, but with maybe fifteen hundred craft watching I had a feeling of the sort that Dunkirk will always evoke in me, except this was for fun and not in dead earnest to save the world.

* *Olin Stevens, great yacht designer.*

And I wondered if the names of the British Dunkirk craft included one called *Hey Baby*. Penelope will have to tell me what kind of people give such a name to a boat—even a powerboat.

Back at hotel around eight o'clock. I may come back during the week if there is a real blow, for then *Sceptre,* carrying more weight than *Columbia,* may win. A couple of small-boat-racing addicts were on board. I wish I could understand the people whose hobbies, recreations, sports—whose so-called leisure—is compounded only of winning, beating a record or some person, with practically no relaxed test of joy for the thing itself.

Sunday, September 21

We drove home with Al Stanford, who has a new gadget. He can adjust his speedometer so that it buzzes at the speed he selects. He fixed it at sixty, and what a start we had when the noise interrupted our talk. Al then told me that he loaned his car to a friend who said, "I resent that buzz. I'm against controls by government or anyone." But Al suggested that the friend set the control, and asked if he really resented controls he fixed for himself. The answer was yes—showing how far a glandular preference for freedom and liberty has gone for some people in our culture.

Later in the day I walked uptown instead of taking the usual Sunday stroll to Chinatown, the water front or parts of this big city of New York that should be split back into separate villages of intimacy, where people can experience a "concern" over their environment.

Lever Brothers constructed a striking, setback, glass-walled, simple office building. Now we have one archi-

tect after another trying to copy the Lever beauty with
only slight variations. Park Avenue is a bore. It lacks
distinction. Too much glass and metal and straight lines.
I'd like one building to go up with some frills and
furbelows—angels carved under porticos or even devils
standing at corners like gargoyles of old. Even a slight
curve might be enjoyable. Since when is a curve dé-
classé? I thought we had been taught that a thing of
beauty is, or could be, a joy forever. Why do the architects pursue vogues like the output of Hollywood? One
hit movie on one subject produces a spate of imitators.

But in Manhattan we don't let things stand long
enough to love them. We are a society without tradition
or affection. The old Ritz was, to many, a treasure. It
was torn down—I forget for what. The new Ritz just
isn't entitled to the name—and it doesn't have it.

Tonight we tried out our treasure game on some
people who dropped in for coffee after dinner. If a bomb
were to fall on Manhattan, name the four buildings you
would save if you had the power. Empire State—nonsense! It could be rebuilt. Radio City, ditto. So this time
we agreed, more or less, on Fraunces Tavern, our City
Hall, Gracie Mansion and the Jumel Mansion. There
are a few more, but if we added all the choices of all
present we would not exceed a dozen. Too few for
beauty, too few for love, too few for roots from which
traditions can grow. Stability and calm even in a changing world depend on tradition and tradition depends on
affection and affections take time to gestate.

Tuesday, September 23

Office closed early—Yom Kippur. I'm not a so-called believer, and I wonder if the spiritual meter would show a great rise in inner religious feelings if we could test it for the next twenty-four hours.

No lunch today or yesterday. Why do I ever eat unless I'm really hungry, except to leave the office and to converse with a client or friend? My rational mind tells me food ineluctably tastes better if one has a demanding appetite. Why do we reduce the pleasure of this basic urge? Is it only to reduce labor and indecision, which are the purposes of all habits? What of the eating habits of unattached boy or girl bachelors? Or does regularity, without thinking, simplify and fill up their lives?

Wednesday, September 24

Last night I read John Tunis' new book. It's an important sociological review of the changes in the American attitudes toward sports, and he pulls no punches about the dollar aspects of big business in athletics. Much of his nostalgia I shared with him—as far back as Honus Wagner and my early heroes. Incidentally, I imagine that baseball is the only great teacher of mathematics in our land. Kids discover the reality of the concept of percentages through baseball.

A great day at the office—nearly cleared of lawyers. Rhoda* is in to do some typing for me. She's an interest-

* *Rhoda St. James, typist, writer.*

ing human being. About a year ago I heard that she was going to quit work in order to write a novel. I sent her to kindly Herb Mayes,* who advised her to keep her job and write at night and week ends. She would have none of it. Like most people, she didn't want advice—she wanted confirmation of her decision, which lawyers soon discover is the purpose of most clients. Herb spoke reasonably, but I endorsed Rhoda who decided with unreason to live on the $307.00 she had saved, write and only go back to work when she had no pennies for food. The work is completed and an agent with integrity thinks it is good. I'll be interested to see what has come out of what many would call Rhoda's sacrifice. She and I know better—there was no sacrifice, only a choice between conflicting preferences.

I read in the dailies a brief and confused story about a shift in education in Russia. When I returned from there in 1956, I reported the creation of a new class through the mass desire for higher education. Every parent wanted every child to get into college. It meant high standing in the eyes of the people and three to ten times the average monthly income. The scramble had already produced the most striking of symptoms— a suicide rate that scared the commissars. I explained that suicide is a concomitant of freedom—as are dreams and frustrations. Only a dozen nations have any suicide rate to speak of if we exclude suicides to escape physical pain. It was clear then that a new class was being created, for if a lad flunked exams for college he was shipped to a mine, or a farm or a factory at five hundred rubles a month for life. The increase in the suicide rate, the demand for privacy and the great demand for voluntary travel without permits or limitations struck me as very

* *Editor of* McCall's Magazine, *formerly of* Cosmopolitan.

hopeful trends toward regard for the individual, and so I reported to my government on my return from Russia.

Thursday, September 25

Last night we went to see Buzz Meredith's* Production of *Ulysses in Nighttown*. It was showing at one of our twenty-eight local theaters in this downtown part of town. As I went up in the elevator to the theater, I recalled the fight against LaGuardia's perverted desire to suppress Burlesque—for this, I believe, was the site of Minsky's, the most famous of the public outlets for the sexually starved.

Even apart from the wisdom and luck of casting Zero Mostel as Bloom, this is one of the most valuable and improbable of all theatrical productions. We were fascinated that anyone could put into about two hours the essence of Bloom's conflict and the guilts of James Joyce. Surely if Joyce had kept his religion, he would have been more impounded with Hells than with Heavens. As the old saying goes, "The Don'ts Outdoes the Do's." His God was a pre-Hosea one, when man educated his God toward tender ideas. The frankness made me wonder if there is not a kind of separate immunity adhering to Ulysses because of Judge Woolsey's decision, which fends off any public interference or even protest, whereas the same words and purposes derived from any other book would probably produce attempts at censorship. I must look for literary immunities of writings less than "classics." In other words, how long must an author be dead to be a classic?

After the curtain went down, Buzz asked me back-

* *Burgess Meredith, actor and director.*

stage to tell the cast a few stories of the original defense of the book in the courts—the need of overcoming the fear of dirty concepts in the four-letter words, and, above all, the rare chance I had to act out the double stream of consciousness. It was decades ago when that young attractive hick Meredith first came to the big city and had dinner with us on Eleventh Street. Attractive then—more so now that his treadmill is not running him around at such a high speed. Later brought Leonard and Ellie* and an attractive, calm-looking friend home for a glass of wine. Lights out at about two.

This morning ran into one of our few inventive publishers—Zevin† of Cleveland. I think he would be in danger of orthodoxy if he moved to New York. The swim in New York is in turbulent waters and at a speed at which swimmers are pushed along in one direction. Upstream takes peculiar muscles.

Saw a young lad twirling a hula hoop. Went up to ask him how he got it started. He was suddenly silent. The doorman of the apartment house in front of which the wiggle was in operation explained that the lad was out for a record—neighborhood, I assume, not international or interplanetary. The hula boy had been going for thirty-five minutes, to talk would interrupt the rhythm. So I must wait for the answer, but I must get it soon. The first time I tried to get the hula started, the hoop immediately took the form of sidewalk halo—an imagery which, I suspect, has nothing to do with spelling.

It's a good fad—far better than the guns and what-all we have had a dose of for years past. Morover, it shows how easily a fad can be put over, and I can't believe that

* Mr. and Mrs. Leonard Bernheim, cousins.
† Ben Zevin, president, The World Publishing Company.

this variation on an old-fashioned "bump and grind" has any hidden sexual connotation.

Turned on radio for news—heard a couple of my favorites: Collingwood from England and Sevareid from Washington. Both have become mental orthopedists; they told millions of people that most people in England and most of those Sevareid saw in Washington believed "in their bones" there would be no war. Nonsense. Let's go back to the Gallup poll, which predicted Dewey's election. Why do sober commentators have to make exaggerated appraisals equaling the puffings of advertisers? Oh, for one commentator who will just once say, "I don't know. I can't find out." Or even, "I have only a hunch that . . ." And then pronounce his dooms, which the hopeful people of our land are presumed to demand.

Friday, September 26

Up, as usual, a little before seven. Took in papers. I go through the *Times* before Maggie's eyes are fully open. Read letter column first, then glance at editorials to see if I can find one with some evidence of strong feelings—just a little hotter than tepid. Then read Gould on television, then business page and then news headlines—particularly from those cities I have visited. Thus does travel pile up the expenditure of time for years afterwards!

I had an exciting luncheon with Richard R. Salzmann, executive vice-chairman of the Institute for Mediterranean Affairs. He brought along Samuel Merlin, their director of political studies. Their proposal to empty the Arab refugee camps is a contribution toward peace, and they are wise enough to know that any concrete proposal has value only to the extent that everyone recognizes that it can be improved by criticism. All that is necessary is to find someone high in the government who has not lost courage and has a spirit of adventure. This particular approach cannot succeed if either the Arabs or the Jews endorse it. In this situation I am reminded of dealings between employers and labor. Although in every strike both sides know there will be a day of settlement, if either party shows his hand with too much enthusiasm, the other side must resist. As in all negotiations, no one ever believes an ultimatum—take it or leave it. An ultimatum is meaningless.

Joan, Irving and Steffie at our house for dinner. She is an easy child for me to cope with—most reasonable for her age. It is fascinating how she, with hearing, handles her deep responsibility of acting—on the telephone and otherwise—as the communicant for her deaf parents.

Saturday, September 27

The hurricane is on the way to some other shore —others will be made homeless, but they are not readily in sight so distance makes the heart grow duller. The Arch outside my window will be no more than wetted by peripheral winds. Not even the pigeons will be disturbed.

Lazy morning. Maggie made breakfast—a kind of holiday feast. Then a Churchillian hot bath—over an hour, but without the glass of scotch or the cigar. Read "Topics" in the *Times*. A delightful column—in the real sense of the word, full of light. This is usually the real editorial of the *Times,* filled with decency.

Readers can enjoy it, can leave it alone, but cannot really disagree. I wish we could honor the writer, but maybe this is one of those many situations in life where the mere disclosure of his identity would destroy the tender whimsey that stems only from the anonymous. It's the best of the editorials because the writer does not try to make everyone happy and offend no one. If I'm not mistaken, the column has a tradition of the pen of Finlay and Strunsky. Surely these unsung Homers must have had some outlet besides the essay—where matters of importance to them can be spread with a little unconcealed stir of the blood. The column today was about bowling, and no one can be against bowling—and still the author dared in his paper to say that the people of our republic spend more on bowling than on baseball. What happens to him if ten letters come in from baseball fans? Does he walk off his inner high feelings, as did Finlay? Didn't Strunsky take it out in music?

Dropped in at Abercrombie & Fitch—the only floor I go to: the boating department. It's sad that we have so few good ship chandlers. None as good as Watts in London off Piccadilly. And so few books on boats compared to the British. But we have few new books on any subject. For years the British new titles have run over twenty thousand—about double ours, for a quarter of our population. Maybe the explanation lies in our damnable accent on the vogue of best seller—a concomitant of a nation our size with its distribution problems. But why do the best-seller lists have to be less than honorable and so easily created artificially? Above all I'd like to find out the relation of reading (more than a chapter) of best sellers to the total number of copies purchased—a discrepancy particularly wide, I suspect, with nonfiction. Often a purchase and only a riffle are needed to get into the chatter at a dinner party. It's like the social pressure to see a play early in its run. We used to go to opening nights, but soon found the batting average of enjoyment was too low. So we wait for plays and movies. If they are good, they are likely to be around months later. As for books, Maggie makes lists and has parcels of books sent to Nantucket for the following summer. Time enough, what with rereading.

To the Gate Theater on Second Avenue to see *Héloïse* by James Forsyth. Brooks Atkinson raved about it. For me it had a great head start: curtain up at 6:30, dinner after the theater. This makes social sense—and not only for commuters and folk who live far from theaters. I've liked it ever since decades ago in Europe I found the joy of going to the theater on an empty stomach (juices not used to digest food) and dining at leisure later when hungry.

In the first act, the love story of my youth was spoiled by the leading lady who asked, "Is there any other love than sacred or profane?" I was tempted to shout, "Literary love." It started off stilted, with all the noble characters quite objectionable and all the evil ones attractive. I'm sorry the author—far to be preferred to Fry—submerged the incest theme. How does man cope with sordid problems if they are only insinuated? But it's too good a story to be spoiled and as it goes on it gets better.

I first read the story of Heloise and Abelard, I think in Stephen Phillips blank verse, fifty-two years ago. It was during my first and hence greatest reading jag. I love the emphasis of a jag. In one month, with the needle of Lew Perry, my teacher, I read all the plays of Ibsen, Shaw, Henry Arthur Jones, Pinero, etc., and the great love stories. Some day I'll look at the old library cards if there're still there. I remember the alcove to which, in my suppressed adolescence, I hied with a volume instead of a girl. Nothing but a girl or a substitute for a girl could have produced such a drive. It didn't have anything to do with giving birth—which I have experienced in later years. To finish at the lathe in the shop makes eating meals unimportant, to sail against a stronger tide or wind makes me kill the physical need for sleep, to be in the middle of inventing a legal theory to bail out a client's misery makes me deaf to the noise, telephones or even the most telling of sounds—the call of my own name.

Reading in bed. Over 1300 people tested on ESP; on a run-through of cards, 1200 give one clear conclusion, which I welcome: subjects who believe in ESP achieve scores consistently higher than chance and still higher than the disbelievers. The Schmeidler study separates the "sheep" from the "goats." The difference in scores is slight but gives additional proof that faith can move cards if not mountains.

Sunday, September 28

All predictions were for bad weather, but it's just perfect for fall. Rented a Hertz car. Silly to own a car in Manhattan—no place to park and impossible to drive. Off to Nathan and Helen Straus's* at their Quarry Lake home for lunch. They are good—a simple word, only four letters. In the Oxford dictionary there are fifteen columns on *good*. The original meaning of the root, suitable for any use, is, among others, "to bring together." About a dozen other guests at their gracious

* *Owners of radio station WMCA.*

and elegant home. I did not know till Maggie told me on the way home that none of the guests knew each other or, save us, the Straus's. It's part of a hospitality program for UN officials. Most enjoyable—New Zealand, Holland, France, Japan, Denmark represented. Peter and Ellen* were my main delight—a couple who for a decade have seen government service abroad and in Washington. They are dominant in one of the city's biggest and most dignified parishes—radio station WMCA. What a responsibility—to have access to a million minds, twenty hours a day. I told them it is a bigger audience than that of any cleric, even of Cardinal Spellman.

Much talk about Little Rock. As usual, few knew that many schools have been integrated within a hundred miles of Little Rock. My real irritation was with the reporting of the election news from L. R. The way it was carried in all media, people failed to realize that only a minority of L. R. voters were really steamed up on the issue. Interpreting the stay-at-home voter, I conclude that less than a third of the total population feels strongly against integration. What a difference it would have made if the headline writers had seen this side of the medallion. I'll check the final figures tomorrow, if the press is still interested in the vote.

Drove back along Bronx River Parkway—less crowded, slower, more beautiful, curved and rolling than the efficient thruways. Efficient for what, we always ask.

Stopped at Bronx Botanical—almost all closed off although only five thirty. Odd, we thought, as Sunday is a day set aside for play. Water lilies and dahlias were worth seeing. Much better than the shabby flower ex-

---

* *Mr. and Mrs. Peter Straus.*

hibition in Moscow, more elaborate and less intimate
than the indoor show in Vienna a couple of years ago.

Looked for an outdoor restaurant on the highway.
None such—until we got to our neighborhood. This
and the absence of bookstores must bewilder the people we lunched with; also the size of our cars. It's my
guess that this year Detroit is in real trouble. Many
people will think that the model for 1960 will be small,
sensible, novel and popular—so why not hold off for a
year. Maybe the Madison Avenue advisers have not paid
enough attention to the desire of our people for a ve-
hicle designed for transporting people rather than estab-
lishing social castes.

Monday, September 29

These days at the office are full of drama, challenges and excitement. Unfortunately the stories that
come over my desk do not belong to me and cannot be
put even in a sealed diary. The public gets only a squint
at that part of law that appears in the courtroom, and
the press for some odd reason has never realized that
the great stories of love and hate, of passion and design
are often resolved outside the courts. My desk and the
chair opposite are a stage set for life in the raw. Hence
I feel no constant need for the theater or for reading
fiction or seeing movies.

Lunch with Herb and Eddie. What a threesome.
With L. S. G. we were the most incongruous quartet
ever to start a partnership at the bar. Not one of us
would be able to say for sure if we were held together
by differences or likenesses. But with one thing I'm content—the essence of the endurance was attested to for

more than a score of years: we never had a written partnership agreement. Not until court decisions made it
awkward for inheritance-tax computations did we provide instruments such as we demanded for our clients.
This isn't as perverse as it sounds. The best of relationships need no writings. Among people of honor, documents are needed only to support memory.

In late afternoon, to meet John La Farge, whose new
book comes out shortly. I rather think that this year's
writings of eminent Catholics will help reduce the gap
between Roman Catholics and others in our society. A
spate of such books seems to me to be less rigid and
adamant than I expected. Above all, they *invite* debate.
I don't understand why so few of my friends don't know
that the Catholic official position permits family limitation, sterilization and abortion under certain defined
conditions. If this were known in our culture, the debate could proceed to discuss the defined permissible
areas, and the philosophy underlying the—to me—still
ill-defined exemptions. Incidentally, in Anchorage,
Alaska, a Citizens' Advisory Committee on Literature
has been appointed by the Mayor. This committee is
to make clear the dangers of censorship. But, I ask, are
the dangers the same in cold, dark climates as at the
equator? Surely the long, dark seasons in Scandinavia
must have had an impact on the sexual desires and fears
of its people. How else explain the "advanced" positions on illegitimacy (practically freed of stigma),
avowed premarital sexual intimacies, condonation of
the use of contraceptives, etc.?

As we were reading in bed, Maggie mentioned that in
Lindermann's Daughters she read that as far back as
the eighteenth century Norwegian boys and girls engaged to be married lived together sexually. Isn't it odd

how we are inclined to believe that new knowledge implies a basis of recent events? The Scandinavian sexual folkways in the last half century have been made to appear as a recent development. I imagine that this updating is to save us the scar on the ego resulting from having to admit that our previous knowledge was incorrect or inadequate. Maybe this is an explanation also for the Soviet claim of all man's prior inventions.

Tuesday, September 30

I looked in my left-hand office-desk drawer. It's nearly empty. Maggie must go to Shackman and restock.

My only memories from going down to my father's Liberty Street office about sixty years ago are a letter press—still the best duplicator—and a supply of rubber bands, clips and pencils I was allowed to take home with me. These were great treasures, the right size for my age, workable and, above all, from the adult world of my father. They were not meant to be toys and hence were good toys—they were part of life. As a present for Nicholas when he was about three, Connie and I made a board to which I attached a hinge, a latch, a cord, a door knob and several other little pieces of apparatus that children see and scarcely comprehend. These tidbits were all usable in real life, and they belonged to Nickie alone.

Today the six- and nine-year-old kids of one of the lawyers came to the office and were brought in to see my treasure drawer. For thirty years the left-hand top drawer has been kept stocked by Maggie with toys for visiting kids—make-believe money, crayons, marbles, cards, models of autos, airplanes and other small toys.

Each child of a client or member of the staff rushes for the trove. Each must go through the painful period of decision. He can take two or three things, but is urged to look over the field before making his final selection. It's been fun watching the different types of affirmation, indecision or even return for change of mind. Most of the kids will never learn that indecision is the greatest five minutes to decide the brand of whiskey or flavor of killer of energy known to man. Some of my friends take ice cream. And more often than not, any decision is better than none. I have seldom fretted over any decision and no doubt have made more than my full quota of mistakes, but I still doubt whether my percentage of mistakes would have been appreciably reduced had I pondered the pros and cons of my decisions. It occurred to Penelope that the other great destroyer of energy—regret—may be peculiarly a characteristic of people who suffer from indecision. This I first fully appreciated when, during the F. D. R. administration, we were so often at the White House and saw the President and the First Lady, two affirmatively decisive people, argue and differ on big and little issues, with a decision reached with little left hanging in the air. Any decision is often better than none.

H. S. T. was so right when, as Chief Magistrate of our republic, he put on his desk a sign reading, "The Buck Stops Here." Maybe each of us in our own way should use a tiny replica of that symbol.

OCTOBER

Wednesday, October 1

Once more I have something to report to the U.S. Government—the results of my gull experiment. For eleven years we have hung a dead gull at the end of our pier. Copying this stunt from the Maine coast fisheries, we found we could keep the gulls off the pier —thus we didn't have to trample on the shells they dropped to extract the food, not to mention the excretion, which by September looked like a coat of whitewash on the walk and float.

It had occurred to me that I might work out a kind of antidecoy gull. If man can attract ducks by wooden replicas, maybe a stuffed gull or a wooden model would do the reverse trick. After dry rot and rust, gulls are one of man's greatest nuisances, even at times a burden. My taxidermist promptly showed his horror at my suggestion that he stuff a gull. "It's illegal to kill a gull without a permit!" Hence my elaborate correspondence with Uncle Sam. I'm still thwarted, because I'm not sure what keeps the gulls away. I'm told gulls have no sense of smell. Is it the sight of a dead one? Does it make a difference if the antidecoy is long dead? Hung by the neck or the feet? What of sex? age? color? species?

I spoke about the problem to one of my favorite sailors, Al Stanford, who admitted that he was also plagued by gulls. He is running a similar, equally successful experiment on his dock at Milford Harbor on the Connecticut shore. Do these animals have innate memories of death? As far as I know, they don't go off in solitary fashion, one by one, when about to die, as is the myth about elephants, exaggerated into that entrancing imaginary forest in Africa where all elephants are supposed to go to die, promising vast profits in ivory. Incidentally, toward the end of a summer the young generation of gulls *will* drop shells on the pier. Maybe they have not accumulated a memory of death sufficient to scare them off. Next year I will try my dead gull in a familiar standing posture. I must go to Muskeget Island, too, the isle of the gulls where the population increased at such a pace that helicopters now spray the eggs to kill off a part—as if man could ever keep nature in tune by killings.

Man accents death by celebrations: music to scare away devils in Chinese funerals, Jewish marches in zigzag patterns so that the demon can't follow. To Catholics in Spain processions are so important that Protestants and Jews—of whom there are fewer than 100,000 —are not allowed to have street processions.

Margaret can talk to flowers, our theosophist friend Mrs. Sellen could detect the cauliflower at the grocer's that had the most recent reincarnation, Maxo Vanka* whispers to birds who live in his vest pockets, like St. Francis who had no vest. Somebody—probably the daughter of a fisherman—can interpret gulls for me. Maybe we can get the answer in our garden. We have

* *Nephew-in-law, Yugoslav-born painter.*

a cowbird, brought up by a song sparrow. The cowbird loves people and doesn't like birds. It comes into our house, follows people around, takes toast out of Maggie's mouth. And why not? There are people who love cats or dogs or birds more than they love men and women. For me, I'm all for people—not all people, but all who can articulate. Babies bore me very quickly and I'm nervous and uncomfortable with them. Bad upbringing?

Friday, October 3

Abel Green, the boy-wonder editor of *Variety*, once again asked me to write a piece for his January anniversary issue. Last year I wrote a formula for ending the wasteful suit against Broadcast Music, Inc.: preserve competition for ASCAP, expand the market for music lovers and get the networks out of the music-owning licensing business—a business they were ill-advised to go into. Abel refused to run my piece, which I had written in good will. I forgave him at lunch when he couldn't explain his timidity, and this year I sent him a series of suggestions for a cultural utopia. Some day I may expand each of the items, and another score that I have in mind, into a book.

I might as well incorporate the piece into my diary—then I'll be able to find it in the future, if I want it:

This is the time of year when people make what they call "resolutions." What they are really doing is editing their dreams and ambitions. Only old men have ever written utopias, because they alone know that dreams are potent makers of history. I thought I would jot down very briefly a few of my dreams, all easily attainable, to help the culture of the people of our Republic:

1. Let's get on to subscription television. This may be an instrument of value in the race between quality and quantity. At least let's allow Zenith and others to gamble their millions to see if the experiment will find favor with the American people.

2. Half a century ago we decided that no railroad could own a coal mine, and now we won't let a railroad own an airline. Let's divorce the radio networks from the television networks. Anyone but the present owners can make real money out of radio. The present owners cannot do so because the top radio management looks across the hall at television and says: "*There* is the field of gold." Just look at radio personnel turnover.

3. Let's divorce ownership of radio and television from newspaper and movie ownership. This is particularly important in areas where the same person owns all the radio stations and newspapers. Democracy depends on diversity of opinion.

4. Why should we allow newspapers to own their source of newsprint supply? What a cruel, unfair market this creates, particularly vis-à-vis the dominant position of Canada on newsprint.

5. Why shouldn't we abolish all tariffs on First Amendment materials—books, movies, etc.?

6. Can't we break up the big museums in metropolitan centers so that, with many branch museums, artistic wealth can circulate into the local areas which comprise each big city? The big museums, moreover, might ride circuit with their art to the towns presently starved.

7. We should prepare at once for the evil day when Russia joins the copyright convention, since under that odd document Russia may join only to *prevent* the publication, for seven years, of its technical books in

English in our land.

8. With very little persuasion the censorious groups, which are mainly Roman Catholic, might shift their censor activities from a negative to an affirmative approach. We should help them shift so that they will tell people what to see, to read and to hear. They might enjoy the comfort of affirmation instead of negation.

9. Let's hope that some foundation will make studies to find out what causal relationships, if any, exist between the publication of obscenity or sadism and human behavior.

10. The government might well examine the injury to the market place of talent through concentration of power in two entertainment agencies which in the main control talent and operate in many cases with conflict of interests.

11. Bar associations should explore the illegal practice of the law by lawyers in the offices of the big talent agencies, and at the same time re-examine the position of the bar in relation to lawyers whose primary function is to act as entrepreneurs and agents for talent.

12. With Alaska our forty-ninth state, we have a chance of developing sufficient water power to use those vast forests to increase our paper supplies for books, magazines and newspapers.

13. How long do we have to carry the absurdity of a tariff on paper used for magazines and books, while newsprint comes in free of duty?

14. Let's reduce the international postage rates so as to add to the spread of our culture. All international mail should go by air, but the subscriber or reader throughout the world should pay only the modest postage rates required for transmission by boat and train.

15. Why shouldn't copyrighted material, a form of

governmental monopoly grant, get the same capital-gains advantages as are now lawful for any useless gadget patented under our monopoly patent laws?

16. When will the FCC come to grips with the philosophical problem of whether a license to stations—and thereby indirect licensing of networks—does not create a duty on the networks to invent and control the programing, rather than abdicate programing to the advertising agencies and sponsors.

17. Is there no way of creating public pressure so that the prestige symbols of the networks shall not be limited to guns and Jayne Mansfield's breasts?

18. Since the book trade, unlike any other industry, consciously helped abolish its retail outlets by supporting book clubs, can't we use our remaining eight thousand weeklies as cultural outlets for books in small towns?

19. The magazines of our nation are granted vast subsidies. Last year *Time* magazine got over twenty million dollars from the U.S. taxpayers by way of postage subsidy. Shouldn't we give greater subsidies to the small and new ones, and maybe provide that after a magazine has a circulation of one or two million it might stand on its own feet without further subsidy from taxpayers?

20. Our tax law should be reappraised. At the moment all entrepreneurs are given great tax advantages. Surely discrimination against creative people and other performers in the sports and entertainment field—writer, painter, opera singer, baseball player, etc.—should be abolished.

21. In the field of music, the networks should trustee or otherwise dispose of their stock in BMI, at which time the million-dollar annual drain arising from the

present litigation would be reappraised, and with good will we will approach a settlement for the benefit of the *users* of music.

22. There is a myth in the U.S. that we have lost a thousand dailies and five thousand weeklies because communities cannot economically stand the cost of competing papers. All that I ask on this score is that the misguided who subscribe to that myth should take a look at Nantucket Island which has two competing weekly papers serving a winter population of only 3500 without unbearable economic burdens on readers or advertisers. If anyone is really interested, he can there see how competition enriches the market place.

I could add another score of suggestions. I am persuaded that our leadership in the world depends on what we do to encourage the creation and diffusion of knowledge. Creative people have the best and most dramatic lobby in our nation; any time that they want to be imaginative and daring, they can lead us to a spiritual revolution.

Saturday, October 4

October in New York is like June in England. Town a little on edge because of third game of world series. And still a resentment is evident—why should Greater New York have been so dumb as to lose the Dodgers and the Giants? I hope this means that the people hold in disdain the owners of these properties, who had so little local pride that they ran out for a little more profit.

The danger of figures is evident everywhere, not only in legal documents. Three times as many tornadoes per year are recorded between 1950 and 1956 as in the years from 1916 to 1950. The way this is reported, the reader might infer there is a basic change in weather. Not so, I imagine. Maybe just better recording, plus a changing definition of "tornado." The cancer figures are given to us in similar shocking form. What did they call cancer in my youth? Ditto for insanity. Only recently have low-income groups been included in much of our statistical knowledge. Aunt Millie, just plain nuts, still roams a village street, hurts no one; in a big city most likely she would be considered a nuisance and be put away as a statistic, if for no other reason than that the family is crowded into an apartment or, if it has plenty of space, is rich enough to buy a sanitarium room to be relieved of a nuisance which embarrasses the family. So I really resent figures, particularly those from Africa, India and all backward nations.

I'm also cynical about factual material handed out to our people. The Truman election in 1948 was a good example. All polls and prophecies were wrong, yet no one *wanted* to be in error. Thus we should worry, because, if we continue to pump into our minds vast errors, we will surely develop cynicism to such a degree that no one will be willing to die for Freedom of the Press. Correcting this becomes increasingly difficult. If we had enough competing papers and radio and television stations, the very competition would in time create its own corrective. But we have lost a thousand dailies, and have only three significant radio and television networks. And in the main each publisher thinks it is ungentlemanly to mention the error of his competitor. Maybe this diffidence derives, not from manners, but from fear that one's own mistakes will in turn be picked up by a competitor. In the days of the Founding Fathers, editors went out and horsewhipped each other. Maybe even that would be preferable to our market place with its decreasing diversity and a monopoly of silence on errors in all media. If someone got out a sheet of daily errors of fact, there would be no way of distributing this information to the public. Maybe some day one radio station will think it good business to do a daily fifteen-minute broadcast listing important mistakes. CBS tried it once for a brief time. The story of the pressure for its discontinuance might make a good tale for *Harper's* or some such gazette. A worthy, honorable paper should encourage such a program—a kind of Inspector General of the press—conducted preferably by some anonymous reporter.

The conviction of Marie Torre of the *Herald Tribune* has been upheld on appeal. She rested on the valuable privilege of a reporter or author not to divulge her source. The issue arose in an irrelevant case; Torre had made reference to material that Judy Garland thought important in order to sue CBS. I do hope the case goes to the Supreme Court. I'm sorry our professional relations with the *Times* precluded me from accepting an invitation to join in the case. But the issue was not fully exposed by the Torre-*Herald Tribune* attorneys. What about Reston who got the Yalta papers, what of the leak on the Gaither report, what of the significant jobs done by Drew Pearson—including his recent alerting the public to the Adams-Goldfine mess? Some day the reporters who get these leaks may be called before congressional committees, refuse to squeal and go to jail. The Restons, the Torres, the papers *et al.,* are unimportant. I would have loved to argue the case for the only important client

—the market place of knowledge. How can biography or history be written if there is the danger of having to divulge sources? It's all another aspect of the ethical problem of squealing, tattletaling—otherwise called Fifth Amendment—sophistries.

Sunday, October 5

Maggie fixed the breakfast. Her art of making a dish of eggs and chicken livers is of a high order. Chicken livers are as difficult to prepare for individual tastes as are boiled eggs. Grabbed the Sunday papers; Reston and Alsop gave us real joy. Their techniques have no similarity, but they stand out as reporters who have strong feelings and care about our nation and its welfare.

Musicians in the square. Not one big orchestra, just half a dozen spontaneously created groups, each with four or five bongo drums and guitars, and an audience. Where else can this be found in Manhattan?

Saw the fourth world series baseball game on TV. Dull as cricket. The announcing could take place only in our culture. Every player is described in detail. His place of birth—who knows where the Vice-President or any senator was born? Warren Spahn's age is made an asset, and every statistic is put into favorable perspective. "Joe Zilch—his thirty-second appearance as a world-series player—the only one of this record who is six feet one and weighs only a hundred seventy-two pounds." The kindly intimacy of the historian-announcers is a virtue we might try to use in our appraisal of college presidents, mayors, scientists and artists. We must make other occupations of societal value as glamorous and intimate as we do those of athletes.

Saw Aga Khan IV on television, and a grand impression he makes. I am a great admirer of his father, and help him whenever he calls on me; and I have been worried because our people are so unable to understand that he and his father could work hard as well as play hard. Few of our citizens do both—so we are not ready to believe that anyone who plays much and hard can also be a great force by great effort for the common weal. Aly* at the UN in one year, I think, has done much to educate our people on this score. Maybe just because he enjoys horses and sport he is peculiarly able to speak the language of the average man and thus be effective in his effort to bring peace to Pakistan, and educate us as to the real conflicts between India and his country. In time our nation may develop some citizens who can play and still be something besides playboys. So far I can think of none such.

At Seafare on Eighth Street for dinner. At next table an inviting-looking young couple; we chatted. People *are* friendly. He was on his way to Berlin as architect for a U.S. hospital. They were obviously from the deep South. Montgomery, in fact. Important—they had been to Uniontown, Ala., which I have not seen since 1890. They made the town of my birth seem gracious and civilized—ante-bellum houses, one main street, population around five thousand. I guess we will have to go there in the spring—then we can compare it to Maggie's Natchez.

Wandered around our dear streets, saw the lights were on at the Katz's† and so dropped in to hear their usual story of disaster in a small sailboat. Some day they

* *Prince Aly Khan.*
† *Joel Katz, attorney, and wife.*

will become humble toward the power of wind and wave. They have still to learn the need for precision and care in dealing with nature.

When, oh when does anybody find time to look for answers to all the exciting questions that flood one's mind? Electric felt beneath a carpet will create, I'm told, a floor temperature of about 75 degrees Fahrenheit. Does moving furniture damage the heating element? Can you drive a nail through the carpet and felt? How does it feel if one goes barefoot, my usual home habit? Insects have waterproof covers to prevent their drying out. What makes the coating? Do all bugs have it? The butterfly doesn't look as if it had a plastic covering. At just what point from bug to bird does the danger of drying up the water content of the body disappear in relation to intake? Is the coating or veneer of different thicknesses in different climates? Is it true that water is the only liquid which becomes lighter when frozen? Do porpoises protect human life, or does the porpoise chase off the sharks without any deference or kind feelings for us folk? And so it goes by the dozen—all amusing and all proving my ignorance. For some years I had Marie to bat such questions to, and most often she would fetch back the answers.

A telephone service to answer all questions might be profitable at a modest fee, say twenty-five cents. The entire telephone system in our land has been less than imaginative on this level. I have been in cultures where you can call up and find out the lunch menus at schools. Call up and get the tuning-fork A for musicians in Vienna, the city of violins. Times of movies, concerts, etc., cost a call. If you want to practice stenography, you call a number and get so many words a minute. For race track news, you don't have to wait for the radio announcement. And the best of all—a fairy tale told to a child about to go to bed. All these amenities are yours in Vienna or Copenhagen by lifting your receiver and dialing a number.

Although radio does supply some of these services in our country, there are clear advantages to calling on the phone. You get what you want, nothing more, no waiting—and no commercial nonsense. Possibly all such services were denied to us because the telephone company originally owned a radio network. So much of the market is reduced in services by interlocking of interests or conflict of services!

Monday, October 6

While in the courthouse recently, I dropped into the courtroom when scores of aliens were being admitted to citizenship in our republic. What a tawdry mess. No dignity, much confusion and not a sign of our great spirit. We are a nation of immigrants—even though only thirty-five million people have come to our shores.

Here were some people who had fled to freedom and others who had made the difficult choice of giving up membership in nations to which they and their ancestors had been attached for centuries. A pedestrian speech by a bored judge, a tired clerk murmuring names, etc. What a chance our nation is missing! Don't tell me the United States of America can't set up an initiation ceremony as glamorous and impressive as the Elks or the Knights of Pythias or the B'nai B'rith. Have we lost our pride? Have we no sense of tradition? Does it take much imagination to say to an Alien: "I can imagine that to shift from Denmark [or any other free nation] to us took a lot of sober and painful thought. It is a tough decision. Of course you should keep up your folkways. Don't be pressurized by some of us who think the idea of a melting pot is to burn out all of your past— art, dance or song."

Tuesday, October 7

My daily ration of indignation was drained off early today when I reacted to an advertisement of nylon produced by the Chemstrand Company. The advertisement showed half a dozen good-looking young boys and girls with guns aimed at each other, with some silly legend such as "After the battle cools off, buy our nylon." Kill-shoot-destroy—these are the association images sold by some stupid advertising agency to a substantial American corporation. I wrote to the company and asked whether the president, who probably never saw the horror ad, had any children of his own and whether he insisted that they be conditioned to become delinquents or addicts of violence. When will the presidents of our great corporations stand up to Madison Avenue? I find little difficulty in getting my prejudices into the minds of big-business officials. They realize the need for quality as well as quantity with no necessity for inconsistency between the two. The top officers know that our corporate mores will deteriorate if the fiber of our people is made shabby by such ads.

Spoke to Harold Gardiner about the next meeting of Catholics, Protestants, Jews and nonadherents. We must go further with our program dealing with "affirmative" persuasion of youth with regard to books, radio, television and the press. Such diets cannot be controlled by negation. Caveats invite perverse curiosities. Surely such men as Edward R. Murrow, John Hersey, Dr. Karl Menninger, who have been at these meetings, can exercise leadership in the fight against vigilante attacks on newsstands and at the same time shame the networks and editors into some regard for the harm they are doing to the youth of our nation.

Looking out of my office window brings pangs. Even the East River, with its fierce currents and its despoiled shores, invites an urge for sailing on a day like this. And what a gem Manhattan Island was, and could have been at this very time! A curse on the short-sighted leaders who allowed our shore lines to be cluttered with dirty, indiscriminately planned buildings! Even the necessary docks could have been used to beautify our island. I recall Liverpool in 1905 and during World War II. It makes me sick at heart to remember Bergen, Stockholm or Oslo. Why couldn't we, with our vast acres, have retained the beauty of our gem of an island with its streams, hills and rare coastlines?

Alan Schwartz for dinner, and after dinner Peter and Ellen Straus. I envy this couple. Heirs to one of the important radio stations of the area, they have enough wealth and education to feel no compulsion to be cheap in their programs. We all agreed that ten years from now people will look back at radio fare in 1958 and be bemused and astonished. How could that generation stand for all that rubbish?

Cleo* is a joy. No matter how many extra for dinner, she always smiles. For nearly forty years we have always had agreeable help in the home. No relations are as important from day to day as are those with cooks, maids or nurses; and Maggie has a real knack—a waiting

* *Cleo Crawford, our cook.*

list of people who want to work for her. Someday I'll try to define this very special art.

Much good talk, but the emphasis always returned to the invisible power of the Central Intelligence Agency in our foreign policy. With Allen Dulles we are fairly safe, but who follows? If men were angels, there would be no need of laws. I didn't realize the size of the CIA —it needs a building bigger than the Pentagon. Then again, it fulfills a basically corrupt function—excusing, on the level of national interest, lying, cheating, etc., as with all secret-service agencies. I must get in touch with Senator Mike Mansfield, who has spoken about his concern with this secret, unsupervised arm of our government. Why not, suggests Ellen, a Senate watchdog committee, as over atomic energy, which operated without a leak. Spy we must in an era of Communist expansion, but how do we spy without having the spies corrupt themselves? Government officials who use wire tapping soon tap themselves down to the ethical levels of those they try to catch.

Mag* flew in from London today. Yesterday she had lunch with Connie in London.

Wednesday, October 8

Alan used the spare bed rather than go out to Jamaica. We worked on a short article for the monthly publication of the New York City Bar Association. Today a lawyer arrives from Goodie's† office in London. Dick Ader from our shop is already in London. This minor Fulbright exchange of lawyers will be exciting.

---

* My sister, Magdalen Stetten.
† Arnold Goodman, British solicitor.

If the bar had any imaginative leadership, fifty lawyers a year could be exchanged between New York City alone and the bars of other cultures. What better adult education for all the lawyers in our shop? Interviews are better teachers than books. As we wrote in the article, a few of the questions which we will raise are:

Why and how is it possible that in England the prosecutor turns over all evidence of innocence to the attorney for the defendant in criminal trials? How effective, in terms of our advocacy system, is this concerted attempt to get at the truth? How extensive is the protection of ideas against theft, as shown in recent English court decisions? How would this apply to protect ideas against mass-media pirating in the United States? What are the comparative virtues and dangers of having accountants mentioned in certificates of incorporation? To what extent does such practice convert these accountants from employees controllable by directors or officers into people who owe a duty only to the stockholders who hire and fire them? What is the history and practical effect of the general British practice of having no briefs in court? Would such a system work here? How do British barristers feel about the rule permitting unlimited time for argument? Could our bar be skilled enough to aid the court so that the judges, as in England, would render opinions on the close of the evidence and "off the bench"? What is the real basis for the separation of barrister and solicitor in England? Does it weaken the lawyer's relation to his client? And, if possible, would such a separation in this country help to resurrect the trial lawyer in our metropolitan centers? How does the treatment by the British bar of indigent defendants differ from ours? Finally, and perhaps most important, why do the leaders of the British bar have no hesitancy in representing, either in or out of court, the most unpopular of clients or causes? Surely here is something we could emulate with great profit to our prestige and power in the community.

Off to Si Rifkind's office to set up machinery for the operation of the Jerome Frank-New York University Law School Fund. After Jerry's death his friends gathered at Will R.'s* apartment at the Plaza. A majority grew sentimental and pedestrian; that sector raised money to give more comfort to Jerry's family, since he had used up his life's savings while in Washington in public service. A few of us—Rifkind, Schachner and I —wanted to do something typical of Jerry. We raised enough money to give awards each year to a policeman who did an outstanding job in behalf of civil liberties and due process. A kind of "man bites dog" episode. Today we activated the machinery for locating the recipient of this year's award. I hope that Ed Murrow will hand out the money and plaque to the winner; spurred on by such a ceremony, we may find, all police associations will make nominations in future years. We may even create new attitudes between cops and people. We heard of a police officer who came into a court out west to advise the judge that his testimony of the previous week was untrue—the policeman had learned that he had identified the wrong man as the robber. Wonderful and wonders! Great decency lies behind any public admission of error. Then, also, there is the police chief in the South who kept his head in a race riot, and the other one who reports to the federal government every complaint of violation of federal due process. We are all enthusiastic,

* *William Rosenblatt, banker.*

and even though Yale Law School rejected the project, despite Jerry's devotion to it, the New York Law School, under the leadership of Edmund Cahn, will do a great job.

Thursday, October 9

Once more today the point and counterpoint of news struck me as most dramatic. The Pope, a man of good will and peace, died. And I heard that Alvah Sulloway had finally arranged for Beacon Press to publish his great manuscript dealing with the theological shifts of the Catholic Church on family limitation. For possibly fifteen years I have tried to get him a publisher, but they were all timid. The worst turndown was when a publisher wrote that just because he was so strongly in favor of birth control he should, as a publisher, cancel out his personal predilections and therefore reject the manuscript. I then arranged, through Dr. Kiskadden, for Aldous Huxley to write a foreword. Out of the mouths and writings of Catholic theologians, Alvah has shown the ease and dignity with which the R. C. Church accommodates to life as life changes. Now Dr. Rock, a Catholic communicant, is the leader in the research for a contraceptive pill, and in Italy legislation is under debate to repeal the Mussolini birth-control laws.

Another item. I see fine buildings being torn down in our town. New and bigger ones will go up. This process raises hell with city budgets. When the population increases, new traffic, school, police, and street-cleaning burdens must be put into tax collections—without any direct contributions by the realtors who tear down and build, making new expenses necessary. Cities now control height and setback of new structures as well as uses of areas—homes, manufacture, business, etc. But now Penelope calls to tell me that a proposal is being developed in detail for permits to tear down buildings in certain sections of big cities. It's an extension of the historic-building controls of New Orleans, Nantucket, etc. A need for permits to tear down would at least give a pause and time for consideration and debate. This basic compromise between freedom and control by the sovereign states will continue to be a battlefield as cities and nations get bigger.

Then again, a new hurricane is coming up the coast, spelling destruction of homes and—still more important —of trees and soil. But in terms of counterpoint, I read in a British science magazine that by 1960 one million Boy Scouts in the U.S.A. will be engaged in saving trees, etc. Already six million trees, one million feet of hedgerows, half a million food-bearing shrubs have been planted by our youth. As a footnote, I see that 55,000 nest boxes have been erected. So we are doing more than holding our own. Voluntary effort, the best of human effort, does more than offset the ravages of nature.

In Si's office yesterday I saw a set of beautifully bound big volumes. It was the Talmud in Hebrew, financed by our Treasury, done in Germany—a form of PWA made-work for scholars unemployable after the last war. It's odd how often good comes from evil. From war, scholars benefit. City corruption often leads to beauty —note the Thompson regime in Chicago and the lake waterfront development, and we in New York got Central Park as a shrine during the corrupt days of Tweed. The only offset for graft is that political forces—taking off a little of the cream—need patronage and often leave society with social advances. Note excellent hospitals in Jersey City, erected under my friendly enemy, Mayor Hague.

Friday, October 10

Whenever I am at Joan and Irving's for dinner, my mind goes to the essential difference between the home of a totally deaf couple and the homes of hearing folk. The difference is equally acute if applied to the homes of people who have lost their hearing late in life. The latter are pervaded with suspicion and always show a lack of ease. But the deaf must treat their parlors with a different emphasis. Dancing outside of the home, though possible by getting the rhythm through the floor vibrations, is difficult. Hence, as little drive for dancing as for U.S. movies. Reading of books, surprisingly enough, is no passion for many of the scores of deaf couples we know. Long ago I thought of reading as a great outlet for Joan, but the mere burden of learning grammar and gathering a vocabularly is totally different from learning these tools by mimicry, as hearing people do. But the home is not only the core of the family, it's the social center. Joan thinks little of preparing and serving a meal for ten or twenty of her deaf friends. Although most of her friends have learned speech, conversation is usually by sign language. Why use sound when sight is more convenient?

Saturday, October 11

Leisurely day. If I remember leisure's history it means only "allowed." No compulsions. Catching up in office, lunch at Voisin's with Alan. Maggie comes up to join us for coffee. More anonymous telephone calls on Galindez case.

Plane with Maggie to Washington. Slept from the minute I got on till we landed. What a lucky guy I am to have this Churchillian knack of mental and physical refreshment by napping. I have a hunch that the more uncomfortable my posture is when asleep, the better the sleep. Is it because I must go deeper into the unconsciousness if all crunched up in a chair than on a downy bed? I'll ask Penelope if the psychoanalysts have any knowledge of the ability to recall dreams as related to comfort or habits of sleep. What of the Japanese who use wooden bolsters, or our children who use no head support until they follow the adult pillow habits?

Jean served her usual elaborate meal, we played with Debbie and David and after they went to bed we talked of dynamics of government officials and need for more daring if we are to lead the world, etc. Then to Roger's proposed move to a bigger house, which we will see tomorrow. No one should try to advise another family on the purchase of a *home*. Too many conflicting values involved—better house, private schools for kids, trips abroad, cooking and household help—all choices that cannot be appraised by remote control.

Then for the night at the delightful, peaceful Kenwood Club on River Road. I've never wanted to join a country club, but if I did this swankless place seems to show values not planted in ordinary conspicuous expenditure.

Sunday, October 12

One more proof that October is the month for the northeast sections of our nation: the leaves have turned as much here as in Westchester. Why, I don't know—maybe it only looks that way with fewer pines.

The news is full of the moon. Thus do our people who lack adventure live vicarious adventures. But there is surely a sorry element in the reporting: Russia shoots up its Sputnik and we go into jitters—the Soviet has the lead; now we go for the moon, so there is a presumption that we have taken the lead. This kind of competition is thoroughly invalid. The victories have little relationship to military superiority and certainly no relationship to the contributions of science to the enrichment of lives.

J. Donald Adams, in the *Times* book section, brings his engaging urbanity to bear on the consideration of the cultural renaissance in our land. This is the first comment of this kind I have read that takes the position I took in my *Utopia*. And Adams is low in his estimates —for example, he talks of only 160 symphony orchestras, whereas my figures showed around a thousand. But I welcome any rounding up of figures on cultural growth in book reading, painting, woodworking, etc. I recall how the Russian commissars were skeptical of my figures on cameras, etc., but took notice when I showed them that one fourth of all our homes had some kind of woodworking power tools, used, I told them, not only by fathers but by sons and daughters. The one fact that troubled them was the story of the sewing machine in our land. Many of the villages of Russia and the East have one sewing machine and a village tailor. "Singer" is our best Point Four propaganda. They were fascinated when I explained that in our high standard of living the sewing machine is no longer an instrument of need, as in my family in my youth, when little ready-made clothing was available. Now, I explained, it is a tool of art like the easel or the darkroom. The new machines with hundreds of contraptions are bought by upper-income women to create clothing of unorthodox and unique design. Russia and all of the East has not started to reach the stage of ready-to-wear clothing. Just as my mother, fifty years ago, sewed the nightgowns and the pillow cases, so Russia and the East are about fifty years behind us—and I assume I am right in the value judgment contained in using the word "behind."

Maggie wants to get me a new toilet bag for traveling. What a row. My old one has a hole in it, a small hole not big enough for razor or comb to fall through. Nix on the new. I love the old one. It is a friend. It understands me and forgives my oddities. I won't throw it away. I'd be embarrassed. It would be cruel. Maggie suggested I leave it in Nantucket for unexpected and occasional use. Of course not, it would be heartbroken as a relegated, second-best old relation put aside for an expensive, untried, stranger upstart. I think I won the debate and my friend of more than a decade will travel to England with me next month. Footnote: If our economy depends for survival on disloyalty to old friends like shoes and cars and bags, then let's go the whole hog and start a lot of fires—they also make work and keep the factories and mines busy. Moreover, what a silly world. There are no *new* cars except those in the showrooms. The minute I buy a new car it becomes second-hand.

Monday, October 13

Gray day. One of those grays that makes the world seem quiet and subdued. Two pleasant items. I heard of a parking lot that advertised, "No Cadillacs." They were too big and the lights were too likely to break. I enjoy man's daring to stand up to our cultural god—Gargantua. I also read that our Vice-President will not use Cadillacs in California because he does not want to give an impression of "affluence." Thus does the symbol of Cadillac work in its mysterious, conflicting ways. The other item is the idea that we should lend our atomic submarine to the World's Fair at Brussels. All we would have to do is to plug the lighting system of the Fair into the atomic-power supply and it would light the entire Fair—for free. This gave me the idea that a circuit-riding atom plant could be shipped to cities and towns that would then be hooked in for free power. Of course there are always problems implicit in giving away anything, just as butter to India hurts the dairy export business of Denmark. So here, which cities are to be preferred? Will the gift benefit the users of juice or only the utility stockholders? Such are the problems of plenty.

More evidence in press that in most of the world only a small percentage of the population has over 2500 calories daily. Surely these minorities must run their worlds—they are the only ones with enough energy to run anything. The historic problem: how does a backward nation stop its increase in population and also accumulate capital, when the only sources are the masses —undercaloried and hence incapable of creating capital?

Another item of good news. Bishop Mosley of the Protestant Episcopal Church declared that in the last half-century more than fifty mergers have taken place among non-Roman Catholic bodies.

After some private business with government agencies, I went to the Supreme Court. It's always a vibrant thrill to watch the judges walk in, usually on the dot of twelve, to hear the opinions spoken and observe the lawyers admitted to practice. I was interested in two cases—one which our office had pleaded for the Farmers Union, and the other the Costello case, concerned with a decade of wire tapping, bugging of his mail and the right of a prosecutor to examine the tax returns of all persons on the jury panel.

The acoustics are unbelievably bad, and I have for years regretted that Jefferson, in his zeal to drop patterns of our mother culture England, caused us to drop not only titles such as "Sir" but also special, colored clothes for our jurists. I enjoy and believe in the nonplebeian patterns of the Queen in her gold coach and horses driving to the opening of a Parliament in London. Ceremony as ceremony can have values even greater than statutes and regulations. It helps mankind to respect proper authority. What would Nehru be without his white Congress hat and his flower? The Supreme Court is a great court and has authority even though it has no army to enforce its decrees. It's a rare institution on our planet: authority by tradition.

Tuesday, October 14

It's interesting how my machine changes its rhythm. In town, though there is no conscious pressure to make me wake up on office workdays and even though most people come to work after nine thirty, I'm usually up and about at seven and at the office by nine. On Saturdays and Sundays I break the pattern and sleep later, and when I am out of town I not only sleep later but develop a reluctance to wake up and get up. So it was in Washington the past few days, and today a kind of hangover developed. I dozed until eight instead of being wide awake at seven. What power Old Man Unconscious has to create a series of irregular patterns of sleep and awakening!

Good news. Since what the courts decide affects millions of lives, and since most papers give the impression that courts are only engaged in trying divorce and murder cases, it was heartening to note the new kind of reporting of Supreme Court decisions. The *Herald Tribune* started its fine experiment of interpretative comment by thoughtful lawyers, and now the *Times* has done a brief summary—omitting the names of litigants—of the important issues accepted or declined for review, as well as discussing the opinions rendered. Of course it will take time before the gutter sheets will find news in anything but sex and sadism.

Many decisions relate to "color"—the problem of the century. Throughout history, white has been deemed good and black evil. Penelope suggested that this derives from the danger of darkness in the cave age and the joy of sunlight. And still there are deviations, such as in one place in Borneo where white skin is held inferior to dark skin. Maybe the first sight of a white man was frightening—just because it was unusual. But in Puerto Rico light-skinned people do not loll on beaches because of the danger of getting tanned.

Frank Calderone calls to tell me that his hydrofoil boat is in Puerto Rico. This excites me because—with reduction of friction—this big vessel can go forty-five miles an hour and carry food with such speed as to reduce man's dependence on refrigeration. Refrigerator boats seldom get to little islands and food for export cannot wait. F. C. knows the Caribbean, having cruised the waters in his great schooner, *Tradition*.

For drinks at "21" with Margaret Mahoney, a careful Carnegie Corporation gal. I think they are really excited about our national default—dissemination of knowledge. Our scholars are creating a deluge—much of the best financed by foundations that have had little concern with the diffusion of the knowledge. The book publishers, including the subsidized university presses, cannot individually afford to make a survey or experiment to find more readily the market for a particular book. The book section of *The New York Times* is the only effective tool for distribution. Advertising is pedestrian—but the publisher with the best reputation for cute and wise marketing makes little, if any, profit on his ordinary trade-book sales. The organization bails itself out by profits on children's books and subsidiary rights, such as movies, television, etc. I have yet to hear of a foundation that finances the creation of knowledge inquiring in advance how the publisher proposes to hit his target. A good example of the debacle is *How to Get Better Schools,* a book by David Dreiman with a foreword by Roy Larsen. Written by a skilled popularizer, distributed by Harper's—none better—and practically no sales. No one really studied the 45,000 school boards and 10,000 PTA's and other audiences assumedly literate and interested in the problem. Books are the historic instrument for enduring values in our culture. The increase of sales of books is heartening—but all too fortuitous and haphazard. Any foundation could finance a survey and invent new techniques for a great expansion of book reading in our nation.

Wednesday, October 15

Spent hours digging into the scandal that touches quiz shows. Unlike the ordinary procedure of District Attorney Frank Hogan's office, much of this scandal gets into the daily press. I imagine we cannot stop witnesses from talking, and maybe we should not want to do so. I have little doubt that the quiz shows have been as phony and lacking in high standards as is much of network television. Whether a crime has been committed should await determination by some court. But, unfortunately, acting as scared and guilty men, the dominant persons in the networks have run for cover, at times discharging competent personnel even before an indictment, and on no occasion taking a firm position to rebuild some degree of faith in network operations as such. I hope the FCC will explore this form of rigging of the market—even assuming that the behavior involved proves to be less than a penal offense.

Now I become concerned with the competition of U.S. oil companies in the Near East oil fields. I wonder if our oil companies can afford—for the free world— to engage competitively across the table against any single government-owned agency. This is the difficult position freedom is in when dealing with statist nations. Our competition breaks the market to the advantage of the dictator—or any government-owned operation.

To the opening hockey game with the Austin Fishers. Loyalty is important in professional contests. We have stuck by the Rangers for twenty years—and mostly been stuck. But no hockey game is a loss because of the beauty and the grace of the skating. Furthermore, I do drain off some sadism when a real fight takes place; I'm amused at the men and women who never stop giving instructions to the players or yelling at the referee. And there is Gladys Goodings, who since man can remember has played the organ and sung the national anthem. After the game, out to dinner—wonderful to eat when really hungry, which is late at night.

Thursday, October 16

The bus going uptown in the morning is civilized, in the evening it's obscene. Once on a crowded evening bus a driver took out his irritation by saying, "Will the more intelligent passengers move to the rear of the bus?" This bit of rational thinking created a stampede. This A.M. I entered the empty bus to the office. It's like a small town or a club car. I often meet the same friends.

Downtown to lunch with Russell* for my fortnightly refresher. I wish I knew the origins of his wisdom. Maybe the rejection of the less important. I doubt if Russell has a television set or listens to the radio. Years

---

* *Russell Leffingwell, formerly a leader of the bar and now a member of Morgan Guaranty Trust Co.*

ago I wanted to send him the records of the Churchill-Roosevelt speeches—only to find he had no phonograph. But he has a vast library and is a poet at heart, and he knows that all real poets are perpetually in love, a fact that makes their letters or autobiographies inviting.

What a pocketful of ideas I garner whenever I am with R. L.! Endless new approaches to old problems must be played with. The financial market is increasingly dominated by the shift from individual ownership of securities to pools such as investment trusts, union funds, etc., added to the traditional portfolios of insurance companies, savings banks, etc. Will not the relegation of individual power to a position of practical impotence lead to increased government control—whether wise or not—over all such funds? On quite another topic, what value has the rule of privilege as to communication between lawyer and client if people are tried in the press and not in the courts?

Roger telephoned that he bought his new house; he also told me when he and Jean would cruise the Maine Coast with us next summer. So I'll try to charter a Controversy and range the Penobscot—that hundred-mile area with hundreds of harbors—from July 15 to August 15. That's worth living for during the intervening months.

Saturday, October 18

Beautiful day, too warm for me to wear my new cashmere overcoat. Too bad since, although I think I like my old clothes best, I always want to wear new ties, suits or coats as soon as they arrive. Maybe one of my dislikes is the very act of purchasing. I know I hate to shop, feel bad, in fact, if I have bothered a salesman and then walked out without buying anything. I ain't no shopper. In fact, Maggie has always bought all my haberdashery. I am not to be trusted to buy even a tie. And as to socks or shoes or shirts, I buy identical ones by the half dozen. Maybe my clerkophobia comes from disgust long ago when important friends, men of the theater and arts, shocked me by yelling at waiters. I'm scared of store-keepers except in bookstores or art galleries—the two most frightening types of tradesmen to most Americans who live away from Eighth Street where such emporia are village centers.

Swapping headlines with me in bed this morning, Maggie suggested that our great nation might invite the UN to give us ideas on how to solve our color prob-lem. The objections to the idea are many, including that few of the UN nations are without their own bigotries and the nations of the East are far behind us in even a campaign for racial and religious equality. And still something might be done along Maggie's line in order to reduce the international evil results of Little Rock.

From bankers and industrialists to chat with Frank Costello before he goes to jail. I shall continue to believe that he was tried in the press and that the law made in cases such as this one is bad law and will have to be reversed—wire tapping, mail bugging, hearsay evidence for indictment, decitizenship standards, etc. etc.

The attack on Carmine De Sapio in the press is get-ting out of bounds. No details—just a cry of *"Kamerad"* by the press supporting Rockefeller as a Rockefeller, and not as a Republican.

I must get others to join in a letter to the press along the following lines:

Political freedom depends on a two-party political

system. With only one party, people have dictatorship and with many parties they have chaos that leads to dictatorship. It is unfortunate that in our culture the owners of mass media of communication, and in the main people who make public opinion, spend little or no time in the support and development of political parties. Naturally, therefore, in part out of a sense of guilt, they must look with disdain on those citizens who take political party-organization work as a serious responsibility. Outside laggards, in which group I include myself, have little right to complain if there are shortcomings in our political parties. Party government is entirely unrelated to the final fanfare of a Madison Square rally. Absolution of guilt should not flow even from money contributions during the campaign. As is so often the case, real trends in our culture can be discerned by phony and false symbols used by our people. For a time we stigmatized all those engaged in the financial markets of our nation under the disparaging term of "Wall Streeters." We might attack the false values of advertising agencies in better ways than by the isolated tag, "Madison Avenue." In our own community we have discouraged thoughtful young people from joining political party affairs by calling the head of the Democratic organization a "boss," even though the active head of the Republican organization is called the "leader." All of which leads me to observe the total indiscriminate unfairness of the attacks on Carmine De Sapio. The attacks are, to my knowledge, never accompanied by a bill of particulars—the simplest of the steps known as "due process."

We are faced with a bit of dishonorable irony in our political life. It is good and right and proper that Mr. Rockefeller should try to persuade the political leaders of his party to endorse his ambition to be a candidate for governor. It would be arrant nonsense to suggest that Averell Harriman, with a similar worthy ambition, should be so stupid as not to try to get the support of the political leaders of his party. In the absence of issues, we find the mass media increasingly supplying their default with the word "boss" for Carmine De Sapio. It would be just as cruel and indecent to talk of Boss Reid, Howard or Sulzberger, or—in another field—Boss Blough of U.S. Steel or Boss Curtice, formerly leader of General Motors. I wish your paper would set this issue straight, so as to encourage greater participation, particularly by young men and women, in the political-party life of our community—a life that the wealthy and those with social prestige have seldom explored and still more seldom aided.

Sunday, October 19

This is one of those days that dilute me. Personalities have their edges removed by rare temperatures and lights. It's the opposite of lunacy—sunacy. A great day for an expedition for Nicholas. Off we went in Alan's perfect Morris car to the hills of Suffern to dine at the new Japanese motel. All the Nippon architecture and décor show the diminutive stature of the people. Typically Japanese dwarfed trees and low ceilings were adapted by the architect to get U.S favor, and still there was respect for what is seen below the eye level more than for what is seen above. Also delightful use of fast-growing bamboo, which we fail to raise, not to mention the sensory pleasures of rice paper. Both are too simple for us, I suppose. Any relation of height and slanted eye to the written language, which is vertical?

I have long had a hunch that the early Jews (as even today) had a dominant strain of left-handedness since they wrote, convenient for the left hand, from right to left. And what of the Latins who alternated the lines left to right, and then right to left, and no doubt had many cases of mirror writing? Is there some writing on astigmatism in relation to art? El Greco—long, tall people; Rubens—horizontal as to his bosomy ladies; and our own Thomas Hart Benton, as if his astigmatism were extremely up and down, and wavy.

Monday, October 20

At lunch I sent Jack Jessup of *Life* magazine, an ardent Civil Libertarian, a note that I would like to do a piece on the migration of animals. Storks go from Africa to Jerez in Spain to nest, eels to the Sargossa Sea, salmon beat out their genital organs to go back up the Columbia River to hope to spawn, elephants to secret places to die, etc. A world migration map of animals would be amusing to ponder. How dissimilar to man's migration—to the west for centuries. And, as Karl Marx already wrote around 1850 when he was a London correspondent for the *New York Tribune*, we in our land would not realize the extent of the westward migrations of man and would bottle up these people on our eastern seaboard. This is just what we did—with the result of disequilibrium and cultural concentrations. In fact, this prophecy of Marx is one of his few correct guesses, even to the point where he estimated that a million people would migrate to our shores at the turn of the twentieth century.

For dinner with Loths* and Lena Levine† at Nicholsons on Fifty-Seventh Street. It's attractive in the sense that it has the modest overdecoration of an old-fashioned bordello—unintentionally, I assume. Good food and good people with a sober concern for the trends in our society. Lena is a wise psychiatric counselor and Dave is the best popularizer I know. They both seek quality and have pride in their work. They point up the difference between "work" and "labor."

Our Advent cards arrived from Zurich. I'm not sure I like the business aspects of Yuletide, but if cards are to be sent at all they might as well not be pedestrian and like all others. Maggie still uses for memo paper the cards we received last year. It's neat. We get a second chance at remembering the sender and a retake of the pleasure that personal messages on cards gave us last year. In addition, they make excellent paper for notes to Cleo, or between us or for recording telephone messages or making out marketing lists.

I just located one of the real sources of *The New York Times* science stories—it's my favorite magazine: *Science News Letter.*

Tuesday, October 21

Hurrah, just heard that in Japan the main supports of the Civil Liberties Union are the newspapers. Why not in our culture? The main enemy of individual freedom in Japan is authority, an understandable situation because in that culture, except in relation to those in power, people adjust relationships graciously by the

---

* *David Loth, coauthor of books with me, and his wife.*
† *Dr. Lena Levine, psychoanalyst.*

process of "saving face." In fact, all financial as well as emotional accounts are kept in balance, and one dies in debt only to parent, teacher and Emperor, the images of authority. Complete balance of accounts in other relationships makes it easy to accept the authority unquestioningly.

Lunch with Alan Collins*—one of those unusual Williams College graduates who has continued his education, attained a real cultural attitude with its necessary ingredients—the open mind and hobbies: keeping bees, selling honey, selling sensible wooden blocks for children. Our talk recalled to me the great impact James Harvey Robinson's *Mind In The Making* made on me decades ago. On reading this volume, I first learned of the growth of the mind. And now that we have learned the trick of making mind, we can continue to make more and more of it.

A day full of law practice, which is, stated in other terms, the clash of desires between different persons. Increasingly one "person" is government. This must be so as we find an increasing number of projects that man has decided can be better handled by the cooperative power of government than by private enterprise. This trend is not new: in 1776 fire departments were privately run for private profit; I once saw a broadside reading, "No money, no squirty." The oddity of our way of life is that the biggest advances toward government operation are urged by big business, and usually under Republican presidents. It was President Hoover who set up the RFC, that vast government bank whose early loans were to big business. Vice-President Dawes pulled down more than seventy million dollars for his bank in Chicago. It's my friend Henry Luce who sees

* *Literary agent.*

no irony in shouting against subsidies while the U.S. Treasury annually gives him more than twenty million dollars as a postal subsidy. And what of banks that would go broke in a free competitive market because of interest rates to borrowers or interest paid to depositors? A wise savings bank could pay four per cent on savings at certain times, and thus suck out all the deposits of neighboring institutions. Free enterprise can't afford such competition. And so it goes. When the financiers of the Cape Cod Canal lost money on the venture, all they did was to sell it to the U.S. government. Hundreds of such events, nullifying free enterprise, are generated by men who shout fiercely against the growth of governmental power.

In the evening, dinner at the Bar Association. Tonight the lawyers were gathered to appraise and endorse candidates for judgeships. The reports, debates and resolutions were amusing. They were equivalent to writing secret autobiographies. Totally impotent. No appreciable effect on the votes cast on election day.

But the meeting was a great compliment to De Sapio. Every nomination of the Democrats under the De Sapio leadership was endorsed by the Bar Association as "qualified." The Republican candidates were not all deemed qualified; anyway, Republican nominations have little relation to reality in this town.

Wednesday, October 22

What a joy when book critics are prompted to feel kindly toward an author and his book! This happened today in the reviews of Mark Van Doren's autobiography. I stopped at Doubleday's on the way uptown to buy it, and I am sure after years of warm friendship with Mark and Dot that we will have pleasure reading of his joy of living.

Another cheer we woke up to was the letter from Amman by Purchase in *The New Scientist* discussing "the sickness that never was." He referred to so-called "sunstroke." He writes about the lowest spot on the earth—1300 feet below sea level, with a thermometer usable only in Dante's Inferno. I always enjoy proof that established facts just ain't "facts." What a world if man could be taught to take little if anything for granted without trial and proof. The misery from "trial" will always be plenty, but certainly less than the immobilization of Man's mind resulting from human gullibility without scrutiny.

Women in the House of Lords in England. This is just, and I imagine will prove helpful. That body has great value since, like the House of Commons, it is a debating forum—the best in the world. Commons of course is in no way like our Congress. Members have no secretaries, no offices, ordinarily no chance to introduce their own bills and, above all, the opposition party has only the function of opposing. Its effect on legislation is either total on a vote of confidence or useful only as an argumentative backdrop. The debates add to wisdom and public knowledge. I have never seen any appraisal of the effect of the debates in the House of Lords on the position of the executive-legislative policies of the party in power. After all, the great powers in life are those that have the fewest sanctions. Our Supreme Court has no army to enforce its decrees. Hence it must rely on the higher power—the esteem of the people.

The day ends in a drizzle—the kind of quiet ceiling that one enjoys on the countryside where rain is just another thing and where rainwear is not a nuisance. Big cities create a different kind of rain, since this feat of nature must be coped with by crowded transportation and too few taxis. In New York few kids enjoy plastering their noses against window panes to see the drops. Rain is rain only if a kid can see puddles and think of the fun of mud oozing up between his toes. But we are lucky—our tree on the Square was full of happy drippings.

Read in Mark's new book. At least through college, his life was pleasant, but he scarcely gave me an impression of his strong feelings—loves or hates—and little of his drive or passion. He probably spent it all on Carl, his eminent historian brother—as who couldn't. Also heard a radio show, "The Hidden Revolution," which Ed Murrow narrated. It, too, had little iron—or, rather, too much of everything. It roamed too widely, giving me the feeling that the title—as with most titles—was pretentious. And I did so want it to be something new—not only because I'm a utopian, but because Ed must be taking quite a bit of pushing around at CBS. I'll bet the boys upstairs are torn—his new TV show, "Small World," is a hit. They need the dough, but are frightened when their predictions that only the tawdry makes money are proved false. They themselves prefer the vulgar, and so, naturally, must push it and insist that it alone pays off. I'd like a reading-habit survey of network and talent-agency executives. How many and what books or magazines do they read, unrelated to their business? It would be of interest if lawyers also could be interviewed on cultural habits.

Thursday, October 23

Woke up about two A.M. Not usual. Wide awake, I picked up the Van Doren autobiography and finished it with confused pleasure. I didn't hear Mark talking through the pages. He seemed to carry neither the shield nor the spear that in person make him such a good conversationalist. He can be so tartly humorous and so biting in conversation. In this book he is silent on all issues for which he has a deep concern—the education of his boys, his atttitudes—as a teacher—on quiz shows, censorship battles in which he has been a symbol of freedom, the Hiss conviction as related to his Whittaker Chambers episodes, etc. etc. He has another book in him about the Mark Van Doren who can and does get angry —and I don't mean loss of temper. For years Maggie and I used to wander in on Mark and Dot for coffee in the evening. For many years I was closely associated with *The Nation*. I looked for Mark's comments on the cause of the decline of *The Nation*. He must have wise clues, because he and Dot were deeply involved there for nearly a score of years. I have my own theory that, aside from O. G. V.* and Ernest Gruening, the editors were too insecure to write or publish any affirmative proposals to aid our society. They suffered from lack of chin—also

* *Oswald Garrison Villard.*

known as negativism—and hence had a following mainly of grumblers and "agin'ers." How else explain the impotence of all the so-called liberal gazettes? They didn't even rise in status and influence during what to them might have been a Rooseveltian band-wagon era, when people followed only men of hope.

I got Mimi* in for lunch. It's fun listening to alumni of our law office. They are more apt to give honorable adverse comments than while in our employ. She not only has a top legal brain but has carried on her two lives—marriage and law office—with a calm unknown to most women lawyers. She never tried to go up the ladder of this male profession by simulating masculine attitudes. She used, if that is the word, her own femininity. After she has finished breeding, she may return to the law. She will never be able to take up gin rummy or charity work as a total substitute. Thanks to Jerome Frank for sending her to us years ago.

Jan de Hartog† in from Europe. Off he goes again, touring the waterways of our land and writing about our people, their habits and folkways. This will be the best picture of our society since de Crevecoeur in his *Letters of an American Farmer,* written about 1777. Most valuable, because Jan is not a reporter but a storytelling social historian without intending to be one. Much as I like reading anthropologists when they write about other lands, what I seem to need is a book about my own republic through acute foreign eyes and ears. He is neither propagandist nor cynic, and has no passionate feelings about forms of government.

* *Mimi Obstler, formerly of my office.*
† *Dutch writer.*

Saturday, October 25

Thought about last night's dinner at Trader Vic's. Good food, interesting décor and very popular. And I didn't like it. In fact, I have an odd and maybe invalid initial prejudice against the popular—the vogue —the crowd. Maggie says, "But for twenty-five years you were at '21' or The Stork at least three nights a week, and they were the vogue." True, but I come back with what I think is the truth: I went there to hear Heywood, Benchley *et al.* chatter away. And after they died I seldom went to those popular bistros. But the style of the herd does not entice me, and perhaps it is true that my dislike stems not only from this negative attitude but from an affirmative desire to be different—or as kind Penelope once suggested, to be myself. But even her defense may be a rationalization. Who can pinprick the line between wanting to be unorthodox and wanting to be oneself?

I note that our goverment has a rule that a U.S. cardinal does not lose his citizenship by voting for a new Pope. But what would happen if he were elected Pope? This is cute Talmudic material to play with. Is he taxed as a nonresident? Incidentally, do cardinals and church officials generally report as constructively received income the value of their homes, food, autos, etc., paid by their employers? This is, generally speaking, the case with employees of other incorporated or unincorporated charitable or profit-making entities. The entire field of separation of church and state needs rethinking. Concerning the Prato case in Italy, for example, I read that the bishop who was held liable for slandering two of his parish (later they were excommunicated for starting suit without permission of the church) will now appeal to a higher civil court. In our jurisprudence we have held for at least forty years that a cleric gets certain relief if he "persuades" within the contours of his faith, but if, for example, a cleric goes beyond trying to get a news-dealer to withdraw a certain book, then organizes a group not to buy chewing gum from the dealer, he is liable for damages. Just as the problem of permissible boycott is unresolved in ordinary labor-employer rela-tionships, it is totally unexplored in the Church-public relationship field. Why not refer it to Eric Johnston, the movie czar, who works out such problems on grounds of expediency?

Sunday, October 26

How full my life is of fortuitous good turns, chance benefits! On Friday late I was laying out a pro-gram with H. F. P.* to ambush the factual part of our brief in the Supreme Court for the Farmers Union, cruelly hurt as an innocent bystander by a broadcast over a television station out west. I listed all of the FCC regulations, rulings and hearings that we should have someone digest at once. The next morning, out of the clear, by mail come page proofs of a book with a request that I write a foreword. The author is Professor Elmer Smead of Dartmouth. The title is *Freedom of Speech in Radio and Television* and the volume will be published by a gallant house, Public Affairs Press. Thus half of our research work is done. Kindly fate—how else explain these nearly daily occurrences that drift into my life, un-

* *Harriet Pilpel.*

requested, unannounced but blessed? My files are full of what others call coincidences. A lucky guy.

A new batch of Penguin books, mostly on science, arrived. *The Face of the Sun,* and *The Face of the Earth,* to be read up to the point where my lack of education creates road blocks—which was quite soon in the former. *Harper's* also arrived. Little vim in this issue, and why Jack Fischer chose as a lead a pedestrian piece on Harvard I'll never know. It will not be of help to Pusey in his dreams for that cultural center, or raise a cute debate among Harvard men. Was he making a pitch for the men of Eli?

Read some campaign speeches and saw some on television. They are not really on a high level. I doubt if they educate us to any great degree on important issues. Maybe the standards of debate are lower as polls are used more by press and parties. These canned opinions do little more than encourage herd, band-wagon patterns of behavior.

One of the subtle but basic problems of our nation lies in the question, are we a democracy or a republic? I rather think and wish it is the latter. Our elected officials should vote as each one believes best—and not as he thinks his electorate desires. Likewise, the schoolmaster should not give the parents or pupils the educational course they want. He should lead, in nondemocratic fashion. Otherwise, in a plebiscite, education may degenerate into courses on beauty techniques for girls. It's the old problem: do educators and editors lead or do they guess what the masses want and then give it to them?

Monday, October 27

Next Saturday New York City is starting an experiment—in fact, an announced experiment. It is a rare event when a person with power to act poses an experiment to his employees, beneficiaries or voters. Washington Square will be closed for a period of at least thirty days to all traffic except buses and fire engines. What interests me is the government's wisdom in declaring that it has not all of the answers to a problem on which people are divided. Hence: "Let's try it out," says Borough President Hulan Jack. Now why should not the Mayor say to the people of the city, "We have a dozen or so suggestions for handling the traffic congestion problems, and we will make one test after another to get public reaction. For *x* weeks we will try to ban parking in certain areas, then we will try one-side-of-the-street parking, then no left turns, then crossings for pedestrians in the middle of the blocks only, then white-line paths for cars, with strict enforcement"—etc. etc.? Maybe the extent, quality and source of the gripes will be of some guidance. Maybe suggestions will even flow from popular complaints In any event, in what seems to me to be an insoluble problem in Manhattan, the public may take with better grace and with more compliance a final decision reached by the City Fathers after public trials and tests. To take people into one's confidence can be practiced only by a wise politician who knows the essence of democratic leadership. Maybe we will discover there is no answer to our traffic mess. I believe that if we widened every avenue to provide six more auto lanes, the only result would be to suck out of garages millions of cars not now in daily use. I'm afraid we have long passed the saturation point of transportation in our metropolitan centers.

Terribly bored with the weather. Rain, clouds, rain. Weather can be as boring as people, and one can be bored by uninterrupted sunlight too. I should imagine there must be a correlation between boring weather and crime.

Tuesday, October 28

Newspaper repartee with Maggie while having berries and coffee in bed. The ball was tossed from one to the other, just in case either might miss some intriguing item. Do you prefer the tax on off-track betting to an increase in the city sales tax? Yes, for surely the bettors do not include so many of the low-income families, and the sales tax favors the rich, who spend a small proportion of income on taxable things rather than untaxed services and rent. Did you catch great news of recession in births in U.S. in August and September, 1957, with increases in October and decline in November and since? Great news, since standard of living is nothing but total income divided by population. Didn't catch it but do note that the outrageous myth of families—cheaper by the dozen—is being refuted by all census figures. And so it goes and could go on with unanswered queries for hours.

To the dentist. The new drill at high speed cuts out all pain and all pain of noise. I suggested that right-handed people wear their teeth down more on right than left side of mouth. Agreed. Also teeth are stained right or left by smokers depending on right- or left-handedness. Agreed but with doubt.

New Pope elected on twelfth ballot. Since he is seventy-six, all this show must be endured again in a few years.

Friday, October 31

Lunch with Herb and drinks at Plaza with Jess* in from the coast. Jess is a wise and well-informed adviser on movie and television matters. We agreed that the present trend in the movie business is still one of confusion and despair. Maybe the basic trouble was that the tough old nickelodeon people who dominated Hollywood for the first fifty years were so strong in personality that no second generation of management was permitted to arise. On top of this the New York bankers, to their genuine regret, were attracted to movie finance, not by the validity of the business, but through the glamor aspects of the so-called business.

Looked over *Boats* and like Al's idea that a garage for the boat makes sense. A two-car garage—one for car and one for boat. It's good for the boat and good for the owner.

Then read Heyerdahl's *Aku-Aku*. I'm always attracted to authors who try to undermine long-held axioms. This Heyerdahl did in *Kon-Tiki,* and I recall the thrill I had when I saw the raft itself first in Zurich and again in Oslo. This book is not my dish and I would not have read it if I had known that the author is writing a scientific monograph on his discoveries. In fact, at the back of the book he had the list of what I was looking for. Did the people go to Easter Island from the west or

---

* *Jess Morgan, economic advisor to movie stars.*

the east? When did they get there, as now estimated by the carbon-14 test? How did they make and move these fifty-ton statues of which many were recently discovered, covered over by earth even though Easter Island has no brush or trees (the basis of overlays over the centuries in most of the world)? Again I complain about the absence of a minimum number of maps and basic statistics.

Steffie and Joan for dinner. Irving at the shop. With Steffie I found a delightful limitation to the workings of a four-year-old mind. When asked, "What's new?" or "What's the news?" there is usually no response—maybe because to children *all* is new.

NOVEMBER

Saturday, November 1

During the past few days I have been running some coffee tests. Usually I enjoy the ceremonials of grinding the bean in the electric machine Mag gave me, using Shapira's special mixture, very cold water, etc. Usually I fix the setups the night before. But today I used Chock Full o' Nuts ground coffee in my electric pot. Can Maggie discern the difference? What are the realities? Is what we think more real than what our taste buds communicate to the brain? Some relation to my Carnegie Hall friends who think they can distinguish between a Steinway and a Knabe piano on a blindfold test? It's the old cigarette-test racket. Only recently we found many of our friends could be handed a glass of milk after taking two scotch highballs and, if blind-folded, declare it to be whiskey of some sort. It's not easy to control oneself so as to be unaffected by other than personal, inner-directed controls.

To the office to check with Maury* before he flies to Paris, Zurich and back at once. One of those week-end trips that we increasingly take for clients. Then to meet

* Maurice Greenbaum, law partner.

Maggie, Rog and Jean at Divan for lunch. Fun checking up on Washington's activities. We listed the shifts in government in the past few months—in South America it happens every fortnight. Now all over the world the complexities of economics, the pressure on creation of energy to replace undercaloried labor make it necessary for all nations to increase the power in the executive branch of the government.

In the afternoon to the Washington Square celebration. We are on our way, solely by the pressure of thousands of people, to preventing Bob Moses from replacing grass with concrete. I was peculiarly interested in Mr. McCarthy, president of the Fifth Avenue Coach Lines. I liked his brief remarks and his demand for engineering facts. Now we should be able to persuade the bus company to arrange to run their buses to Houston Street, pick up many more fares, avoid the Square, make more money for its stockholders and prove that a public-service corporation can act so as to deserve the affection and thanks of its public. The Fifth Avenue Coach Lines stockholders' support, as I mentioned to Susan Pulsifer,* may be just what McCarthy wants and would enjoy.

For dinner after a chat with Charlie Abrams' intelligent artist daughter, to a new Japanese restaurant on McDougal Street. The owner seemed like one more of those foreign women, like Mrs. Lind of Ugly Duckling, who show such gallantry trying to make a go of a foreign-food restaurant. Maggie specializes in foreign-food hangouts, and it's surprising how many are run by women.

Afterwards to the roller derby on Fourteenth Street. This is sheer sadism, and the audience is even tougher

* *Sixty-year resident of Eleventh Street.*

than at a bullfight or a prize fight. As an antidote took our usual stroll on Eighth Street, and we both commented that the bookstores are as crowded as the ones in Moscow.

Monday, November 3

More dreary weather. After such a spell tempers will be more brittle and I think that even the spirit of adventure declines. Only to the inventors—who suffer from addiction to their dreams—is weather immaterial.

Most of the morning spent with keen minds on corporate policies related to economic facts seldom discussed publicly: (a) The need for a reappraisal of competition, since it scarcely exists on price at the sources of production and certainly not in terms of interest paid to or at banking institutions. (b) Competition in favor of the consumer depends not on the product but primarily on advertising techniques. (c) Price inflation now dangerous only in the area of distribution and not in production. (d) New techniques needed to take care of a large number of unemployed, although no one knows the relation of total unemployed to total number of man hours worked in our nation. (d) Adjustment to an economy where machinery has replaced man hours, and at the same time both machinery and man power are less than fully used. (This is the great advantage of a dictatorship—it can use machines and men on a full-time, one-hundred-per-cent basis, and as machines replace brawn and brain the values, in this sense, of a free competitive society diminish. When have our steel and auto plants been used above eighty-five per cent of capacity?) (e) The perils of democracy in industrial unions, since the leadership must depend for power on the mass—the majority—and hence must disregard the small percentage of skilled workers, thus reducing the spread between pay for skilled and unskilled. If the differential in pay is negligible and the prestige is absent in our culture, we face trouble.

And so it went, with constant endeavors to apply such trends to a particular set of existing corporations.

American Civil Liberties Union for lunch, with discussions on noneconomic trends. But the relation between dollars and freedom is always in the background. For example, the television programs are sponsored—that is, financed—by marketers of consumer goods. Hence, the philosophy of freedom and the standards of taste are in the hands of beer, tooth-paste and perfume distributors.

In the washroom I heard one man ask another, "How long does it take you to get in, in the morning?" The answer was, "One hour." This is two hours a day, or ten hours a week. It takes me no more than twenty minutes by bus or cab. Thus, I'm better off by more than an hour a day. What a harvest—in fact nearly another full day a week—although train commuters do a certain amount of living via reading newspapers, playing cards or reading books, or at best have a peck of leisure for dreams.

Picked up Professor Siepman, who was going to N.Y.U. All-too-brief chat on the subject on which he has written—the clash between public and private interest in television and radio. Too bad he lives in Connecticut—otherwise he would be grand evening coffee-talk company.

Tuesday, November 4

Read in the Nantucket *Town Crier* a brave statement by Bob Mooney, our representative. He came out against a law compelling all meetings of selectmen to be public. With the highly unrealistic demand that publicity be given to all government deliberations, the press has gone overboard in trying to pressurize all government agencies to behave as if in a birdcage. I have long been against open covenants openly arrived at. After full opportunity for public debate, executive sessions are needed for the exchange of thoughts among those with power. Even a newspaper could not be wisely published if it tried to have all its deliberations public in advance. For a candidate such as Bob to take this stand is likely to appear to some as an attack on a free press. I can imagine that Joe Indio will differ with Bob, and it's good also that the press keeps on attacking executive sessions of executive agencies. But the executives above all should resist the demand for, let us say, public deliberation of the Cabinet in Washington.

Voted and then to the office to look at mail, then to new Hulot picture—a charmer. Can we produce one like it in our culture? Can we kid ourselves except in the all-too-rare Thurber-Benchley tradition? Lunch with Maggie at Museum of Modern Art. Pleasant. Home to dinner with Jan and Marjorie.* Jan as a commentator on U.S. folkways was entrancing, and all of us wondered how we were able to muddle through with our archaic system of divided responsibility between executive and legislative.

* *Jan de Hartog and Marjorie Mein, his secretary.*

Up until three A.M., waiting for election returns after a brief trip to Democratic headquarters. The dullest state election I can recall.

Thursday, November 6

At office all day, with a brief lunch with Bill Wolff. Moe* was at the next table and discussed the basic trouble of the book publishers. Distribution costs have risen out of proportion to other costs. It's a miserable market place. Each book is a new, separate commodity; the "brand" of a publisher has no popular following; and above all the only way to apprise the buyers of new books is by mail order, word of mouth or through newspapers. And among newspapers only the *Times* has any significance left. Maybe I should revive the plans I discussed with Helen Reid† for a national Sunday book section to be sold to newspapers in fifty or a hundred cities as an insert like "Parade," "This Week" *et al.* Query: would the publishers cooperate with such an experiment by underwriting advertising based on rate schedules tied into total distribution?

In late afternoon to Tavern-on-the-Green where Syd Baron has arranged for exhibit of Silhouette Mark II, the great new small British sail cruising boat. This will be a huge success, selling thousands, not only because of Syd's ingenuity but also because the distributors have never cruised, have a total ignorance about sailing, and hence are unretarded and unembarrassed to think in channels where most men of the water have been blocked by hand-me-down caveats, cautions and fears.

---

* *Henry Moe, of Guggenheim Foundation.*
† *Mrs. Ogden Reid, former owner-publisher of* Herald Tribune.

Friday, November 7

Perfect weather. No coat needed.

A variety of news tidbits intrigue me. Postal rates for international dissemination have been reduced. Why should there be any postage on magazines, books and newspapers in international commerce? Why should not the federal budget absorb the entire cost? A brave Republican senator, Clifford Case, states that the Democratic sweep should be laid to Eisenhower. This is a small item as carried in the press. Imagine if the cards were reversed and conjecture what our non-Democratic press would have done to the story! A cultured lawyer, Judge Breitel, dares declare that courts have the right to consider social and economic factors in reaching decisions. He is right and brave—brave as shown by the fact that this simple axiom gets a big story in the press. John Frank, convicted of failing to register as a Dominican Republic agent, will be tried again, says the Department of Justice. But why did the UPI release cite as the only ground for reversal the improper remarks of the prosecutor trying to connect Frank with Galindez? The opinion of reversal also referred to a press conference of Congressman-Lawyer Porter, during the trial, as a ground for reversal. Why was this omitted in the press story? Fear of a congressman? Fear that the press, having rested heavily on Porter, would undermine its pet congressman as a lawyer who ran foul of what the courts declared to be a fair trial? Joe Alsop also gives a bill of particulars on the point I have been making, that those who got respectably large votes last Tuesday were men with personalities—Herter in Massachusetts, Goldwater in Arizona, etc. Are we running into a personality cult in politics instead of debating issues? Maybe taking Ike as a genial friendly uncle, if not papa symbol, is the tip-off.

Saw three sailboats on the East River—two with the current and one against. What a difference if man can play with rather than against all tides, winds and currents of life, as wise sailors always try to do. I once figured out that if I started from Pollak Rip at the end of Cape Cod and could make nine knots I'd save about twelve miles from the Rip to Hell Gate. Wouldn't it be fun to hit such favorable currents in life itself? Some people think a fair wind makes people soft and is corrupting. Shame on the residue of Mr. Calvin.

Dinner at New York Yacht Club. Rod Stephens* spoke on the Newport races, the boats and the crews. An exciting analysis by an expert. The gathering showed a repetition of the spirit of the Newport races audience.

This lecture was not remote from the Kevin Sullivan† talk at the Joyce Society. Both audiences would be insulted if anyone said they had anything in common. I'm quite sure that the drive for completion, perfection, the last word, is the same with both lecturers and their audiences. These bands of addicts are important in our culture.

Home. Found Maggie with a bent, bruised or broken ankle and in pain that needs codeine. After a night's sleep will see about X rays, hospital, etc.

* *Yacht designer.*
† *Joyce scholar.*

Saturday, November 8

This was our doctor day. Maggie, in great pain, taken to hospital; doctors, technicians, X rays, wheelchair, crutches; committed to bed with foot higher than heart. A senseless situation. Trip on curb, broken bone and no one to blame. How much relief from pain there would be if someone else were at fault! A kind of cleansing absolution follows from pointing a finger at another human, or even a horse or dog. In fact, animals serve this purpose even better than humans, and strangers fill the role better than friends. If there is no identifiable fault, and man can blame only fate, this for me is the worst of all states. In most of the nations of the world the Fates—or dogmas—bring comfort whether man is stricken by blindness, malaria or typhoid; but in a culture where man thinks he has some slight control over his life to have to say, "How stupid of me to fall"—this in no way hastens the mending of the broken bone.

To the office for just a glance at some intriguing mail. A letter from Jimmy W.* was even tender. What a sad life on the *Post*. He suggests he wants to see me and I'd enjoy it. Lerner† also states how he voted and tells of his independence as a columnist. I did not expect the sophistry and evasion Max displayed. Surely the question is not whether he has had conflict, but rather how much his pen hesitates to write for fear the owner would not like it. Max must know that an owner has

---

* *James Wechsler.*
† *Max Lerner, columnist.*

a "right" (i.e., power) to be wrong-headed and cheap. I'm not surprised he said nothing of the degree of independence an editor should have from the whims or taste of an owner. How far could Max with decency go in the area of his freedom? Assume that some day he gets a slight revulsion at the amount of crime-sex tawdriness in his paper. Comment with feeling? How much feeling before the Boss says, "If you feel that way, give up your so-and-so-many dollars a week from my check book." Do his limits of freedom place him in a position where he feels his lips should be sealed in opposition to Dolly's* column? I do think that Max, Sylvia† and other *Post* columnists will have to dig deeper before they can continue with comfort. I wrote Jimmy I'd like to help him out of this confusing mire. What he said in his signed editorial may be a lead. I recall the days in my youth—or at least I think I do—of signed editorials, and I learned much when I spoke for Heywood in the Sacco-Vanzetti case and the Lippmann dispute, and many other situations for Dorothy Thompson, Drew Pearson and other columnists.

Alan's Ma and Pa dropped in to pick up our theater tickets. Glass of wine. Great stuff—that gal now going back to classes to fill out her education. I understand she cried when she was told she stood near the top of her class on her first examination. Good adult tears, and the difference in tears is wide and great as one gets older. Penelope suggests they can taste differently—depending on the length of time they were bottled up, the atrophy of the unused glands; maybe a salt test would be amusing. In twenty-five years I've bawled like a baby on only two occasions—once in a train, and once

* *Dorothy Schiff.*
† *Sylvia Porter, writer on economics.*

on a crowded street. On those occasions I shed tears
that neither public nor private shame could dam up.

Sunday, November 9

Ordered a remote-control TV set for Maggie, in
bed with a broken metatarsal bone, to help her while
away time and go on with her Spanish refresher course.
It occurred to me while watching the programs that
there is no effective way the public can express its pressures on Paley and Sarnoff, the responsible publishers
of television. The press is timid even to the point of
not criticizing each other except on rare occasions; much
less would they risk being stout of heart in editorial
crusades against P. and S. So why should not the Parent-
Teacher Association or the Public Education Association or even the leading educators and clerics picket
CBS and NBC? The placards might say: "Are you
happy when your own children or grandchildren view
your product of sadism and the tawdriest aspects of sexual love? In fact, are your own youngsters controlled as
to their television corruption?" What would happen if
instead of picket lines there were on the sidewalk a
parents' newspaper addressed to the duo who dominate
our folkways? They, more than all the presidents of all
our universities, determine our social attitudes.

At breakfast I went back to the gold-edged coffee cups.
It's good that trifles are important—short of tyranny
over a person. Elsie* cups—as we have called them ever
since we got them as a wedding present—are designed
with flowers and a few flying bees—delicate and clean
and clear. Maggie has said for nearly thirty-five years,

* *The late Elsie G. Cullman, intimate friend.*

"Stop pouring when the bees' wings are wet." This is a ritual of pleasure—a shared trifle. And made enjoyable by the beauty of the cups—more important to me than any picture I have ever owned. The Mergentime* table-cloth with Presidents' signatures, the initialed Ferber† oversized bath towels, the bamboo iced-coffee glasses, the smooth wooden cork remover from France, the Spanish hand-baked plates—dozens of items of daily intimacy point to highly appreciated places for art at its best. Whereas the Swiss may have few great painters, their well-turned and smoothly finished woodwork and their hand-woven table sets may be a far better expression of design and color than is so often exhibited by reproductions of paintings of even great popular works.

Bill Wolff reports a top success on his trip to the State Department in Washington; Frank Hogan comments on my letter about his high standards of civil service; Jim Bennett writes about some new ideas for a Public Defender system; *The New Leader* shows the danger of comments on South American politics (the piece on Venezuela was just two days too late, enough to make it ridiculous, since events change more speedily than type can be set in the U.S.)—and so it goes, from illumination by Fowler Harper on the new Connecticut birth-control cases, to review of the Bob Gessner-Buzz Meredith college movie-making plans of 1947, to a new difficult will-contest matter, to an improbable person who has new ideas on Galindez's disappearance. The mill turns over and over.

Maggie has invented the damnedest funny method of locomotion I've ever seen. She has a chair by her bedside, she puts on one slipper, puts her bum leg from the

---

* *The late Marguerite Mergentime, designer.*
† *Edna Ferber, author.*

knee down on the chair and pushes the chair with her arms on the back, hobbling along on her good leg. Oh for a movie camera—blackmail her later.

Maggie says, "Your hair needs cutting again." Is it possible that as one gets older and loses some of one's hair the remaining crop grows faster? I have an impression that growth applies also to fingernails. They need most cutting as a baby or in very old age. I'll ask Penelope to find out if there is any research on such tests for age.

Saturday, November 15

The big adventure was taking Stef and Nick to Idlewild to await the jet bringing Connie and Mike. With minds like these, every detail is an eye opener to me. The leaps of their minds put me to shame—so little hindrance or interference. The taxi driver was pleasant. Stef says, "You better not drink milk or you will grow so tall that your head will hit the taxi top." Nicholas explains that the Ginger Ale building is not where they sell it but where they make it—"And, Steffie, do you understand the difference between selling and making?" We are up on the observation deck—a double helicopter, dozens of four-engine planes, the trucks, the stairs. And, above all, the new jet lands and taxis right under our noses. Every blessed thing—every noise, every person, every iota—is a matter of novel impression. Nothing resembling boredom or even the bored question falsely attributed to youth, "What'll I do?"

Connie and Mike are surprised and happy. Brief reports on de Gaulle, Allen Lane,* Fleur Cowles, books,

* *Head of Penguin Books.*

agents, authors and many of our friends. The most worrisome item was the question to be put in Parliament next Friday by Labor, for MacMillan to defend the retention of publicity firms—one from U.S., J. Walter Thompson, I think. This might carom back to us and let us review the wisdom of sellers of tooth paste as the marketers of political philosophies and programs. We had better search ourselves soon, as England may do, otherwise a huckster may say, "If I can elect a president, why should I not be president?" A generation ago, P. T. Barnum was the counterpart of the tribe of "Given enough TV time we can elect Gargantua president."

Tuesday, November 18

Shabby day—gray, drizzly and defeatist. So: I fixed a lush breakfast—raspberries, several cups of coffee, hot rolls and a fried egg on roast-beef hash; even honey and jam for the rolls. A repast worthy of my special small iron frying pan. Maybe good cooking depends on the size of the utensil. We really ought to have two small frying pans and cook dishes separately for each of us, since the uniform spread of the heat is basic. I should think a special breakfast is for a man in our culture the counterpart of a new hat or hairdo for a woman.

Each day I discover an item that excites me so that I assume, probably falsely, that all others would be equally thrilled. This is my headline item for today: in Marie's scientific journal I learn that my dream plane is in operation. A vertical take-off has been made in England by the Short SCI which is a "completely orthodox" airplane with wings and tail. I have always been skeptical about helicopters because the entire weight of the plane must be carried by the rotor, and I'm told by my aeronautic friends that the whirling wings can't get to or through the sound barrier. Hence, helicopters have a speed limit of 225 miles per hour. So now this new plane, about which I can find out little among my friends and clients, may be the answer to airport congestion. In New York we have reached the saturation point of airport departures and arrivals. Just think—the rooftops can have vertical-lift small-plane garages. What a neat revolution, even to the point of small planes of "up and on" types. With a wise planning board we should *now* provide that every new building must have space for landing, hangar if space permits, and tie-down facilities.

Another item that concerns clients is the rapid advance in synthetic textiles. Surely no more cotton will be planted by us for our clothing. Men's shirts and underwear are already through with cotton as a base. Dacron will be outdated in a year or two. And as for wool, sheep will be relied on for eating and not for warmth.

Had lunch alone. Good once in a while—at least when I can have more pleasure with my own ideas than with a pleasant but idealess client.

Dave Loth in to chat about my notes on "the just society," an attempt I have made to find out just why for three centuries our standard of living has climbed at a greater rate than that of any other nation.

Wednesday, November 19

The Bernsteins* were delightful last night and, as was inevitable, talk moved toward the effects of the mass media, the press and more particularly the *Times*. B. understands the high compliment implicit in the fact that thoughtful readers are more critical of the *Times* than of the press of lower standards of honesty and taste.

Heard from Frank† and his hydrofoil-boat project. Maggie also told me of the use of such a fifty-mile an hour watercraft on the rivers of Russia. More and more I am disturbed about our economy's slipping behind those of the dictator lands in that ever-growing area of enterprise that is neither admittedly governmental nor concededly free enterprise. Our subsidies to the transportation business show the extent of government concern and the incapacities of private investment to take care of capital needed for grabbing hold of new arts and inventions. Frank's dream is in this in-between realm.

Now for a truly significant item: The Sound Yacht Supply Co. is marketing a waterproof Fiberglas twelve-inch-high owl that, they assert, will scare off sea gulls. If true, it satisfies my dream of an antidecoy for gulls. I'll suggest that Maggie get me one for a Christmas present, and then I will find it difficult to wait for May when I can test it in Nantucket.

Incidentally, someone last night alerted me to two U.S. companies developing vertical-plus-forward jet-

---

* *Theodore Bernstein*, New York Times *editor, and wife, neighbors.*
† *Dr. Frank Calderone.*

motion airplanes. He suggested we were ahead of England in this new air era. Must check.

Thursday, November 20

Lunch at University Club with Jim Armsey and
Alfred Wolf of Ford Foundation. Sober-thinking, informed men. As we went into the handsome Stanford
White-designed high-ceilinged room I said, "I always
enjoy eating here—because I like to eat with nonbigots
in this club that no Jew may join, no matter how many
university degrees he has garnered."

Ran into Norman Cousins*—chatted about Kashmir,
the adamant position of Nehru on the UN plebiscite,
the pacifist Nehru's use of troops and, above all, about
Norman's statement that a recent survey in India showed
the belief that Russia had done more to help India than
had any other nation. Shame on our government, since
we contributed probably twenty times as much in
money. Today in press I read Nehru gathered another
eight hundred million dollars, or some such sum, in
loans from our economy. Norman agrees with me that
Russia will capture another Indian state, in addition to
Kerala, in the next two years. We both guessed it would
be Madras—that section from which we got our first
concepts of free public education in the early nineteenth
century, and from which we may learn much about a
new contraceptive—in the tale of unfertile mice that
eat certain peas!

Home with hobbling Maggie and her new wheel
chair. A broken bone anywhere but in the foot can be
treated lightly—in finger, toe or rib. But each little bone

* *Editor of* Saturday Review.

of the foot carries a mountain of weight—pain, trouble and a long time to mend.

Here is an odd one. In Wortman's Double-Crostic there was a quote from a poem by one Ann Coe Mitchell. This rang a faint bell. I wrote to Mrs. W. and she graciously gave me Miss Mitchell's address. To satisfy some hidden urge I telephoned to Montclair, New Jersey, and spoke to Miss M. Yes, she is the gal I recalled meeting at Smith College fifty-two years ago when both of us were on the editorial boards of our college papers. I remembered what she looked like. As far as I know I have never thought of her since the meeting at Northampton. Her hair, she tells me, is no longer dark—it's white. We had nothing to say to each other, of course. She didn't recall me or anything about me, which did not surprise me at all. Why should she? But my query was, why did I remember her? To be sure, I was a shy lad—a virginal (regrettably), phlegmatic youth, afraid to talk to any girl. I looked at their ankles but not their eyes. My unconscious might now speak up, if I let it, and indicate that this girl really created some kind of a yen in my—wherever yens are born and die. I'd like to see her for no reason other than to tickle and tease some brain recess, to recall the true dimensions of this unique experience. Anne Coe Mitchell was my something of 1907—but by remote control and remote recall. How silly, tender and futile life can be for delayed adolescents!

At a party last night at Mary Lasker's, a generous liberal businessman, relating an event of years ago, said, "That's the year when I made my first million dollars." A sorry human; insecurity covered up with an announced dollar sign. I prefer my Anne of 1907.

Friday, November 21

While on way to the office, got my hands filthy again reading the newspaper. What mobile ink! Can't something be done to prevent all the ink from rushing to a reader's fingers? I have a hunch that before the merger of the printing-ink companies there were inks that didn't smudge. Mergers, I believe, do not always raise the standards of products.

Lunch with Vic Lasky and an Indian friend. We discussed new techniques for international communication about national folkways, different patterns of corruption condoned in our nation but abhorrent in another. I threw out my idea of a travel book on each nation dealing not with tangibles—Taj Mahal or Eiffel Tower —but with attitudes and daily conventions. These could be told in simple terms, without the use of value judgments: the French relax for hours over an apéritif for a few pennies, we are ashamed to use a restaurant chair and table for an equal length of time over one cup of coffee. Incidentally, our shame if we do is absolved by a bigger tip to the waitress. A great book can be done on patterns of corruption in different nations. In our land many of my clients can get theater tickets for hit shows, hotel rooms and airplane seats when I can't. In other lands they prefer the more direct corruption of money under the table. What the world must understand is differences without any necessarily ensuing value judgments. So Holland has villages without movie theaters but with string quartets; so what?

Finished Daniel J. Boorstin's *Americans: The Colonial Experience.* Plush in oddities of early colonial folkways. But what a blind spot—just no concern for behavior patterns that touch on love, love-making, marriage, parental authorities and challenges, leisure outlets, dance, drink, play. How is it that the author, with a sophisticated background of education and travel, omits references to these elements of early life on our shores? Might it mean a kind of blockage because he himself minimizes the values of these outlets of men and women? Or did he have the information and decide it was irrelevant? Or—more likely—did he collect and then suppress because he could not get himself to write about these sectors of life? I'd like to see his notebook.

Saturday, November 22

To office. The usual pile of material in the mail. Some time I'll figure up the hours it takes each year to make the selections for the trash basket. Out of seventeen publications in one mail—all subsidized by taxpayers through second-class postage—I kept only five. *Carnegie Quarterly*—on defense—not up to usual standard of writing or bite. *CIAI Bulletin*—the usual waste of paper and brains of American Jewish Congress. I'll wager no one ever appraised the effect, if any, of such propagandist public-relations publications. The same money spent sensibly might have illuminated for many people the idea back of the figures of recent decline of Jews in China. A trade journal for lawyers—*New York County Bar Bulletin*. Must read "advice" of an insurance lawyer. Is it to his client to reduce calendar congestion; is it to lessen corruption of insurance officials, claim agents, etc.; or is it, as I suspect, a delicate defense of the shocking uncriticizable patterns of behavior of

insurance companies? The Union Bank of Switzerland
sent me another of its reports. This one is on the Italian
economy.

Sunday, November 23

Pounds of Sunday papers in bed with coffee and
juice. The four Bessies arrive, and the kids enjoy the
wheel chair and crutches more than any toys we have
on hand for them. It proves my theory that the equipment of the adult world is the toy of the child. Doctor
looks over my cripple and gives a blessing, so I take her
out—chair, crutches and all—for lunch at the Brevoort
where the waiter, on serving the kippers and eggs, says
to Maggie, "Enjoy it." And we did doubly because of
the unexpected friendliness.

Returned and finished reading *Canadians in the
Making* by Arthur Lower. I'm shocked. How come in
school and college I was kept so ignorant of our northern neighbor? Is Canadian history taught today? I doubt
it. Do we think that nation negligible? Or are we
ashamed to let our people know that we lost the war of
1812? It's an entrancing story, of a land less formal than
England and more formal than the U.S. The Canadian
desire not to become "American"; the comparison between our Founding Fathers and the MacDonald period
nearly a century later in Canada; the failure of cricket
to get a real foothold; the feeling of superiority during
our periods of hysteria such as McCarthyism—it's all
exciting, particularly because I have been so ignorant.
This man Lower is my kind of social historian—little
about techniques of government but much about shifts
in attitudes away from Victorianism in the early years

of this century, problems of illegitimacy (which runs higher than ours) and, above all, constant conflict of pressure for and against a federal system of government. Thanks to Bob Fowler I had a good day with this new area of knowledge. I wonder if it will be reviewed here?

Just as Canada spent millions to bind itself into one nation by east-west railroad instead of submitting to the cheaper north-south transport, I hope it will spend maybe a hundred million dollars on radio and television to have its own transport of ideas by ether instead of allowing us to take over the culture of Canada by stretching our ether fingertips with the typically U.S. product—from Zsa Zsa Gabor to Victor Borge, not to mention Benny, Gleason, Monroe and the favorites of our soap producers, the shooting westerns. Maybe just because Canada has two cultures and two languages it will have a chance of not being taken over by us. And surely it will enrich us to have a distinguishable civilization to the north. Can't we get out a northern-hemisphere history-geography book for education in Canada, U.S. and Mexico, and maybe one hour every two weeks set aside on radio and television for joint programing? It could, to simplify, be only in English, since many in Mexico speak the language of Canada and the U.S. Maybe George Allen of USIA could inspire a start.

Monday, November 24

Nice note from Anne Coe Mitchell, who seems more than bewildered—in fact, scared. Made a date to lunch with her in December, when she comes to New York. Conrad in Search of His Youth—beware, Leonard Merrick, I may fool you.

Spoke to Bennett Cerf about the censorship in his shop of the Freud *Leonardo da Vinci*. I wonder what he will report about why his substantial firm did not dare print a da Vinci drawing that appears in both the German and French editions. It is not a very attractive drawing—cross-section view of a man and woman in act of copulation. It's the footnotes that Random House cut out that confound me, for they are the core of the Freud argument that da Vinci was homosexual—an inference from which Freud explains the smile on the face of the Mona Lisa.

An interesting woman client: married for twenty years, no children, pushed around by a stern, tough spouse. And now, without her having a lover, the bloom is off the peach and the marriage is to be dissolved. So far not unusual. What is odd is the rather sudden dramatic and pathetic attempt of a woman to change roles deep in life—a violent shift. No longer does she want to be the sacrificial lamb. No longer does she enjoy being the underdog. Can she make the personality somersault? Will she pick for a second spouse an underdog or another tough human? It's never my duty to favor or oppose a split-up. Still, I do feel it the function of a lawyer to pose all the questions—what happens to you after divorce, will you be lonely, won't you miss even the persistent pain of your husband's sadism? These are acute examples of life in its peak of risk-for-risk decisions. I can help by displaying the competing hazards. The client must decide on the gamble—for better or worse. If as much attention were paid to wedding as to unwedding, much misery would be saved for the four thousand people who enter our divorce courts every day the courts are open for business. And still, what of the misery of those who "play" it out to the bitter end—

with every day a bitter day?

Edie and Maury Benjamin* drop in for a jiffy. I ask, "Are you still painting?" She says, "Are you still breathing?" Touché.

Good weather—good eating—good kidding with Cleo, who would quit working for us if I didn't maul her around. I guess in her home she seems so solid that her friends don't dare shove her even a tiny bit.

Teddy† dropped in from Chelsea Gardens up the Avenue, and educated us on the market place of music —the increased diversity in the recording business, which today includes hundreds of firms, whereas twenty years ago it was in the control of a mere handful of giant companies. This interested me, particularly when compared to the loss of a thousand dailies and five thousand weeklies, further concentration of controls in the hands of three radio and television networks, reduction of press associations, etc. Only music, book publishing and theater have been able to maintain or increase diversity among creators, distributors and producers.

Wednesday, November 26

Gray, dismal day. Lay abed late—at least late for my habits. Amused at story that Moscow is in giant drive against Freud. Comparable to ancient drives against Copernicus, and later against Darwin. But it's a good sign. Freud is to the communist thesis the symbol of individualism. Is not this anti-Freud pressure in direct relation to the Soviet drive for privacy—a bedroom of one's own, and the right of voluntary travel? Both of

---

* Edith Bry, painter and ceramicist, and husband.
† Theodora Zavin, lawyer.

these drives were confessed to me when we were in Moscow. But little about such social moves or even strivings are reported in our mass media!

Received Anne Coe Mitchell's book of verse—*Mark of the Tide*—with a welcome dedication: "From a girl of the Long Ago." I sent her a copy of *The Best Is Yet* with the inscription, "To A. C. M. who says falsely that she never met me a half century ago." Let's see what happens next.

To E. R.* for lunch. It's a puzzle to me that after about thirty years of warm relationship with Mrs. R., I still find new aspects of her thinking and approaches. Her approach to Israel as the matrix of noncommunism in the Near East shows clearly her hope that Israel will end up nontheocratic and her belief that the country should be treated by us not as a religious problem but as the one nation of the area least susceptible to communist allurement. She liked my angles on television and due process, and I think was warm toward the idea of raising in U.S. dollar bills for a Churchill Statue in Grosvenor Square to face the statue of F. D. R.

Dinner at home—peaceful in our simple elegance, and time to look consciously at the Jonah on the top of the Whale—that optimistic wood sculpture by Isabel Case Borgatta that I was lucky enough to see, love and buy in the space of a few minutes a few years ago at the Galerie St. Etienne.

* *Eleanor Roosevelt.*

Thursday, November 27

A doubly perfect day because all the predictions were unfriendly. It's on a holiday that man is apt to think, "So much to do, so many excitements, so much to examine—and so little time and so little training or education." I confess to myself, more than any other embarrassment, that I have not even the capacity to choose values for use of time and mind. Is there any school or class that would help me establish preferences —or, as an alternative, reduce my total appetites?

Off to House of Detention to see Frank Costello, whom I do not represent at the moment but who is pushed around by the federal authorities, I suspect, as a headline camouflage for the failure of the Department of Justice to get other malefactors of respectability. This is unrelated to patterns of corruption in our mores, but surely every person with authority or power prefers to find people of his social set innocent of running counter to the law, just as my friends in the civil-liberties field are not exhilarated when they find themselves compelled to defend the rights of free speech of employers.

Wheeled Maggie to movie. First gay evening for her in weeks—if Brigitte Bardot is to be called gay for man or woman. Alec Guinness a real talent and particularly in underplayed British script. It's good he has not been taken over by Hollywood.

To our Chinese restaurant for dinner—ate too much as usual. I'll never learn to reject complete table d'hôte and take just one dish.

Back home, read odds and ends—and peculiarly delighted with piece on television in *Fortune*. It was intemperate and quite inaccurate, but all the more amazing that the Luce-Larson presses should not realize that the assault on the networks is as sacrilegious as an attack on the Republican Party. I'll bet that *Fortune* will apologize obliquely by choice of letters it prints. It's all to the good, even the attack was for a good end but for the wrong reasons. What a benefit to our republic if Sarnoff and Paley would permit criticism of the press, and the TV czars have plenty of ammunition.

Friday, November 28

First snow is on the way. It feels that way, and increasingly my bones are wiser prophets than the weather bureau.

Today's papers show Ernest Gruening's* picture. He is, I do believe, my earliest friend. Sixty years ago we went to Camp Marienfeld near Keene, N. H. This was one of the earliest of camps for boys, run by an educator-author, Charles H. Henderson, with Harvard undergraduates as tutors. I recall little of it, except that at this camp we lived in tents or partial tents, ran barefoot, wore scant or no clothes, climbed Mt. Monadnock as Hilary climbed Everest, and had morning chapel without religion. This isn't quite true, because at the morning meetings we kids would ask questions, and questions point to mysteries of nature, and unsatisfied queries require the growth of faith. I recall only two queries: why is the sun larger when it approaches the horizon? and, how do snakes change their skins? These oddments are excavated from circa 1898-1900—just because I start thinking back to my early Gruening

* *Senator from Alaska, former governor of Alaska.*

period. I skipped over the era of trips with Ernest to the Virgin Islands when I tried a case for him, trips to Puerto Rico, early work with Muñoz long before he was even leader of the P.R. majority party, sitting between Ernest and Ickes in the days when Ickes tapped the wires of his associates, fun with Ernest and Oscar Chapman,* etcetera. Ernest has been a good public servant and will be a delightful Senator—delightful meaning "full of light." A good way for him to top off his career. It's lucky for him he left *The Nation*.

Across our Square a solid-walled building is going up. It looks like a warehouse but I'm told it's for N. Y. U. students. These architects use either all glass or all brick. So I wrote to Owen Grundy, of *The Villager*— why should this not be used as a garage for the Fifth Avenue buses that now congregate in our Park as their free, open-air garage? I wonder if buses idle in great numbers in any other park in the world. Maybe we care too little about people and too much about machines and brick and mortar.

Saturday, November 29

We woke up on this crisp day singing to each other. Only difference is that Maggie can always rhyme every line. No wonder *The Times-Picayune* hired her to write poems to order for holidays and other celebrations, forty years ago in New Orleans. I thought back to a day of similarly brisk weather, a special day with a special feel. I thought of sitting at the first tee of the Greenbrier golf course, eating my first off-season, semi-artificial strawberries and thick cream. It was with

* *Secretary of the Interior under Truman.*

Jerome H.,* my only rich relative, at White Sulphur Springs thirty years ago. I genuinely liked this unhappy, outwardly successful banker—who liked me because, as he said, I was his only uncowed acquaintance. What an episode. For a week we had personal twenty-four-hours-a-day caddies, horses and bellboys. Elegant, elite, show-off and unnecessary—but my first look-see at "elegant" living. We took these hegiras year after year to argue, disagree, call all off only to try again the next year.

Then to a long dreamy hot tub. If I were ever to run an experiment in elegant living for a Foundation (they have spent money on every other idea!) I think I'd start with two adjacent bathtubs. What's more congenial? I'd rig them for food service—say iced coffee—book-rack, soft rubber headrest; and, above all, I'd have painted an Archimides ring in each tub, to show dis-placement changes, and the rings could be painted peri-odically and dated just as all the kids' heights have been marked with pencil on the walls in Nantucket for the past twenty-five or more years. The bathtubs *de luxe* must have fittings for transistor nonelectronic radio, nonslip soaprack, reachable washrag, eyeglass holder, etc. In honor of the Great Bather, I'd call it The Churchillian. I do recall the delight, disdain but envy with which I saw my first private house with a bath-room with two washstands—Lewis Strauss's house on the east side. Luxury—elegance, but no chrome plate.

Odd talk before going to the office. Maggie says, "We have run out of white wine, which you love best." Morris says, "Cheer up, for Christmas we get loads of wine and champagne." "Yes," says Maggie. "We are overstocked on champagne, so whatever cases of cham-pagne friends and clients send us we will exchange if

* *The late Jerome J. Hanauer, of Kuhn Loeb & Co.*

possible for white wine." How's that for a conversation to show our good fortune and how difficult it must be for us to develop sober imagination sufficient to be in tune with our peers in the vicinage? It's a long way from the bathtub gin days and the era when I took R. L. of J. P. Morgan into his first and probably only speakeasy. It was, I think, Tony's on Fifty-second Street—the dark, dismal hangout of Thurber, Ann Honeycutt and our then talk circles. And it was good—dark, smoky, dirty, crowded but intimate.

Sunday, November 30

Connie made reference to an aspect of conformity I had not discerned. The present youth gangs may demonstrate a desire for conformity in a world that looks on youth as undisciplined, unregulated, with no "bodies" to adhere to. So the gangs are organized to have a group feeling—some people to "form with"—which, in turn, gives the members their real pleasure through the inevitable needs of exclusion. Fraternities give pleasure not so much through association as from the satisfaction of exclusions. Fraternity "high-class" warfare was formerly run with dirty rushing tactics, expressed in a form of upper-class kid-glove gang warfare. The upper classes can hurt each other by upturned noses instead of lifted knives, but the comparison with gangs remains.

DECEMBER

Tuesday, December 2

Christmas shopping is out for limping Maggie. All by catalogue or through Joan and Connie. As I hate to so much as enter a store, I can't quite believe that Maggie, though less than most women, enjoys looking at styles, samples, designs, and comparing, feeling and selecting her final choices. Somebody some day must explain the mental operation to me. I know that men formerly did all the shopping and that it is only recently —certainly since Paul Revere's day—that we have let the women do any shopping. But this does not explain an enduring excitement. Or is it a path to power just as women do the storekeeping in some lands such as Burma and thus evidence influence in the family. I hate it all, and if I had my way I'd never allow an advertised item into our home—if an unadvertised equivalent could be found! Why not start an affirmative campaign for the unadvertised? Get Jayne Mansfield to state, "I do not have a single advertised item on my body or in my home." It's a cute idea, but no newspaper would run the story—so back we are where we came in: the antiadvertising position would have to be run as an ad!

Wednesday, December 3

Last night the oddest telephone calls showered us from ten thirty P.M. on. A client called just to thank for the job we had done; real appreciation. Joe Indio called from the island. Several other unexpected messages, and then a lady wanted to know if we would meet her and a friend for a cup of coffee. They came to us, and we met a remarkable man—teacher of philosophy, priest in the Catholic Church. He was truly interested in Heywood's* conversion which he wrongly thought was on intellectual grounds. Heywood was my fast friend for decades. He always needed certainty, and although he never accepted much of the Catholic dogma, he did get great benefit from his nominal adherence. He had spent ten thousand a year on psychiatrists and cardiograms, had always worried about death and carried all through his life the fear of his father and his boss. To his dying day he called Herb Swope, Mr. Swope. Everyone—and that was thousands—called gregarious Herbert Bayard Swope, Herb or at the most formal, Swope. We covered the canvas—censorship, the bad era of Father Coughlin and his present life, the Christian Fronters and of course the presidential nominations for 1960, discussed with nothing more than uninformed casual attitudes. I opened a bottle of champagne and all were talkative and gay until far into the next day.

Maggie's birthday tomorrow. I know she has already bought several presents for me to give to her. A good reverse of an Indian giver. Amused always that she gets

* *Heywood Broun.*

just what she wants but that on the natal day she is not at all surprised—it's always I who am. Long ago we came to the end of our desire for possessions of all kinds. Hence, it becomes difficult for anyone to give either of us a hunk of material wealth, a commodity or a thing.

Thursday, December 4

This day carried throughout only one dominant theme—a real recurring motif, such as Wagner first tuned up for me. That the day was gray and rainy, I think, has no bearing on the events. It may have magnified everything, however.

In brief, nearly all reactions fitted under the caption, "Cruelty by Kindness—or, It Saves Pain to be Ruthless." A person I have befriended for years—truly showered with kindness—was outrageous and, when confronted, admitted, "I hate you because you have helped me." It was the story of going rowing: a man falls overboard, you save his life, he can't take it—the indebtedness—no matter what the saver's attitude might be.

It's tough being an employer. A lad is hired. He is decent and able but doesn't fit into the echelons of the organization. He should leave—for his sake and the clients' sake. After three or four years of employment he should have been advised that his future was elsewhere. The boss (my client) had been kind—kept the lad on into manhood. Then the client says, "Look for another job." In this case it turned out to the good—the employee bettered himself, the boss gave him a big check as severance pay. The size of the check was to assuage the feeling of guilt—but guilt for what, for telling the man to seek another job? Oh no, just the opposite. The guilt arose from soft, gentle kindness: the boss had not dared tell the lad to go elsewhere years ago. The scar was the prior consideration and kindness.

A man is finished with his gal. He does not want to hurt her feelings. He carries on after the bloom is off the peach. So now he suffers, decent human that he is, because he was not more frank—yes, even ruthless, when love had flown out of the window.

A very rich client wants advice on what is called Estate Planning. Wife—so many millions. Foundations— surely. The son—to get a big hunk, at least $30,000 a year after taxes. I remind the client that he had just told me that his greatest joy was when he earned his first $12,000. After he was wealthy, the fun evaporated and he never knew thereafter whether people liked him for himself or for his money. So I suggest: "How mean you are to your son. You deny him a similar joy of proving himself." "Yes," he says, "I was too kind. A pony at eleven, a Cadillac at eighteen, a first-class trip to Europe at twenty-two. So, regretfully, now I must do harm because I was too kind toward my son all of his life. Now I must hurt him and deprive him of his greatest pleasure —testing himself as a person in the market."

In the evening there was no purposeful kindness, no doing of favors, no relationship of obligation—and so there was easeful fun. Birthday dinner for Maggie: The Goldsteins and Mag; wine, Cleo's chicken and a birthday cake. Warm, all friends, no one being helpful, kind or anything, no *quids*, no *quos*—just living. To top it off, a letter from Marie, whom I miss greatly.

A welcomed voice out of the past: Ben Sonnenberg telephoned, to congratulate Maggie. Only the improbable about Ben is true. I hope we will once again have breakfast in his mansion, as we used to—just chin while fresh from sleep, toss ideas around, no matter where they land. Much more fun tossing an idea than a ball—to which Penelope adds, "A green salad?"

Friday, December 5

Great news for mankind: a new drug to reduce man's desire to fight, destroy and kill. This may be a turning point of some kind, and I usually like turning points even though only detours. This drug has been tried on cats with mice. Penelope says, "What's the residual effect? Does it store up destructive energy?" I'd like to be a guinea pig to try this drug. I'm not a physically scrappy type and as far as I can recall never had a fist fight in my life. I rather think I always ran away from physical danger of any sort except on a sailboat— a danger Maggie says I don't recognize. So maybe I'd not be the best one to test it on. So I said, "Penelope I nominate you." Women do not fight to leave physical scars but they can kill without fists or guns. This may prove that they are the superior part of the species. They carry on life—so oddly called "the race." Maybe, suggests Penelope, we should change the name "the race" to "the peace"—or "the relax." People are influenced unconsciously but deeply by nomenclature, and "the race" has the connotations of speed, effort and lack of repose.

Jack Fischer wanted to see some more of my fiction, having run a few short stories with mild acclaim. So I sent him my attempted start of a series about a new fictional lawyer, Roger Taylor, who is interested in *why* instead of *what,* in the real reasons rather than those glibly given by clients and in compensation rather than damages.

Lunch with Cornelia. How difficult it is to use her first name only! Her dignity demands a big, full, sonorous appellation: Cornelia Otis Skinner. I think of her as Nellie, but never get myself to so call her—although I can't believe that she is as mature and grown-up as she looks. Like many people, she is more akin to her writing than to her outward daily patterns of demeanor. I'll bet her original notes and drafts of her monologues would be worth thousands of dollars. It's an art form about which little has been written.

Saturday, December 6

Temperature down to the point where I'm inclined to shift from iced to hot coffee. Iced coffee in winter involves jibes from waiters and friends. My reply line is simple: "How do you drink your scotch in winter? Iced? Well, I like coffee iced." That clears the confusion.

I am of the opinion that either Batista or Castro would be better for the Cuban people than a division of authority between the two. My basic reservation goes to a distinction between Communist International controls and all other types. The CP setup is of a different quality; with Soviet support, a CP dictatorship cannot, with any techniques known to the free world, be overthrown; all others can and are, every week of the year. There is no doubt that Castro is Communist-supported or infiltrated, which increases my concern at the support our government has given to him and his group. I'm afraid that the U.S. policy of neutrality is not "hands off" but "hands out to both sides."

A Dr. Bromberg is headlined in the *Times*—a long story about parent hatred in Communists. I must get his speech. Some years ago Dave and I published *Report on the American Communist* and the interviews we had showed clearly that in our economy—unlike low-standard countries—the CP members join at ages from eighteen to twenty-three, come from middle-income groups, stay on the average only three years (same as turnover of *Life* magazine subscribers) and are fighting their parents. Boys versus papas, girls versus mamas. This was not even news at the time we wrote our book. I wonder what Bromberg has in the way of samples, and whether his patients were fellow travelers or card-carrying members. If, when the Carnegie Foundation financed Professor Gabriel Almond's deep study of psychological impetus for joining the CP it had been concerned with the spread of knowledge, the Almond volume might have saved work for many a Bromberg. Why should Ford, Carnegie, Rockefeller *et al.* be unconcerned with popularization of the learning they finance? I guess they prefer the rarefied atmosphere of scholarship and feel that marketing and distribution are dirty business. This is a hangover from the snobbery of our early history of quill-pen days. The old priests had a monopoly of manuscript writing and naturally did not run an open-end union.

Wrote Aly Khan, who came through more genuinely than most of Ed's patients on "Person to Person." Also must talk to him about Raoul Dufy and find out if his Dufy was painted before or after Freddy* saved Dufy's hands from crippling arthritis.

Three P.M. Beautiful white cargo boat is going to midstream to go down the East River. A speck of cold sun comes through the clouds to spotlight the vessel pushing

---

* *Dr. Frederic Homburger.*

against a three- or four-knot current. A satisfying sight, one that makes me look up to see that it's only 166 days before we get to Nantucket and on board our own sailboat. From now on I check off each day in the direction of our island and its intimacies. Two separate pigeonholes for our lives. It's not difficult—easier than fabricating two different but concurrent lives.

Tuesday, December 9

Loraine C.* in for late lunch to go over Connecticut birth-control cases and policy questions in general. Only through Fowler Harper's friendship are we able to help Planned Parenthood's national body. The national organization has no legal standing in the Connecticut cases. It's just another example of the prevalent confusion seen in all federal experiments—our government and its 49 states, and all organizations like ACLU, Planned Parenthood *et al.* that operate through branches, whether state or city. This problem of centralized policies and local autonomy needs a first-rate bit of research and guidance. It's most important to resolve these twilight zones of authority and action, since in the absence of clarification everything tends to go into a pattern of complete national control. In a small nation such as Sweden or Holland the problem is of a different quality. With our three thousand miles' spread, we are in trouble. Not that the same quandary is absent in most of the operations of any big corporation. I surmise, without intimate study, that General Motors and du Pont have been able to clarify the powers and duties of the separate divisions; and to some extent Chevrolet, Buick

* *Loraine Campbell.*

and Cadillac really compete as if they were separately owned. Some day Chevvie will be spun off to stockholders of G.M., and then we can for the first time appraise the success, if any, of G.M.'s capacity to run a federated business with autonomous divisions.

After dinner fidgeted around with several books new and old, leafed through *ABA Journal*. Then, just before midnight, went to WMCA to go on Barry Gray radio program, which now, according to our less than meaningful polls has an audience of two million. Stayed on until two A.M. Fun. Before I left, Maggie cautioned, and correctly so, "Don't be stern, smile." Discussed unreasonable attacks on Carmine De Sapio; with the producer, the censorship of *'Tis Pity She's a Whore*—so that papers now say " *'Tis Pity She's a . . . .*" (this for a three-hundred-year-old masterpiece); excessive power of Brooks Atkinson, of which José Ferrer is latest victim; Israel defense problem with Shimon Peres, recently arrived Minister of Defense. I fear we men didn't give Rosemary Clooney and Mimi Benzell much chance to cut in. Wires showed that hundreds of calls came in but, in our variously intense ways, we allowed no one to butt in. Went to the Stage Delicatessen with Barry, José, Rosemary and a few others for a bite. Then home, picked up a *Times* and an extra one for office because of strike—and so to bed. Good, full day. In H. B.'s days would have gone to Texas' or Stork for a last snifter with Broun. Now, no Broun and no liquor for me—other than cold, not-sweet wine. When I came home near four A.M., a note on my bed read, "I loved the way you smiled, open window."

Wednesday, December 10

Two provocative and amusing events. I went over to Newark to talk to the Rutgers Law School on the right to counsel. I spoke along the same lines as I had at Columbia Law School to a group of similar size. In each case I explained that the only fun a lecturer can have is from the questions and that no question could be impertinent although my answers might be. I am still bothered because the questions in Newark were, from the point of view of my prejudices and education, so much more direct and provocative. The group seemed more on its legal toes and far more concerned about the future of the law than was the group at Columbia. I wish I had a recording of my remarks and the questions. Maybe my attitude was different on the two occasions, although I don't think so. Maybe the difference arises from the fact that the students at Columbia come from a wealthy sector of society and were more on the make, with an eye on the big law shops, while the Newark group perhaps comes from small towns and will practice law in small towns. In any event, my guess is that there is more spirit of adventure in the law at Rutgers than at Columbia.

On the way to a party at Aly Khan's, I stopped at the *Tribune* and bought a few copies to take to Aly, and as I left the party I drove to the *Times* and picked up Thursday morning papers and brought one back to Aly. What other present can anyone give to Aly than a newspaper at a time when the papers are on strike!

Thursday, December 11

No newspapers being printed except *Wall Street Journal*. What misery for men at newsstands! It's a suitable backdrop for a variety of experiments. Maggie says this should be the key day for books. At every subway entrance, on every newsstand books, books, books should be offered to the millions who ordinarily read papers in transit. Papers from other cities should pour in—thus making us less provincial. Television should cut out gun shows and do a real, complete newspaper of the air, with book reviews in length, movie, concert and art criticisms, sports stories. What a great experiment. Ditto for radio. Television and radio should give running news on the strike—the causes, the tactics, the differences. We might even be shown charts—what the hourly, weekly and yearly take-home pay of newspaper delivery men was ten years ago and is today, compared to truck drivers, taxi drivers, etc. What a chance for the education of our public! Leaders of other unions should address the public. Why do the other unions cross the picket lines? What is the delivery cost to the entire cost of a paper? How could this mess have been prevented? Who are the dominant leaders of both armies? Where is the federal government's arbitration and mediation service? Some radio station might report on the meager job done by radio and television.

Cheer up, Penelope says—nothing factual, dramatic or adventurous will happen in the ether media. Why take a chance on disclosure of knowledge? For someday the tables may be turned, the press could get back at the owners of the ether pipelines. And so the city goes along in a less keyed-up mood—people joke about, "no papers" and the censorious will hope that the crime rate will depreciate as a result of less crime news; the stock market kibitzers will prophesy the effect of absence of Wall Street price listings on the bulls and the bears; the new books, plays and concerts of the pressless days will suffer in audience. And the city folk will have a better look at the snow in the parks, go to bed a little earlier and sleep a little more peacefully. It may even be that some people will wake up and learn that man can entertain himself and that rereading nearly any book provides more news and entertainment than the average newspaper headline. Some may admit that the papers are no longer for news but for games and gossip.

"Maggie, please will you telephone downstairs and see if Fred did stop at the *Trib* to pick me up my Friday paper?" P.S. I'm an addict—so I'll go to Forty-second Street and get a Washington *Post.*

To Connie's for dinner. A small bottle of champagne in the icebox. Told Nicholas a new old riddle, warmed at Kathie's* smile, ate in my favorite dining room—the Bessie kitchen with the butcherblock table. Home early to my crippled spouse.

Saturday, December 13

For lunch with a Southern Lady who deals in guns—and lives a life more adventurous than the gals who fight elephants or sail the seas in small craft. She has five sons, runs a home and family—and knows more about the munitions-smuggling game, legitimate and illegitimate, than anyone I met in my Galindez re-

---

* *Katherine Bessie, grandchild.*

searches. If she weren't so Southern I wouldn't be so amused and surprised. Must inquire how she got into this dangerous and romantic world of hers.

A large roasted beef for dinner. We are a Spratt family —I like the outside pieces, Maggie likes the inside, and so we eat the bones bare.

As we do several times a week, we watch bowling on television. Several reasons: once we saw a 300 game and hope for another, but above all this is a game where we are in tune because we used to bowl. Everything is meaningful to us—techniques, chances of splits, in the pockets, etc. By listening to the fall of the pins I can tell whether it's a strike or not.

Also heard last few minutes of Toronto Ranger hockey game. What a job it is to be loyal to the Rangers. Into the third period behind 3 to 1, then ahead 4 to 3 and ending with a tie—the usual story. A Ranger in the penalty box and in last two minutes Toronto tied it up. On radio the pleasure is one based on loyalty. In sports, unlike news, television gives dimensions absent on radio.

Monday, December 15

Slept late, good dreams unrecallable while Maggie keeps traveling in boats in lagoons in remote parts of the planet. This dream stuff is like smoke or vapors of old. It must be boxed fast or it gets enmeshed with other used-up or newly made stockpiles of memory.

Wrote to Muñoz that he should have talked more while appearing on the Murrow program on Latin America; he's the man who has carried a people toward the democratic process. I must say Milton Eisenhower made sense with facts and thoughtful comment—although I can't explain why no one made any mention of literacy and education. As if standards of living depend in the long run on anything but the growth of human imagination. Curiosity is the greatest enemy of dictators.

ACLU for lunch. Irv* reports on Washington. He would not be easy to replace, as attorney and lobbyist. Old-line, class-conscious liberals don't understand his ability to be on friendly terms with Nixon, Fulton Lewis, Eastland, Jenner *et al.* They believe you must hate those with whom you disagree. I recall an incident after the argument in the case of The Newspaper Guild versus The Associated Press: when I went to the Carlton Hotel for a drink with John W. Davis, attorney for AP, some guildsmen—mainly communist—spread the idea that I must be selling out, else how could I be friendly with the attorney for AP? What does this mean other than the fact that most people find it easy to define people and issues in terms of black or white, so they go through life quite blind to the all-pervading shade—gray.

Irv is invaluable in the army of liberalism. He is a diplomat, one of the few liberals who practice or believe in quiet diplomacy. Liberals in the main are evangelists and not really operator personalities. This is our greatest infirmity.

Good hour with Eddie on Farmers Union brief in Supreme Court; chat with H. A. W., Jr.† about the fabulous Grandma Moses; talk with Doughty of Chicago about his son, an embryonic barrister. Part of today's business, about a proposed merger of two worthy papers, brought up the point that lawyers must often ignore their personal prejudices. I'm serious in my opposition

* *Irving Ferman, ACLU representative in Washington.*
† *Herbert A. Wolff, Jr., junior law partner.*

to merging papers; we have so few as it is; we are nearly finished with competition of the press—and then I'm called upon to counsel with a newspaper company that wants to sell out to another.

Home and happy. A beautiful tree under the arch, and all lit up.

Tuesday, December 16

Must buy a new suit. What a relief I have had since Hong Kong in 1954, when I stocked up on suits and shoes. The latter will do me for the balance of my life—all the same model, all comfortable and all at about a third of the price identic models cost in New York stores.

Wednesday, December 17

Christmas cards came in by the score. For the last few years we have sent Advent calendars, which we found in Switzerland. We send them out before December first so that kids and adults can tease themselves by the daily opening of the little windows, which show appropriate pictures. It's interesting how many recipients never appreciate the windows on the cards despite the clear daily numbers.

Delightful, odd—if not queer—lunch with Ann Coe Mitchell. It was all autumnal. She showed me a picture of herself in 1909. That girl I never met—that is, I have no memory of it. We spotted the time I recall as after May, 1908, when she became editor of the Smith College paper. We checked and cross-checked through my classmate Dick Eurich—all to no avail. It's all under the waves of half a century. Maybe under hypnosis the originals may become developable. I had an amusing time— sort of a flirtation, not with a person but with my own past. She had read *The Best Is Yet* and had curiosity about Joan and the other kids and about Margaret. But she was frightened. I was too remote from her devout Presbyterian upbringing. She didn't like to hear me say I'd like to live forever and may even decide to do so.

Such chance rays are not unlike auroras and those zips of light that break through leaks in the radiation belts of our galaxy. Thus does the mind have leaks that are breakthroughs to one's past, just as some have openings to the future—prevision, in which I believe even though as yet there is not even a speculation as to a scientific basis therefor. All this kind of thought is more akin to liquids than gases or solids. In solids the molecules are tightly wedged together, in gases they are freewheeling; but as yet I have never heard of even a theory of behavior of liquids.

Thursday, December 18

This is a sad day—impersonally sad. I spent ten years sitting as a member of the Banking Board of the State of New York. At the cost of much time, I received a good look at our banking system. Ever since we worked our way through the Hoover Banking Holiday, all the banks have been secure. Even apart from the insurance of deposits, banks are not financially risky businesses. They are scrutinized by the government and freed by legislation from most of the perils of free enterprise— that is, competition. For clients or myself I have person-

ally used many of the banks. For a short time I was director of one and for years counsel to another.

About twenty-five years ago, in connection with the
Paramount Picture Bond Holders Committee, I met
Russell Leffingwell—a fast friend, to use his term, and
my wisest friend. For decades I have been at the Morgan
shop for lunch with Russell or other partners. This
bank was a unique symbol of quality as contrasted with
quantity. A sober judgment led me slowly but surely to
decide that there was one pre-eminent bank—J. P. Morgan & Co. It's a small bank—less than a billion in deposits, no branches and the wisest niche I have been
privileged to see in New York, in or outside of banking
circles.

And now this institution merges with mammoth
Guaranty Trust Co. It's a sorry day for me. It's as if this
were a symbol of surrender to statism. Morgan Guaranty
will merge and merge and merge. In a decade or so we
will have a handful of banks, which for a land of the size
of ours and with our lack of traditions cannot be anal-
ogized to the British five or six that spread over that
island. Competition will be further reduced—all these
big ones will take on the same coloration—and all become impersonal, faceless money houses. I have never
felt lower about the liberty of the people of our republic.
Why didn't Morgan's take on another billion of deposits
if they cherished size? A mere announcement of such a
desire would have brought lines at the receiving window
(I think they have only one).

My only glimmer of hope is that Henry,* who will
head the combine, may invent new formulas for autonomy and insist on the retention down the line of incen-
tives for cautious daring and safe unorthodoxy. I must

* *Henry Alexander.*

see R. L. soon; maybe I'm needlessly sad for his sake.

R. L. must stay, although his modesty will prevent him from realizing that the bigger the institution, the more it needs the symbol, the mood, the spirit of a single lonely person to pervade the mass of treadmill people. I hope Henry will keep his eye on people, and will remember how valuable it is for officials in one organization to know on intimate terms at least ten per cent of their own echelon of slaves.

When the old Ritz Grill was torn down, I was hurt—nothing of quality is permitted to last long enough to show that there are values other than Gargantuan ones. How soon will Harvard and Yale merge because of some phony nonhuman argument that professors can be more cheaply exchanged after a merger?

To a party for Alva Johnson at the New School for Social Research. He was one of those symbol men—he pervaded the New School. Then in the evening to Jimmy R.'s* exhibit—what a guy, at eighty: the same drive with oils that he had at the bar, or building trout pools at his home in the Adirondacks, or in his sporadic activities for Jewish affairs.

Saturday, *December 20*

A little crotchety, what with cholera inoculation this morning preparatory to flying to London in January, and on to Israel and Pakistan. This is a day without highs or lows, no occasions for excitement or fears, one of those complacent ones that are so prevalent with Maggie but seldom with me. It was topped by falling into a sound sleep bathed in the music of the Met.

* *James N. Rosenberg, lawyer, painter.*

This kind of placid, musing day, without a slip into debate even inside myself, reminds me of cruising anywhere from the tip of Florida to the coast of Maine. Not until we sight the blue hills of Camden do we see the first rise of the shore line. These are the first coast mountains from Mexico northward—and all the more exciting because our entire shore recedes, with at most a low ridge or a high skyscraper, until Camden. Camden-to-Northeast is for the cruising man fulfillment of all desires. Nearly every year since 1935, we have spent a month in that Penobscot basin. I'm all set for July 15, 1959—shoving off from Farnham Butler's yard on Mt. Desert Island.

Sunday, December 21

Local newsboys are giving their regular customers a free copy of a Newark Sunday paper. Such minor reflections of the strike are of interest. The deaf and hard-of-hearing get no news—they can't read lips of people on television, and radio is always out. Great saving in collection of city trash; new jokes, such as that fish sales are off because no newspaper to wrap them in.

It might benefit us if the FCC provided that at least once a year the officers and directors of each license-holding television station make a public appearance; have the order apply also to the as yet uncontrolled network owners.

Our new Supreme Court Justice, Stewart, speaks out on his own for the first time. The case involved the right of a wife to testify against her spouse. This is an area of a semi-humorous, changing bit of law. Will families break up if one spouse appears against the other? What if one "must" testify against the other? Should the rule of law be written with an eye to maintaining good relations in the home? To all of this the court gave its answer by sticking to the rule laid down before the freedom of women in our land, but says times might change the rule. Here Stewart agrees but adds what seems a good idea. In the present case, the wife had been held as a material witness by the prosecutor (the evil practice that Dewey made so popular and acceptable), and Stewart points out that it scarcely looks like a *voluntary* bit of testimony by the admitted prostitute wife against her husband, who is being held under the Mann Act. This idea helps nudge us nearer to the British system of seeking justice—to hell with the tricks which we make respectable by such phrases as "contest of wits." I wonder if any prosecutor ever had a witness held in jail in order to testify to *innocence* of the accused? Or are witnesses held only to have the district attorney win his case?

Off to lunch at the Brevoort with the Goldsteins to celebrate Joan's birthday, and then Maggie and I take care of Steffie until tomorrow morning. She is such a reasonable four-year-old that it's no bother—in fact, a pleasure.

Monday, December 22

Steffie tucks herself into my bed for breakfast this morning. It's cold, but we have eggs and cereal and this stokes us up. We spoofed about the little ring that I found, which was the baby of her new ring. What better way to get across the idea of the life stream in the animal kingdom—a feat the mineral kingdom can't perform, although it can have a metamorphosis, which we can't enjoy. Wood to coal for example, although some changes take less time than that.

Nick and Connie to office and Nick raids the drawer, selecting a ping-pong ball and a ruler-papercutter and sheath, the latter chosen, I thought, because of the damnable television emphasis on instruments of potential pain. Gave N. an honest-to-God five-dollar check so that he can open a savings-bank account. He endorsed it and Connie is taking him to the bank. I think he understands the checking system, which one learns only from life itself. He was impressed with the idea that he will get fifteen cents interest for the loan of the money to the bank. Thus check, interest and loan take on meaning in his mind.

It's a good day. Many people I met live with me within the gospel of R. L. Stevenson's "task of happiness." Why does not man learn the value of this pursuit as an affirmative mood of man?

I rather like the idea that magazine advertising linage has fallen off about ten per cent in 1958 over 1957. Would we not have a better, though more expensive, press if we paid directly as readers rather than be relieved of two thirds of cost through advertisement income to publishers? It would be the easiest way to establish books (minus ads) in our folkways. Some argue on Madison Avenue that books should carry ads to relieve direct costs to readers. I don't like it at all, even though in my schoolbooks there were Stollwerk Chocolate ads at the back of the book.

Tuesday, December 23

Big day for Maggie—the cast came off her foot and she had the longed-for bath. In cultures that have no such concept as that of the bathtub, what is the substitute yearning? I have been in lands where a bit of shade is the deepest passion of the unconscious. Do the Eskimos live in hope of higher temperatures, as the people of Sweden are sun worshipers after a dark winter? Do the birds in the northern lands wait for the sun before they wake up and lay, or do hens there accommodate their laying of eggs to darkness (while we in our clime artificially get more eggs by use of electric lights when the sun does not accommodate itself to the cock's crow)? Query: Are there any blind birds and, if so, can they migrate and, if so, do they follow the flock by echo sound waves?

Heard from H. H.,* who at this moment is my very personal leading candidate for President in 1960. He has the background of a professor—which he was—and the sense of adventure that fears not the changeable while recognizing that the face of change is as important as the concept of change. I'll see him with Roger before I go to London and the East.

* Hubert Humphrey.

Wednesday, December 24

Maggie sends to the office some lily-of-the-valley pips for "your nature study group." Viennese cookies come, specially prepared for me by a file clerk. Good— on the order of Alan's mother's concoctions. Presents pour in; the one that amused me most was a two-portion bottle of fifty-year-old Napoleon brandy accompanied by an ancient button bearing the inscription, *"Je garde la nation"* under a painting of a nude man pulling a cannon cord.

Gray day, but folks pay no mind to it because the eve of Christmas is office-party day. An odd custom of recent origin—not, for example, observed in England. Songs at office party quite different from former years—fewer darts at bosses, fewer sly cracks and much more sentimental, international and tender. This stemmed from the Lionel-Dick international exchange, London-New York.

In evening at family dinner party at Connie's. Usual horror of mounds of packages for children. It would be much better to spread them over the year. No kid— or adult—can fully comprehend and appreciate a dozen gifts at one time. Each impression is diluted, each object is minimized. So the lasting impression is that of an *over*-whelm.

Thursday, December 25

Slept late, woke up to sunlight. Used the new small frying pan that arrived from Marie in London. It was a challenge to learn the shift from iron to copper. Liquors, candies, haberdashery—all to an excess. An orchid plant from one client, the annual poinsettia from Ernie, Mary down the hall leaves a candy angel at the door. People are good to us. We are lucky, lucky folk. Even to the powder for bubblebathing—what more could a barrister want, particularly while reading Sir Patrick Devlin's essays on criminal prosecution in England. What a wise lawyer. He knows the acute tracks made when an excessive amount of power is given to anyone—while the donor takes the chance that the holder of the power will be able to restrict his own use of the power. We in our land dare not give great powers —in fact, must precisely define the power granted because we have no background of tradition that would inhibit the powerful from using all their powers all the time.

My favorite cold-weather food (and why I forget it for weeks on end I'll never know)—is Bovril and crackers. A little "nasching" of food goodies that came for Christmas. But most of day—say eight hours—was peaceful with a book and a little shut-eye.

Saturday, December 27

Early plane to Boston on what is called law work. Northeast Airlines does well by me and I had an hour of pleasure with myself. I don't know how I got to it, but I tried to fathom out of my tiny knowledge pile the communication system between man and animals. To dog, cat, horse and cow communication is in terms of simple requests or, more likely, commands. Where communication is most fun is not where we use sound but where we need other agencies. Man often wants to communicate the idea, "please stay away." For example, in *The New Scientist* of a few weeks ago I saw an article about the starling nuisance. In a few weeks I shall look at the National Gallery façade in London to see if man has really won a round in the antifouling battle against roosting starlings. Some time ago they had been scared from Duck Island in St. James Park, only to appear on Buckingham Palace a few days later. But now a compound is used, better than the oft-tried and difficult-to-apply narcotics. We in the U.S. tried loud-speakers that seem to do the job after a week of treatment, just as Alan Klotz's ship's clock has a chime spaced in intervals to which gulls in Oyster Bay don't seem to adjust and hence stay off his boat. Man can attract or repel fish by underwater sounds. But the most we do—or care to do—is to say, "Come close" or "go away." And even that much communication is difficult. A new St. Francis should be around the corner—one who can use or better electronics. He would add to our knowledge of bees, for up to date we can do little more than upset a bee's sense of time by electric shock of its antennae. Decoys that fool the eyes are devised, but man is slow to learn even the sign language of other animals. Maybe a deaf boy or girl who uses both speech and sign language could do a job communicating with deer, pigeon or turtle. The very big beasts or very small insects live in dimensions remote from ours—so far as we know.

Ran into Joe and Connie Indio from Nantucket at the Statler. An important couple. As owners of a town paper, they have been more influential during the past decade than have the seven or eight clergymen on the island. They have left footprints pointing toward better schools, cleaner government and, above all, the need for more thoughtful discussion on all issues.

On to Cambridge to Ben and Felicia's.* Small group; good to meet David Riesman, whom I approached with quite unreasonably prejudiced feelings. Just a brief chat evaporated this unfairness. I promised him that I would urge Marie in London to send a mimeographed letter to her U.S. friends every fortnight or so. Found the Azraels good company and was entranced by O'Connor. Then to a mass cocktail convention, to chat with Jock S.,† chat with Galbraith about early New Deal days and gobble, gobble with dozens of sober scholars. Then to dinner with Kaplans, Azraels, Fainsods and Gerta Kennedy from Houghton Mifflin. I wish Fainsod lived near us in New York City. He's my dish—informed and thoughtful, cautious in expression but daring in thought. I found Gerta K.'s mind entrancing, and she has one of those lovely Eskimo-Slavic flat faces that have always attracted me.

Eleven-thirty plane back to New York. Good, active day. Felt that I was competent at several client meet-

* *Ben Kaplan of the Harvard Law School and his author wife.*
† *Jock Saltonstall, Boston lawyer.*

ings, which, like so many, involved treating with the unseen Great White Father—the Treasury of Uncle Sam, the biggest partner in all law deals from the cradle through divorce or merger to the grave by way of estate planning.

Chat with Maggie, having brought her a present such as she yearned for: the standing of the hockey team, with our Rangers in fourth place—but only one game behind Detroit and Boston. Maybe Maggie's foot can risk the crowd at Madison Square Garden Sunday night.

Sunday, December 28

Maggie, waking at three A.M., found me awake too, and told me her dream before it evaporated, as it does on full awakening. Her mother, long dead, visited her, looking very well, and told her, "No harm ever came from loving too much. The only hurt to human beings is in loving too little—in withholding love." Maggie inspects her own guilt feelings about her mother's last years. But she, as many, was brought up to assume the admission of guilts—a kind of heritage of the early Bible days, when the God of the Jews was cruel and there was no one who would teach Him tenderness and tolerance. Not until the time of Hosea did the Jews start to educate—that is, refashion their concept of God. Only when the Jews started to bargain with God—save a city for one or five or ten men—did the Judeo-Christian get near to the idea of mercy and create values of forgiveness. And now, with the rewards of heaven and pains of hell no longer usable as societal correctives, forgiveness is the great function of all religions in the land. So few can forgive themselves, so many

need an outside Papa and none seem to forgive by twos
—without landing later in a law office for divorce of
home, family or business.

To the hockey game—and a real one it was. The
Rangers got a satisfying lead of two goals and ended with
a great victory against the leading Montreal team. No
real fights, and I enjoyed the officials immensely. Some
day I'd like to work with a sports writer on a book about
those judges, who are in a sense more important than
all the robed jurists—I mean the baseball, football,
hockey and all other sports umpires. These are loved
and hated by millions of us. They are cursed and
shouted at—and never reverse themselves, and can't be
reversed. What do the players say on the occasion of an
objectionable decision? What training is needed to be
a referee, what does one earn, what happens after he
retires? I'd like to know what these men think of the
players, and the audiences. Do they, the next morning,
alone and nude in the shower bath, ever admit to having made an error?

Then to Lindy's for pancakes, home to the Ed Murrow radio roundup, finished Susan P.'s* delightful book,
A House in Time, and read the Pakistan part of Alexander Campbell's book on India. I found it very helpful; I have respected him ever since we met in Delhi
about four years ago.

* *Susan Pulsifer.*

Monday, December 29

Most of my days are full of excitements. As Ruth Hale once said in the highest compliment I ever got, "Your cup runneth over." Almost every day there is a great variety of items that stay with me to record in a diary—that instrument of inevitable incompleteness. But some days a single event overshadows all else—of the mind or of emotion. Then law excitements, science bewilderments, food, music, theater, reading, etc., recede into the background. A bright spot creates a partial blackout of all else. Even to gaiety of *Captions Courageous,* a book of famous paintings outrageously retitled, of which I ordered half a dozen copies to give away.

And again today only one single event remains as a residue: lunch with R. L., my wisest friend. He had called me for lunch—and as always had an idea that I'm busy and shouldn't be bothered to come down to chat with him. He couldn't be wronger. Life is always a game of preferences—ex- and in-clusions. And on my list he is tops. Tommy Lamont joined us.

Wednesday, December 31

Good news—I have at last solved the problem of the use of mass media for illiterate lands that have no hope of producing sufficient teachers in this century. Radio and television require power that most of the planet doesn't have; at least the backward nations lack it. The transistor radio is too delicate for use in lands where no one has the skill to repair even a wooden plow. So at last I'm set with my kerosene-powered generator for a 16- to 35-millimeter movie projector for films on literacy, first aid and the use of seeds, fertilizers and plows. Gas won't do for the power—it is rare and expensive in those areas that must have dictators until people are literate, gain curiosity and can communicate. Diesel oil is close to kerosene and I think I'm near solving my kerosene-movie-projector problem. This is important, even though many economies may skip from kerosene to atomic power just as some jumped from whale oil to electricity.

For decades we have gone to Carrie's* for New Year's Eve. Carrie invites virtually four generations of her friends to foregather at this time—the party has become an institution. It is a pleasure to see most of these people on occasion, a few we see often and Lewis and Alice† we wish we saw more of. As a rock-ribbed Hoover Republican, he is important for us to talk to. How else can we genuinely learn the position honorably held against most of Point Four aid, the basic formula of social-security concepts, etc.? As usual I sat with the youngsters, for they are nearer right in their attitudes than we oldsters—they have not compromised away so many of their ideals, and life has not besmirched so many of their dreams.

From Yale comes the discovery that pregnancy in dogs can be halted by drugs made from yeast—a cheap method, available to the overpopulated areas of the world, if the idea turns out to be applicable to humans. Two observations occurred to me. The first: a dog's pregnancy lasts sixty-one days and this drug works—

---

* Mrs. Jerome Hanauer, cousin.
† Mr. and Mrs. Lewis Strauss.

not by abortion—from the tenth to the forty-second day. What will be the comparable period of effective use for women? Further: this may prove acceptable to those religious groups that condemn artificial methods as antithetical to theological dogmas. Hope for our world in the race between food and population, necessary for Peace on Earth, rests on family limitation. Happy New Year to all those concerned with parents' having that number of children they can bring up in health and economic well-being.

JANUARY

Thursday, January 1, 1959

Perfect start of New Year. Didn't get dressed all day. Didn't go to any eggnog-drinking parties. Lolled and loafed. Many telephone calls, many naps, no meals but only periodic *nasching*. I was indifferent to weather, undisturbed by Cuban news, found pictures of looting regrettable but they didn't raise my temperature, didn't care whether Air Academy or Tex Christians won— just as happy that they tied . . . a vacuum day.

Friday, January 2

At noon went to the Public Health Clinic to get a yellow-fever shot. Once more I was disturbed by the policy of our government toward its citizens. About a hundred people came for shots. The civil servants were all efficient and polite and the entire reception was well organized; except—and this is a prevailing exception— a hundred people were waiting in a spacious sitting room for an average of one hour. I should guess that the time of those people was worth about $3.00 an hour, on

the average. That's $300.00 a day for five days a week—
or a least $75,000.00 a year. There was one very efficient
technician who gave the shots. I assume that hiring
another technician and an assistant would increase the
cost by no more than $20,000.00 a year. Now let's assume
that the waiting time would have been cut only in
half. The manpower net saving would reach at least
$15,000.00 or $20,000.00 a year. Count federal, state
and city agencies, and the figure grows to important
dimensions. I see it wherever I go, and even more pro-
nouncedly at the Social Security offices. But to waste
our economic wealth by keeping members of the public
idle seems to be less objectionable than raising government expenses. So, even though we might as a people
save a billion dollars, it takes more political courage
than exists to increase the budget and hence the savings
by even half that sum.

Sunday, January 4

All morning on phone with Castro intermediaries
—about ambassadorship, dislike of present U.S. ambassador, proffers of financial support from Russian interests in Guatemala and Venezuela, and above all the
total absence of cash in the Cuban Treasury. Castro will
enter Havana with no money to pay government employees; U.S. must come through promptly or he will
have to accept loan from Soviet or one of its fronts. The
Castro move is no coup d'état—it's a revolution.

Around noon the Goldsteins and the Bessies entered
en masse. Too hectic to enjoy the family. Worked all
afternoon, then to Mag's for her good coffee and coffee
cake; Edna Ferber and the Armseys of the Mews drop

in for a drink; then to Chinatown for dinner—to that absurdly named joint, The Chinese Rathskeller. That's great food—how so wholesome and filling and at the same time cheap?

The Milton Eisenhower report on South America is now public. In the press report on it I find that the President of Johns Hopkins makes no reference to illiteracy in So. America—only to trade and money and Things. I can't explain this omission. Maybe the full report does relate literacy to higher living standards. Will order a copy. But why should the papers edit it out —if they did, it's shocking. It's shocking either way!

Monday, January 5

What a chance for us in Cuba. I must assume that Castro himself is anti-Communist and that the Communists of Cuba have nevertheless proceeded, as is usual, on two levels—one out in the open and the other by infiltrating under cover, This is a real civil war, with people of all economic groups in the Castro forces. But there is no mood of Lee-Grant when it comes to laying down arms, with a horse returned to every vanquished soldier. What a mess. No money in treasury, sugar about to be cut and gathered, only four months of work ahead in the chief industry—and the big question is, how many Batista followers must Castro kill or put in jail? How tough will C. be? I recall my friend Davila of Chile, President for a hundred days, not cruel enough to hold power—so he was thrown out, although he boasted with pride that he was the only ex-President of Chile up to that time who was allowed to leave Chile alive. Karolyi, whom I knew when I represented him in the 1920's, lost Hungary because he was soft and kind. He let Bela Kun, the Communist, out of jail and the Communists then drove K. out of office and out of Hungary. Such is the story of control of nations in turmoil—of nations without the least tradition of the democratic process. So C. will be head of the army—he says, "for the time being." At least he knows one of the spots of threat to his controls. He will have a hundred days for all his reforms —like F. D. R.'s hundred days after the years of Hoover's well-meaning lethargy.

Jim Armsey last night told me of a friend who ordered the doctor to stop giving him tranquilizers. The patient wanted his own frustrations and in effect said, "How can I adjust to my worries if I'm artificially supported by tranquilizing drugs?"

I have just learned that the essence of my fun in writing a diary lies not in facts, persons, names or even occurrences. Events and people are little more than springboards to record the travels of my mind. In truth, I must always be reminded that narration is pedestrian, while canters of the mind, the intervals between the facts, are the source of the real enjoyment.

Tuesday, January 6

My thirsty lily-of-the-valley is growing handsomely. There is as yet no odor, not a speck of the delicate flavor that will be so intoxicating in a week. The buds are there but without fragrance. I keep testing, hoping that I will catch the whiff of the first moment when the hormone or gene of fragrance will be strong enough to make itself evident to the nostril of man.

There are few grandames left in our society. Today

I lunched with my favorite, Vianda Williams. She talks and looks the part—very white hair, fine carriage, precise manners (not necessarily to be identified with the Old South from which she sprang), dignity of phrase and stature. Despite her wealth and background, she has a truly open mind. On an intellectual level she can't be surprised or shocked. She seems to be a bit above, but not aloof from, life—or at least life as it has brushed off on me.

Wednesday, January 7

Last evening invited by one of the two top spokesmen for new Cuban government to discuss problems of taking over a country with no cash in the till. I guess that the anti-Batista forces are mostly amateurs. I feel that under certain circumstances amateurs are valuable in government. Many of our best cabinet members over the years have been amateurs—that is, had no practice in the art of running a democracy. And still, the Cuban regime is naive, to say the least. It announces that Cuba will never again allow a dictatorship. After this high-minded pronouncement we then read that of course there will be no election of officials for at least eighteen months. So I ask, what is there in the year and a half except a dictatorship? I understand that dictators are killed every four or five years on the average. But this does not mean, as the better press would always have us infer, that if a dictator is killed democracy is installed. The best we can say is that on occasion the people by civil war or coup d'état hope to get a more benevolent ruler. Democracy is a tender plant—it grows as slowly as the redwood, and not as fast as the slash pine. Maybe Castro wants to win the approval of the people by understating his hopes, as did F. D. R.; thus he postulates eighteen months of dictatorship, with the thought that if he can do better and can allow an election in twelve months the people will be delighted.

Lunch with Jack Fischer. Urbane, benign, open-minded editor. I guess *Harper*'s shouldn't have bite, or care too much about anything but taste and decency. Or is it possible for editors to feel strongly and still not be crusaders? What a going-over we gave the book industry—not the editors or publishers, but the profession as a profession. As a group, they are probably on the conservative side of life politically or even socially, and as a group they have not had any strong leadership. Hence book publishers are pushed around as not even the makers of wallpaper, paper napkins or any other paper products, printers and distributors are. George Brett is the only stout leader I have met in the industry. He really *led* the fight on postage rates.

Saturday, January 10

Now that her cast is off, Maggie fixed the breakfast for the first time in about two months. I rested in bed reading my *Tribune,* being served—like a well-kept lady. Used some Christmas bubble-bath soap and by that time really fitted into the pattern of those movies we export—so untypical of our life.

To the office to throw out numerous—as usual—subsidized third-class mail circulars, but received gratifying mail from Tom Lamont, Jones of the Historic Shrines Trust of England, Elizabeth Barber of Authors Society and many other warm and kindly notes from friends.

Some days the mail just runs sweet.

Never a day, however, but my mail brings me letters that I haven't the wisdom, strength or toughness to throw into the basket—requests from jails and mental institutions. Every day some poor devils pick on me to see if I can retrieve their unused lives. "I have been illegally convicted; Mr. Ernst I assure you I was innocent"; or "Here, I have been put into the nut house by greedy relatives. I'll surely go crazy unless you can get me out soon."

These appeals are for the most part unworthy of time and attention. Many are from unbalanced souls. But what is a lucky lawyer to do? What if only one in a hundred has been improperly pushed around by society? So, at a great cost of energy and time and even the time of a young lawyer in the office, I still, after decades of what should have disillusioned me, read every letter, correspond with at least two thirds of the writers, offer to see maybe one out of ten—and all this for reasons difficult to justify on any rational basis.

And yet I must admit that it is a kind of treasure hunt. At certain periods, just when I try to put on a new thick skin, I hit the jackpot. By some kindly stroke of luck I'm able every once in a while to take a young man from behind bars, arrange for the freedom of a harmless mental case. I must admit I have a deep conviction that our jails are by and large little more than production belts for professional criminality. Except in a few specialized reformatories, the first offender must of necessity associate with an average type of criminal, so that at least half the newcomers are conditioned to their new social set—the world of hardened criminals.

Two steps are long past due. Judges expert at seeking truth in a trial have no special claim on our judgment as being wise in the field of determining how to retrieve the convicted man or woman. They should abdicate the function of imposing sentence and turn it over to psychiatrists and penologists—who, of course, will need and deserve the service of the parole and probation officers. Next, our prison population should be viewed as needing education more sorely than all those who are still free of incarceration—even more than the underprivileged who live in slum areas, or the ignorant. I say "ignorant" because we now know that each extra year of schooling reduces the chance of criminality, as criminality is also clearly inversely related to greater retail purchases—which only means an increase in income and standard of living. Why not then as an investment—in reduced taxes—pay the highest salaries to the wardens and teachers and rebuilders who work in our penal institutions? We might find it difficult to recruit the staffs we need in jails. But without the salaries, the profession of teachers of the antisocial, the distorted, the offbeat will never have the prestige needed to induce people with the skills necessary to cutting down our crime rate and particularly our shocking percentage of recidivism. So, I'll send for one of the young lawyers and discuss what we will do with this last batch of pathetic, phony, idée-fixe—but maybe innocent or sane— letter writers.

To Bob Smallwood's apartment. I haven't seen him since he gave up the reins at Lipton's, which he took over as a puny business and built for Lever into what is probably the best single unit of this world-wide enterprise in the sixty nations in which, I think, that Dutch-British industrial empire operates. We of the U.S. have nothing to match it in variety of product and, more important, in the informality of its top brains.

Sunday, January 11

Minor office hangovers handled on phone with Harriet, Alan, Bill Kunstler and others—mostly on the pleasant, ideational rather than the operative side of the law. Brisk walk in our neighborhood and as usual great joys visual and auditory. A new, bright-blue *espresso* restaurant off Sixth Avenue—Pompeii red walls inside, very Italian, built to look like an elegant home in Italy. Not yet open, but will try it soon. These are so good in so many ways and are spreading uptown and, in fact, to London. They are cheap and restful in the terms of other cultures. Even though the French and Italians are supposed to be more volatile and excitable than are our people, when it comes to dining and wining we are the rushed, the restless, and they are the reposed and leisured.

Walking home, we saw an artist-type man (that is, not too well kempt in clothes or hair) carrying a babe of say perhaps a year and a half or two years. The child looked into a window and said something that sounded like "Mama," to which the toting papa replied, "Oh, no—that's the Venus de Milo." To which Maggie says, "Art education at a young age."

For dinner Andrew* dropped in, and we offered him our special nationality foods. Down here we have the best of Danish, Spanish, Italian, Japanese, Chinese, etc., restaurants. We ended up with Oysters Rockefeller at Seafare and then to Peacock Espresso. As a contrast to all the stories of man's inconsideration of man, Andrew told a true and tender tale of a man whose life was saved

* *Andrew Loebl.*

by a surgeon, and who, remembering the skill of the medicine man, each year on the anniversary of the operation sends him a substantial, expensive gift. And then we swapped tales of man's decencies. A quarter of a century ago I helped a poor hat-check girl about to be dispossessed from her lodging room, and each yuletide I get a card and a letter from her. It makes me feel rich and successful when I receive her recurring remembrance. I wouldn't know her if I met her—but she is a friend.

Picked up last period of Ranger-Chicago hockey game on my little Zenith, a good radio. My Rangers came up from behind 3-to-1 to win 4-to-3. It's not always easy to follow the pick-up by radio, but one goal of Andy Bathgate's I could see as I heard it—one of those plays from behind the cage, the puck sneaking into the corner of the cage past the goalie.

Monday, January 12

Whenever man feels overwhelmed or trapped, he becomes irrational and consequently jumps many hurdles to find a seeming solution for his quandary. For example, I read today a proposal to soup up the grain used as feed for pigeons with whiskey or vodka or some other strong intoxicant. The birds would get groggy and come to ground where they can easily be captured and killed—what a plan of desperation! Then Penelope says, what about South Vietnam and its plan to abolish polygamy overnight—or better stated, "overday"? This we did in the days of Sen. Smoot and the fight against the Mormon practice of multiple wives. But Vietnam goes further, and no doubt much too far—it proceeds against "potential adultery." I can't find the strategy for this brash move. Will they abolish potentially adulterous situations? What about fornicatious situations? I would suggest that the plan will fail and probably do little more than drive what is considered the evil underground and increase it. How often we in our culture have pursued the patterns of the Puritan technique of removal of tendencies from public view, only to have them aggravated and compounded by stealth and sneakeries! Thus do we develop cynicism about law and authority.

Lunch with magazine editor Charlie Robbins and Ernest V. Heyn at Overseas Press Club. Maybe they will dig into Galindez case and the real source of the million dollars, which they know did not come from Basque people as claimed by Galindez. Or they will conclude that the story should never be told. What if it were an operation of our own government? Ethical query: should truth be suppressed to help save our nation? Does a lie help our precious republic in the long run?

Wednesday, January 14

Those words "flotsam" and "jetsam" will have to pick up an associate term. This can be in place of "lagan" —the stuff that lies on the ocean bottom, a word long out of use. Now a new word must be invented—Maggie suggests, "orbitage." In a spaceship man can't "jettison" anything. The flot will follow the plane. How can we throw anything out of the plane up there? It won't drop —it will just follow us around. We'll make our own airborne litter pile as we move. And inside the craft, how do we get hold of floating food? What chains it down? Often I have thought that containers on our sober earth should be made of the same material as the content.

Stick cologne is an example: just wear it down and use it up.

For dinner with friends from Pakistan and then to the theater to see *The World of Suzie Wong*. I enjoyed it more than the critics wanted me to. Critics are a source of important improvement of standards in the arts; we often forget they are also a retarding and destructive influence. This is especially true in the theater, where the critic has the double function of reporter and critic, and the economics of production prevent tricky word-of-mouth information. A production costs too much to carry from week to week while the producers hope for an audience brought by word of mouth. In this plays differ from the sale of books.

The core of the play was the traditional plot of the lady of easy virtue who at heart is a girl of sterling character. But most plots are traditional. In this case I was a pushover from the start: the setting was Hong Kong—my dream city. If my Fate said, "You can only travel once more outside this nation. Pick two cities and only two," I'd not hesitate in saying, "London and Hong Kong." London, my old and tried friend—with the coziest memories for me. Hong Kong—the dream, the improbable, the fantastic, the unbelievable.

Aside from this head start, my joy at the theater was in the deft acting of France Nuyen. No U.S actress could have done the role—it was truly the portrayal of a foreign culture. The hurts, the smiles, the hesitations, the impulsiveness were all so unlike the reactions of Anglo-Saxons or Europeans. It was the nuances that tickled and surprised me no end.

Then to Sardi's and home, to pack, and read the last pile of pamphlets before our jaunt to London.

Thursday, January 15

In the Worthy case—to test a reporter's right to go to Red China—I was surprised at the panic in the Department of Justice when we called to get permission to file a brief in behalf of Ed Murrow and possibly other commentators. The Department refused and said it would fight us in court. I guess it is understandable, since all the great newspaper and network owners, who write about the freedom to roam our earth and the divine right of reporters to gather news—all except one or two have fallen obsequiously on their bellies. Not a one is really in there slugging. The ANPA, the Newspaper Guild and the Association of Broadcasters are effectively supporting the State Department by their silence. But why must this be so? Are they too busy to care about liberty? Do they drain off their emotions in favor of freedom by writing platitudinous, unread editorials on the subject? Or is it that the men who write do not own, do not really make decisions? Why, oh why don't they realize that freedom is lost by inaction and not by action.

Dinner at home. The Goldsteins and the Bessies to say goodbye. All packed, all at ease—not a tense nerve left in me.

Friday, January 16

It took as much time from home to plane and from plane to London hotel as it did to cross the Atlantic. We have licked the air but not the ground. Since my first long flight in the Caribbean in 1938 or 1939, I have always been thrilled at getting on a long-flight plane. The jet was all we expected. The machine is wonderful, and six hours to London still seems improbable. The four-hour meal was pretentious, delicious, obscene in amount, well served and quite indecent—and I loved eating my way across the ditch. The literature—pamphlets—with the exception of an engineering description of a jet is pedestrian and totally unimaginative, even the Hammond maps can be improved by looking at maps in Europe and, above all, my old gripe has not been appeased. I have written for a decade to Pan American and the designers of the interior of its planes for one meager boon, a hook under the window where ladies can hang their pocketbooks. I'm tired of picking up Maggie's from the floor.

All this sounds as though the trip wasn't great fun. It was simply great. When we landed I was a little on the loopy side from wine. I renewed my love affair with London from the initial courtesy of the customs officials to the warm reception at the Berkeley Hotel. We were at home in England.

Marie and Austen Albu met us at the airport, drove us to town, came up for a snifter, and chatted until eight N.Y. time or one A. M. London time. I told Marie how often I still looked at her window on Fifth Avenue to see if she were in or out—just as I had done for several years before she married to England.

Tidbit: on the plane several ladies had their feet up
—the usual plaint, blood rushing to feet and discomfort.
I recalled that once on a crossing I toed my shoes off,
couldn't get them back on; there being no shoehorn
aboard, faced with the prospect of landing in Paris bare-
footed, I used the end of my belt. And now it occurred
to me that people who practice yoga, standing on their
heads, probably don't get gout in the foot. And what
will be the effect on foot gout when people fly in upper
space, freed from gravity?

Flowers, fruit, letters, telephone messages—all appreciated on the way to bed; waited for morning to enjoy
the seven-foot bathtub.

Saturday, January 17

The *London Times*—big enough with proper
perspective toward criminal behavior of man, world
items far beyond anything found in U.S. Walked to
Wetherell, was measured for suits, then to Watts to
order a coracle—the Welsh fisherman's lightweight boat,
never seen in U.S., that the kids will be able to carry on
their backs up the beach in Nantucket. What a store:
hundreds of books, fittings that we don't even invent.
We, the gadgeteers of the world, are outpassed in England by pure theoretical science, and now by gilhickeys
for small sailboats. To lunch at the Connaught with
Charles Foster* and Mrs.

To Austen and Marie's for dinner. Home specially
overheated for us Americans and the food whipped into
a banquet from soufflé to zabaglione to show that Marie

---

* *Expert on education by television.*

has become a graduate Hausfrau. Solved all problems, but the idea that stayed with me overnight is that a book should be done on how a young man or woman enters political party life in each of our nations. The differences are implicit in the conditions. In our land a member of the House must live in his district, and he undergoes little discipline by political parties. Whether the British practices to the contrary are better or worse is irrelevant. It would be of advantage to both cultures to understand the arts and techniques of becoming involved in party political life. Home around midnight.

Monday, January 19

The morning was taken up with television matters. The Berkeley has become my office, and I felt a little like the French lawyer who so often practices in his home. I ordered drinks or tea and was reminded of one business custom in France, in home or office: when the minds have met, the decisions been made, Monsieur strolls to the corner, opens the cupboard and gets out two small glasses and pours the cognac. That is the traditional symbol that the business at hand is done and over. In our culture, business is often done at lunch, and on occasion the matter is sealed by a shaking of hands.

The rest of the day was so busy that weather was quite unnoticed. Mostly publishers, among whom Allen Lane is unique. In the first place he is a reading publisher, he enjoys a phrase and has a sense of words, and still more important he is a dedicated person—he believes devoutly in books as the enduring conduit of culture. In a comparatively short time—twenty or twenty-five years—

he has made the name of Penguin known throughout the civilized world. Not one of our publishers has ever attempted world-wide dispersal of his imprint. What has Lane got that our publishers—or for that matter other British publishers—haven't got? I can't define it and if I could I'd try to describe it with such precision that it could be copied by others. It's a secret process, but not intentionally secret. One ingredient is his attitude toward his list of titles. Twice to my knowledge he has rejected immediate sure profits that would have involved lowering the standards of the writings that carry his imprint. He also rejected the abominable selling frauds of so many of our reprint paper-back houses. No guns or breasts on the jackets—unlike those so often found at home even on books that are neither sexy nor brutal. Among our publishers there are many distinguished but few distinctive, and of those I guess only the name of Alfred Knopf really stands for a type of writing and author.

Tuesday, January 20

Lunch at Travelers with Harold Hartley, whom I have seen in London at least once a year for about twenty-five years. The accident he had in Cyprus forty-five years ago is just now penalizing his locomotion. This is a great person—in the sense that George Marshall or Russell Leffingwell are great. Scientist, administrator, director, traveler, he has his influential fingers in more important pies than anyone I know in England or the U.S. We tried to ambush the problem of capital needed for literacy and simple education about fertilizer, seeds and farming. In Pakistan, the average income is about fourteen cents a week. A very slight increase in productivity for all the people would have a rolling, geometrically increasing result in income, and at little cost to our rich nation. He seemed excited about my S. A. projects —literacy through television, radio or movies.

Black tie and off to Savoy for the traditional dinner party set up by Harry Nathan*—a function that he has insisted on, to my pleasure, for at least thiry-five years. Last year I mentioned the need for more dollar allowances' coming to our shores. Harry now tells me that the men present at the party were persuaded and had enough influence so that, shortly thereafter, each traveler to U.S. was allowed an extra $100. So this evening I had to be careful and selective, for surely those present also had access to power for reasonable objectives. Now I can note, not as a prophecy or a bit of precognition, that Prince Philip should visit our shores. He is a thoughtful person and a gracious after-dinner speaker. Let's see what happens!

Here the television reports from Cuba show the trials and convictions, but end with last steps of priest and convicted, omitting—as we do not and should—the blindfolding and shots. Also, here the inquiring-reporter shows are far braver in showing the ignorance of the public on matters such as size, distances, mountain ranges, etc., of India. We, I suggest, are too kind and too considerate in this matter—it's not that our public is better informed.

* *Lord Nathan of Churt, solicitor.*

Wednesday, January 21

The food in England is strikingly better than before the war. I should imagine that this has resulted from at least two clear causes. For one thing, during the war there was a siege, a food embargo; and just as Paris became famous for food because during the Siege of Paris flavoring was invented, so in England sauces and special preparations were used during the last war. The tired old fish was not tossed in lonely fashion into the frying pan, and the nation that discovered other continents in its search for spices became explorers of food preparation. In the second place, England opened its doors to refugees, taking into this tight, suffering island more refugees than distant rich U.S. was willing to receive. Among these refugees were restaurateurs from Hungary, Greece and all the nations of Europe. These people took over Soho and soon set up different standards of taste and preparation. And thus England today is no longer addicted to soggy brussel sprouts, nor does it rely with ancient accent on a thick slice of red beef.

Elizabeth Barber for lunch. She is "what"—if that's the correct English—makes the difference between the Authors Society of England and its counterpart in our land. Sober, nonfanatical—a girl who does not allow detail to becloud policy issues. We had much to talk over, but in the main all subjects circled around the writers' Maypole of Freedom. How come that in this nation, which treasures learning within hard covers, every tax impediment devisable by the treasury has been placed on authors and publishers?

Thursday, January 22

It's been a busy six days—talking at ease to more people than I see in a fortnight in New York. But each day there is one high spot or at most two. Lunch at the *Times* with ample time to talk to V. Smith, Haley (the editor) and David Bowes-Lyon. I was not too surprised to learn that the British papers also failed to report on their newspaper strike that closed them down a few years ago—just as we have had no discerning reporting on the New York newspaper strike. It's an odd kind of omission, to report on everyone but oneself. I'm quite sure that the British strike had no social overlay, as did the one in New York City. It was just the usual scramble for the division of the wealth—and, as in all cases, management is inevitably defeated and must learn to take its licking graciously.

I'm now quite confident, having tapped significant minds from the left of the Labour Party to the right of the Tories, that all are agreed that the great unspoken, unmentionable drag on all free economies is the evaporation of preferences in pay and social recognition for all skilled men and women. To be sure the dictators— particularly Communist—have a class cleavage due to intentional higher financial rewards and public kudos for the skilled people in every discipline. In time, the Soviet will lick us in the world markets, through their inducement to youth to learn skills and through their economies. I am shocked at the amount of dissection, analysis and gobbledegook carried on in Labour Party circles in England. This in itself works to reduce dreams, inventions and planning of the type that accompanied the social-democratic movements of thirty or forty years ago.

Marie for dinner, but she left too early. She had to pick up Austen at the House of Commons. She is still one of my very favorite persons. She handed us a couple of springboards for mental exploration. One the report of a monkey that acted as if it had read Freud, showing a mental decline with all the symptoms of a good Freudian patient, refusing to eat all phallic vegetables—carrots, etc.—except when chopped up; as to grapefruit, Marie did not know; we also never found out whether it was a male or female monkey. The other, that Sanskrit does not have the word "like" in our sense of "resembling"—a kind of admission that there are no identicals in life.

What an exciting city for us. Comparisons are invited. Most retail shops—butcher, baker, etc.—do not deliver; this results in less truck traffic but more time needed by housewife. Some bald men, but those with hair have big mops of it and the mustaches—wow! Hats worn less? Cold climate kills dandruff? On television, speakers use fewer words and fewer spread-eagle flourishes. Letter delivery more predictable than our telegrams, captions in press derived from Dickens, and contests between cities—I saw Leeds *vs.* Margate—in which each puts on half-hour television shows. I'd like to see Troy *vs.* Natchez. Why have we overlooked indigenous cultures outside of New York and Los Angeles and, maybe, New Orleans and San Francisco?

Friday, January 23

At lunch at my club—Savile—with Harper of Law Society and Goodie.* A full discussion of next steps to popularization of our exchange of young lawyers. It ought to be a cinch to get twenty exchanges. We agreed the age should be around thirty, after a general knowledge of the law and before too accented a specialization; better results in smaller U.S. offices than offices with a hundred or more lawyers where partners have only a bowing acquaintance; three months for each is enough; swaps should be spontaneous; the program would be destroyed and bogged down if it were handled on our side of the Atlantic by the New York City Bar Association or the American Bar Association (we should keep an eye on Birmingham and Chicago, or Glasgow and San Francisco). The next move is that Harper and Goodie will send me jottings—or what Hartley calls "flow papers"—and I'll add my notes and get Dick and Lionel to work. We all see a book in the project.

We kept the evening free and went to Coq D'Or for dinner all alone by our own selves. Little packing for the week end in Paris.

* *Arnold Goodman, solicitor.*

Saturday, January 24

Easy flight over. In France as in England airports are clean and well organized, and tariff inspections are handled on the assumption that travelers are honest.

This France confounds many Americans. The only difference I note is that the taxi horns have been silenced. Most of the people of the States think the French are lazy. In fact, they work longer hours than we do, but the lunchtime closing fools us. I hear travelers ask how the French can live on so few francs a week—little recalling that rent is only about ten to fifteen per cent of income, whereas at home we spend twenty-five to thirty per cent of our salaries on rent or home ownership. Maybe it's time the rent controls were relaxed here, so as to encourage building. But the symbol of Paris—in fact, of France—for us is the three-foot-long loaf of bread carried unwrapped under the arm through the traffic. The cars have less color than in England, but neither the French nor the English waste as much of their national income on colors of cars, gadgets and change for change's sake alone. I like their down-sloping car hoods better than ours—gaudy, searchlighted and meaningless.

Maggie and I recall every black can and red nun buoy that lies in the waterways between Camden and Northeast Harbor. After we had ranged the Maine coast the second or third time in the 1930's, all these markers stayed in our memories. We enjoy the experience of looking for these important old friends—much clearer in our minds than the buoys in the sandy Nantucket Sound. It is the same in Europe: odd trifles of no fathomable significance bob into our minds. The restaurant at Rond Point has been repainted, the teatime waiter at Grosvenor House is the same one who presided in that big room during the war, the desk at the Savile has been changed, the coffee pots at the Berkeley leak just as outrageously as ever (Margaret thinks we should send the hotel one that pours cleanly and neatly). Why are the bathrooms in the French hotels so big and so bare of bath rugs or mats on the cold tiles? Why are French cheeses so much stronger than any in the U.S.? Why are there so many dogs in Paris—is this a national answer to loneliness in people with a falling population? The fun of travel is in the whys. I guess that is the fun of living and surely, after some traveling between times, we travel sitting still—with every bit of our reading endlessly creating retakes, from Hong Kong to the Virgin Isles. What an exciting world; and what a challenge for man to cover the mud floors of 800 million homes, to let people in fifty years learn to read and write so that one billion people have at least fifty-percent literacy rate. One world is far off, I'll settle for the next century just for a healthier—in mind and body— world. Someone in London suggested an identical airplane rate between any and all capitals of all nations. It would have to be based on the two closest together —and of course all other travel by air would have to carry this loss so as to average out.

Sunday, January 25

Quiet Sunday in Paris, full of sunlight for about six hours. This is the family day, or at least it appears more of a family day than does Sunday in New York. Off early for about three hours with Aly—a gay person, an emphatic personality, and a human without guile.

In the afternoon to visit with Dr. deLazovert—a fabulously youthful seventy-two, still an old race horse when he smells oil. When he talks with excitement of his past oil ventures and his real smell for oil underground, he seems like a playing child and one would be hard pressed to believe that this is the man who killed Rasputin in St. Petersburg. He's off on new, improbable adventures. He has no expensive habits and ample income and much capital, but must keep busy—never for the sake of being busy, never for pennies, only for millions. He's a hunter, for big game only.

Strolled in this beautiful city, laid out by the same city planner as our only correspondingly avenued city, Washington. How come that no big cities in our land copied the wide avenues, and that we have no beautiful towns or cities in this sense, save some of the New England towns with their "Commons"?

Tuesday, January 27

Back in London. Such odd items come into conversations here, so unlikely to bob up in the States. Uganda has practically no whites, no outsiders save only a few Asians. Uganda, I hear, is slow in moving on and up. It has no visible whipping boys, no outlets for hate, no internal devils. Hence, it is slow in the generation of nationalistic drives. Another: though the papers and magazines in the United States may dismiss with a line or so the trouble we create by offering butter to India, in England we can't avoid knowing that Denmark is up in arms. When will we learn that our ten-billion-dollar surplus cannot be dished out on any bilateral or binational basis? Ghee to India hurts Denmark, rice to Burma hurts Japan, and so it goes. Some years ago I explored with Nehru the wisdom of my government's turning over, say, eight billion dollars of food surplus to the UN, which the UN might then distribute and would turn over to our Treasury any money it might get for this stockpile. The UN would have to juggle the disposal of this wealth and would learn the ungodly burden of being a donor who, for every thankful recipient, is faced with at least one injured producer. It might educate the UN to the simplest facets of the democratic process—the art of give-and-take, avoidance of extremes, compromise on many levels now termed "matters of principle." Or it might wreck the entire UN. I'm for a try at it.

To lunch at Bill Astor's with a gay, intelligent gal— non-Irish Catholic, and not self-conscious, of whom we find so many in the U.S. Bill told the interesting episode of his trip to the Dominican Republic, where he received $25,000 from the Generalissimo for Hungarian Relief, in which cause he was so active. I thanked him for starting my warm relationship with Aly Khan.

Paid a call on Dean Don at Westminster Abbey, left our best wishes on his retirement, and again saw the Abbey. Man will never again build anything so beautiful and so touched with reverence. The cultural background of our nation is told on English statues and funeral slabs. As we walked through we recognized our past—like touching with our finger tips the values inherited in our education, art and slow struggles for personal liberty. Incidentally, *The Manchester Guardian* gave a full spread to the opinions of Judges Whitaker and Douglas on the most recent high court-decision on the question of the police power in search and seizure. Is there a counterpart of reporting from England even

in *The Washington Post* or *The New York Times?* Also
shocked at design of our new Embassy Building in Grosvenor Square—a total disregard of the architecture that
in the main surrounds the Square. Why do we feel we
must always appear different? Must we forever in our
foreign service prove ourselves to others, or do we just
have no concern for tradition, even in architecture?

Wednesday, January 28

Last-minute departure details—pick up tickets;
gets suits delivered; telephone office, since no reply received to dozens of requests for information; farewell
to special London friends.

Fred Warburg* came for lunch. He has an acute concern for freedom of the printed word. In part this is
because he has been in the dock as a defendant. In our
culture our publishers react quite otherwise because
they are seldom, if ever, the defendants in obscenity
cases. With us it's the newsdealers—as in the *Life Magazine* case—or the bookstore clerk, as in most cases involving books. Thus authors and writers buy emotional
comfort by offering to pay dollars for a lawyer for the
defense. But this personal involvement makes a world of
difference. Imagine the reaction if Bennett Cerf had
actually been subjected to criminal process in the *Ulysses*
case, instead of trying the issue by importation of a
copy with an action entitled "People of the United
States *vs.* One Copy of Ulysses." Credit to Roy Larsen
of *Life Magazine,* who allowed me to state in court that,
as publisher of *Life Magazine,* he was the responsible
party, even though the prosecutors had for obvious rea-

* *British publisher.*

sons not seen fit to hand him a summons. It's this impact on publishers themselves that has caused a more
disturbed but thoughtful concern for reappraisal of obscenity legislation in England.

Thursday, January 29

We left London in a fog. We are used to living
in the dark hours and hanging around airports, so were
not uncomfortably discommoded by a five-hour delay.
A real peasoup fog, of which Nantucket would be proud.
So what—memory of Heywood Broun, who turned in
only at sun-up in New York for years. Time, when you're
interested, is of no consequence.

We were "downgraded," as it is called, from first-class
to tourist seats since planes were changed—a satisfying
act of compelled thrift—while other passengers were
upgraded just by being on a plane. Some of the immigrants to Israel from torturing nations are frightened,
not of flight, but of freedom. Others afraid to fasten the
seat belt—a symbol of "cloisterophobia."

A very intelligent Israeli hostess on plane, and we had
several hours of questions. A few hunches, deduced from
this girl and others on plane. A distinction in status between those born here before Israel was a state and more
recent arrivals. Tolerance, in its real sense, for the orthodox—sort of an attitude of "Let them go their ultra-
religious way without let or hindrance." An orientated
condescension for the rich U.S. benefactors who want
favors or influence in Israel in exchange for gifts or purchase of bonds. A new prestige in form of lipstick and
tight-fitting slacks in the kibbutzim. No obstacles to con-
traception, reduction of guilts and stealth as to pre-

marital sexual experiences of young people, reduction
in size of families among those who came from areas of
unlimited offspring, cleavage in terms of attempted or
assumed superiority between European and Eastern Jews
as in U.S., women from necessity of military training
developing hard outward selves with self-proclaimed
soft interiors, the boys not effeminate but soft compared
to women.

The relative prestige status of banker, rich hotel
owner, rabbi, scientist, member of congress, doctor,
etc., will be fairly easy to iron out. Certainly the rabbi
does not head the list, as does the priest in Spanish cultures to the south of us.

The Hotel Dan in Tel Aviv is a clean and good hostelry. I suspect that gadgeteering is not a passion of these
people, many of whom never heard of a toothbrush before they arrived. Things already look disorganized and
run down on plane, in hotel and certainly in bus and
taxi.

To bed tired—a good way to retire.

Friday, January 30

Slept until ten thirty, breakfast with canned
orange juice—in a land whose big business is oranges.
Then a stream of visitors and telephone calls, thanks
mainly to Syd Baron, who in his addiction for doing
favors cabled to the Deputy Prime Minister, Teddy
Kollek, known to even the telephone operator as
"Teddy." The familiarity of the names of high officials
does not bespeak necessarily effectiveness, but affection
it does declare. Ike, Teddy Roosevelt, F. D. R., even
Cal—but Herbie Hoover, Warrie Harding: never.

Picked up aliens in the lobby. I didn't like a single one of them. Some on the make, some prideful as if they had built the land, some frighteningly insecure, such as a rich Englishman who said on the plane, "When you land in Israel you will feel welcomed as in no other port." Such reaction is difficult for us to decipher. In a way we are the most alien of all—neither of us being worshipers, we have not entered a temple for worship in at least 50 years; know neither Hebrew nor Yiddish, both of us when asked "Race" say United States or Caucasian and for "Religion," say none. So we are looked on quite differently than are the so-called non-Jewish visitors, and our deviation (in the eyes of the Israeli), gives us a position for observation where the observed act in less than relaxed fashion.

Took a walk for an hour or so, which was all Maggie's ankle could stand. Started to add up cultural tidbits: more men's stickpins than I have seen in fifty years; beautiful brass-fitted shoeshine boxes; lots of handshaking, but no walking hand in hand as in Morocco; eyeglasses for women as fancy and gaudily decorated as with us; lots of barbershops and many men getting shaved for Sabbath; not as many lush breasts as I had expected—maybe result of military training for girls; no Arabs at all, except in areas of economic segregation, as in Harlem with us; cooking not too good—too busy building a society and still low economic standard as to choice cuts or dishes; above all, too bad these new artificialities, new cities—Karachi, Tel Aviv, etc.—did not have an architectural dreamer, the counterpart of L'Enfant. This city has no distinction in its layout, avenues, or even beautiful waterfront.

Maggie says, "You wouldn't know an Arab if you saw one—the entire population looks Arabic to our eyes."

Saturday, January 31

Arranged for car and English-speaking guide-driver, and off we went into day interrupted by showers and double rainbows. Kept going until we got to Tiberius, Lake of Galilee, where we found, in a gracious inn, an upper-middle-class group of rich, gin-playing couples in the evening. Clean, good hostelry, but it reminded us, as did many other buildings, of Puerto Rico: fast-moving, proud economy on the make, with worthy ambitions but little skill of individual workmanship. Drawers don't quite close, wires are needlessly exposed, even in brand-new buildings many spots need paint—all signs of workmanship that has lost its personal pride.

Of course asked endless questions of everybody, and of course the answers were often diametrically opposed to each other. But across all ran the theme, "It's a tough life, it's a low scale of living, it's a great nation but some day we must stand on our own feet and no longer be a remittance society dependent on charity from Jewish people throughout the world." Maggie and I felt like very distant aliens—as we are—and no doubt those Israelis we met looked on us as offensive people. We should be like their picture of Jews from the U.S.: we should know Hebrew, go to synagogue to worship, at least understand Yiddish, have only Jewish friends in the United States, be in sympathy with those who keep a kosher kitchen (employing a long-outdated dietary code made senseless by refrigeration and modern dietetics). They, from their point of view, had a right to resent us on every level. We don't like Miami, Cadillacs and mink coats. We make clear we are nonworshiping and look on kosher habits just as we do on the cow fetish of India. We can't really understand the segregation of the Arab, and the ban on building a Baptist room of worship in Tel Aviv. Intermarriage is prohibited by law. I conclude at this moment, subject to change of course, that the Extremist Orthodox Political Group may be right when they assert the necessity for a merger of state and religion, claiming that anything less than complete, dogmatic control will in time lead to softness toward worship and the Hebrew dogma; and thus, in the end, to assimilation and the loss of belief that the Jewish path is the only sure one to a good life and a true Heaven. It's identical with the attitude of many of my Catholic friends. I dislike to think of either group in full power over an economy and a body politic. Only the insecure need such restrictions to boost their own egos.

This is a tough land for us. It's not easy to shift over from admiration for fortitude and esteem for great effort to agreement with objectives.

FEBRUARY

Sunday, February 1

Drove on to Haifa, a city of charm, cleanliness and beauty. Of course I'm a pushover for harbor civilizations—Goteberg, Stockholm, Bergen and all the rest. Got some glances at kibbutzim—surely a declining institution of localized communism and immunization of the family. As the general standard of living increases in the land, the disparity between kibbutz residents and the other workers will evaporate. They will become private-ownership cooperatives. Too bewildered and confused by conflicting bits of testimony of what I hear and what I see to dare have a mind on anything significant, save only that it is a God-awful piece of land— as bad as the stretch we drove on the west coast of Ireland. Its rocks laid out for masochists, for those who live on the Challenge, for those who will be in terrible shape if the initial challenge recedes. Like the early pioneers to U.S. who by now are nonexistent, like the fanatic U.S. lads who joined the Abraham Lincoln Brigade to fight in Spain, many people in Israel are already a trifle frightened because the hardest years are in the past. To keep going they will need the burden of a hundred thousand new immigrants a year—otherwise their own standard of living will go up too fast, food will be more plentiful and present housing inadequate. I don't understand this attitude, even though in a way I admire it. It's a little like my enjoyment at riding out a terrible blow in my boat, the *Episode*. I feel invigorated and refreshed, and if I win I know I'm a hero to myself. But all such attitudes do not necessarily make the hero have more grace or charm or be more likable. Expresso and to bed.

Monday, February 2

Went to Bahai Temple, and to me it recalls Horace Holley, whom I haven't run across for near fifty years. Of course this new sect has been persecuted even though it never proselytized, or maybe just because, like the Quakers and the Jews, it never tried to make converts. Intelligent chats with passive members of the sect that creates ire because it believes in one God and adopts the heads of all religions as the Prophets. What cruelty and horrors man commits in the name of religion and varying concepts of God! I dare say religious intolerance is the source of more cruelty than all the economic causes to which we attribute recent wars. Cruelty is also overlooked if committed by members of a nation or race against their own kith and kin. In Ghana, deportations and arrests now made in the name of democracy far exceed anything carried out by the colonial rulers. If England were still a Trustee of that land, the present outrages would have caused loud complaints at the UN.

Myths must be colossal to carry the mobs and have

endurance. They need not be beliefs in any devout terms in order to carry on for ages. Jews throughout the world help Israel, even though such Jews care little about the tenets of the religion. Man seems to want isolation on religious grounds, and in fact invites a separateness that encourages persecution. Little faint efforts of man to worship God or Good or Nature or the Unknown make little stir. But loud shrieks like those of the Jehovah's Witnesses create animosities even though the followers are a tiny legion and a threat to no one. Maybe the advance of science toward the discovery of the origins of power and light and sound and life itself will reduce these schisms that afflict man.

Stopped at an entrancing artists' colony: separate lives and cooperative exhibits, kilns, etc. Here we found gracious living and the pursuit of lives of beauty. I'll bet they even cook with taste, for they are not solely consumed in the conquest of land; much more concerned with the individual emotions of man. Then an hour or so at a Youth Aliyah—a kind of hostel-school-home for children from eight to eighteen—many without parents, some from each of the lands that contributed refugees to Israel, all relaxed, wards of the state or of private charitable agencies. Remarkable scholastic work done. I wonder if such institutions have run long enough to appraise their effects on the personalities of the kids, whether parentless or from divorced homes.

Lunch at Lod airport and then to King David Hotel in the city that David built three thousand years ago. We had been on the Jordan side when we flew down one day from Lebanon, a few years ago. Haifa, Tel Aviv and Jerusalem are each different and distinctive in terms of architecture, layout, culture and stores. For dinner with Moish Perlman, an old friend of Connie's from war days in London. He's a public-relations man in our terms and the most natural, gay personality I have met in Israel. He is a *"Gutschmecker"* and we had an elegant meal; and then to the home of Teddy Kollek. Good new ideas came from the exploration of the labor union setup, which might prevent the disappearance of prestige and pay differentials for the skilled workers. Here the new order arose from a complex of factors, the main one being that, although immigrants had looked on manual labor as *infra dig,* the nation needed hands more than brains and thus conversion took place from traders and *"Luftmenschen"* to farmers and construction builders. I sensed at Teddy's home a coolness—we were more offensive than goys, we were Jews who did not worship, who were in love with our own nation and who, no matter how much we admired the effort and results in Israel, looked with objective eyes on the venture. It's tough not to be chauvinistic in a world mad with nationalism. Particularly do they resent folks like us who do not feel the need for hair-shirt living. They can't look on us as other than traitors to our class—in this case, what they call "Race."

Tuesday, February 3

Room smelling of paint, no hot water, hammering next door early in morning—and still we are living the elegant life in this culture. So what. An American lad now living here after a GI trip came from Moish to give us a tour. Lucky we went to the Mandelbaum Gate at the time when scores of Arabs went through the gate to see Arab relatives. It reminded us of the Hong Kong-Red China Border, where Jock

Murphy of Governor's staff took us when train and mail and people crossed over. I rather feel that there has been little exploration or invention to expand these cross-border meetings. Still, it's understandable that the high emotions—derived from bitter fighting—should diminish the capacity of the adventurous Israelis to pry open more cracks in this curtain.

Tour of handsome beautiful buildings, of hospitals, university, etc. Here the children live and see history, while our kids are far from Bunker Hill or Lexington or even our shrine, Independence Hall in Philadelphia. Here the youths see their past. We saw the Dead Sea Scrolls—couldn't read a word, but a thrill like that we experienced when we saw Book of Kells in Dublin at Trinity College.

We discussed left-handedness and its higher incidence among Jews in our culture, particularly among male Jews, and explored Maggie's theory that left-handed people naturally write from right side of page so as not to blur the writing. No one so far has dope on reading infirmities here, even though probably half million had to be converted from right-handed literacy to left-handed Hebrew. Moish told of a Yemenite group that could read from any and all angles. The reason: there was only one book in the class—Holy Writ, of course—and the class surrounded the teacher and read sideways and upside down.

At lunch at the Katriel Salmons'. The crowd seems more friendly than yesterday; maybe we only imagined that they thought of us as enemy aliens. I like Teddy, the Czech. He is still Czech. Although when I was nine or ten I got a gold medal for Hebrew at Sunday School, I don't remember a single letter or idea of it. I read the Bible when about thirteen, when Al Hellman lived with us on 120th Street and we each read a chapter or so each day. Little memory of that. Once or twice over the years I have read parts of the Old and New Testaments, but only for history and stories or maybe poetry. This might be a good bit of reading on long trip to Karachi or back to New York.

At another good restaurant, Hess', for dinner with the Gerson Avners of Foreign Office. German origin, Oxford education, which made for a less stern rejection of pleasantries of life. He as well as Moish seemed interested in my hunch that Israel is ready for foreign capital, on a noncrusading, nonemotional basis: money not out of sympathy, guilt or Jewish solidarity, but on an avowed basis of saved capital entitled to a return for those who forewent pleasures to save for future reward—interest or dividends. This, however, requires different approaches from the sympathy motive, and unconcern with goodness of the Israel philosophy or magnificence of sacrifices. It will be difficult because the bond and gift campaigns in the U.S. are based on fear of Arabs or need of charity for new refugees, and if capital is forthcoming on straight economic grounds, the donors on sentimental grounds may use this as an excuse to reduce benefactions. Moreover, no Zionist can do the job of promoting such investment effectively.

Wednesday, February 4

Room still smells of paint but warm water is flowing in the pipes and the bathroom heater works. How soft we are—but these minutiae are important. Both of us like comfort in hotels no matter how much we can rough it on *Episode* or any cramped sailboat.

Maggie and I took a long stroll, window shopping and buying gifties for family, Paula* and the girls. Jerusalem is a clean city compared with all of the East or Near East, in part because of shortage of paper and the absence of the usual water buffalo, camel, cow or horse. To the King David Hotel for our first meal there, some writing and reading, and then a visit by Dr. Louis Miller who, in his task of reorganizing the health system, of necessity ran into problems of emotional discomfort arising out of illiteracy, and the great difficulty of shifting from one literacy to another.

One of the best sources for reactions in any country is always the corps of reporters. I learned much from Homer Bigart and Rosenthal in India, Hank Lieberman in Hong Kong, Welles Hangen in Moscow, and so in this culture we went to dinner with the Kings (*N.Y. Times*). It's always a circumspect and different reaction from that given out by the natives—it seldom even resembles what appears in their papers after editing by the foreign desks, so often colored by strictly provincial New York City (not even United States) prejudices and attitudes. I recall an Indian working for *Time* in Delhi, who had a plush job but had to quit because of the torturing of his reporting at the rewrite desk in New York City. Good food and acute insights from both of the Kings. Not only because they look through eyes of our nation but because they are both Christians and, equally important, from the midwest. This is their first foreign post, and I must write to Mike to see if he can't get King to do a book—objective and explorative in this complex neck of the world woods.

* *Paula Gross, secretary for more than forty years.*

Friday, February 6

Up early, warm and sunny day; we walked to station about a mile away, carrying our small bags. Train went through most God-awful stony land, but the train and then a bus in Tel Aviv were, in a way, necessary for us to form a picture. Back at Hotel Dan and then to U.S. Embassy, a moment's chat with Baxter, chargé d'affaires—may see him later. Then to Hobby Exhibit, which was striking because the hobbies were mainly collections of match boxes, perfume bottles, soap labels and the like. Some things dealing with ham radio operations, some hand-made jigsaw wooden toys, and rather unimaginative clay. The great exhibit came from the U.S. and showed the major events in Jewish history —with the most careful attention to detail of costumes, weapons, boats, walls, building, etc. Maggie wanted it for the ten-year-olds at her City & Country School.

The exhibit might mean that, in a society just coming out of an initial egalitarian program, the spare time (and there is plenty because of well-regulated hours of labor) is used to collect and hoard rather than to create. I guess this is natural, although in our culture I rather incline to the Hinkle* theory that anal eroticism is a basis for the collector's addiction. Then we walked back for a mile or so stopping for coffee and cake on the way in a café. Maggie went for hairdo, while I roamed around chatting with many visitors and residents. The visitors—all Jewish—would say what a job they have done with this desperate piece of soil. This was clear admiration. Never once did this admiration turn into,

* *The late Dr. Beatrice Hinkle, analyst.*

"I'd enjoy living here." These visitors, supporters of Zionism and hence Israel, seemed to me to be quite confused. The Homeland—centuries-long dream—Jews can't adjust with other peoples—the final Brandeis argument in behalf of a Jewish State—all such tore the visitors with guilt, since all the arguments and emotions should logically have led them to want to live in Israel. This conflict, a partial confession of weakness, no doubt augments the size of the opening of the purses.

What an enigma we are seeing. Miriam, that attractive fifth columnist, brings Moses to see his parents, and finally Moses, full of high calories from the Pharaoh's table, leads the Jews out of Egypt to the land of milk and honey. He sees it from a distance and dies. I wonder what he looked on, and what was the season of the year. At best it must have been stony—unless over some thousands of years the inhabitants have denuded the soil as we did our eastern seaboard, never putting back into the soil what we took out of it. If Moses had lived longer he might have taken his following to the north, to richer Lebanon. But the tough soil made for hard living, the core for the development of new religions, and prophets. If people live off lush soil, the demagoguery of religious ritual has no great appeal, except for passing faddist cults like that of Aimee Semple McPherson. But surely Israel faces spiritual revolutions in the foreseeable future. The bond is scarcely one of definable race; as for religion: so much is nonspiritual and little more than a prerefrigeration-age dietary code that the social adhesions will evaporate; and already the shift from an initial classless society is going forward at an accelerated pace.

Saturday, February 7

Slept late and took a car to Katriel Salmon's country place. He with the fabulous wife who had a grandfather who went with his caravan around 1880 from Bukhara to the Czar in St. Petersburg with 500,000 gold pieces, and then to Palestine where he bought much of the land. Discussed with Katriel rain making, desalinization of brackish water, the advent of productive hobbies in the culture. The do-it-yourself drive in our land has scarcely been recognized as a great productive and spiritual revolution. Katriel himself alone built a first-class extension to his week-end home, and we had much in common, in terms of carpentry, bricklaying, etc.; while Margaret was in tune when we were shown their fruit trees and garden difficulties.

Driving back, we both mentioned how little grace and elegance shows up in Israel in or outside the homes. Government housing everywhere tends to monotony of line and layout, even though the vast Israel Government housing has more variety than does ours around New York City. Passed "the Kremlin," as the drivers call it—the union headquarters.

The rigidities in this society after only a decade are formidable, but the most threatening one, it seems to me, is the frozen power—by way of job appointments—held by the leaders of political parties. This is invited because the parties—naturally in historic terms—are much more than political persuaders—they run such operations as labor exchanges, health facilities, etc., and hence there is a vested economic interest in the hands of party leaders, far beyond anything reached in our political-party structures.

Back to hotel and then to Esther H.'s* apartment. Esther is on a sabbatical leave from the Foreign Office and finds that being away from home for seven years was too long despite brief home visits. She is now a political-party employee. A teutonic man and wife in for a drink, and then we went to Luky's, good food, and to a Greenwich Village-type coffee house. Exactly like many near Two Fifth Avenue, except girls far less attractively dressed and coiffured. Overheard enough to know that not everyone was solving all of Israel's economic and political problems all the time. Saw the supermarket that helped break the retail food prices, which we are told were kept up by an unwritten accord. But shops here do deliver and give credit—two services not rendered by A&P and other American chain stores. On the street and in the stores there is an absence of grace and manners, seldom a thank you and above all very little ogling of girls by boys. Can't get two answers that agree as to romantic pursuits and pursuers and mood of romancing.

Sunday, February 8

Loafed late in bed, read Scholem Asch's *Moses,* which I must take in small doses. Also read local paper containing World Zionist statement asking for more power over Israel instead of just getting declarations from Israel in return for dollars raised. This external financial help must be a mixed blessing to Israel. Money is often power, and the donors obviously are not satis-

* *Esther Herlitz, Official of the Ben Gurion Mapai Party.*

fied with gratitude—they want to say how "their" money is spent.

Out to Asian-African Conference on corporate-cooperative structure in modern society. This conference attended by about forty, with usual language-interpreter problems. Mostly very black people—Nigerians, Ghanans, Rhodesians, etc. plus a few from Japan. All their expenses paid by organizations who sent them, and after three months of escape from reality many would like, we are told, to stay here. After a very dull session, even for the delegates, there was a typical example of birth pangs of democracy—they tried to establish an alumni association of the group. The names of nominees to propose a program were Ba, Ige, Watanabe, Atiemo, Miss Tayetch, Ayorinde, etc.—names not easily found in our land of varied cultures. I suspect the months were spent in more concern with forms of organization and power than in root problems, such as: under what form is most wealth created? how does society best create disparities so as to reward skill? how does society best induce young people to develop skills? what are the prestige symbols used by a society for various functions? etc. Too often such groups assembled by labor or employers go too soon into the problems of division of wealth, even then disregarding the follies of divisions that themselves create inflated currencies to divide. The gal who took us over ran away from her life in Paris. Surely we need new words—"refugee," one turning to, is not always appropriate: more often here it is "effugee" or "affugee"—one turning *from*.

To dinner at Luky's. Farewell party for Maggie, who goes back to New York without me.

Monday, February 9

Took Maggie to airport. Ran into Lena Levine, who was stuck for a day or so en route to the Planned Parenthood conference in Delhi. We had a good day's trip to Elath with a look at a feeble copper mine, supposedly the same vein worked by King Solomon—the old boy must have worked it out. One trouble with government operation is that it sometimes dares not admit error or failure as readily as do corporate managers.

Back at hotel, loafed around. Increasingly puzzled by the problems Israel will face in next decade. I think they will be far more difficult to cope with than the early ones. To dinner with Esther and Lena. Later to a night club run by actors, singers, etc., to supplement their incomes. Understood little, but the audience was attentive and full of applause.

To the airport. Plane late but finally asleep at four thirty and got in three or four hours of heavily closed eyes. All day I pondered how easily Russia could strike a blow at Israel by allowing, if not forcing, a million or so Jews out of Russia. Israel could not absorb them, and the free world might not face up to the challenge. Even if it did, a real grudge would develop against Israel. This is one of the horrid possibilities of the future.

Tuesday, February 10

Stopover at Teheran after riding over high, snow-covered terrain. Ran into Bill Vogt* and the English delegation to the Delhi conference. In brief chats with Planned Parenthood folk I explained why I thought they were ill-advised in their undignified attitude toward the Catholic Church, and why I thought that the answer was not in the pill alone, for with a cheap, effective contraceptive there would still be the need of finding a simple, understandable motive for its use. I doubt if this group will consider motivation except in terms of theory and generalizations. I suggested the reverse of the French tax on bachelors, which is intended to encourage marriage and offspring. I hope someone at the conference will follow up my offer to act as a clearinghouse for lawyers' work papers from each country pointing to minimal monetary rewards for smaller families—say a rupee a year less in tax, no matter what the form of levy—for families of five or under. The technique would not be concerned with revenue or burdens, but only invoked to begin some discussion in each village.

At Karachi met by Aly's car and representative. To Luxury Beach, which is just as I recalled it from four or five years ago. Aly called up—he is staying at the President's Palace. Took a welcomed bath and was really lonely for Maggie. What a profound habit, bit of environment, part of my reach she is.

Sat down to eat, but after a call from Aly went to his suite at the President's Palace for dinner. The cellar was locked—no white wine; so had to drink a bottle

* *U. S. population expert.*

of champagne. Good talk. He had just come from Cairo. If the Zionists keep on getting, driving or seducing Jews to Israel, that piece of land won't accommodate them all, so the Arabs wonder what then, even though Israel voices no expansion desire now.

Wednesday, February 11

At lunch with Mr. Yusuf of Recreation Association who had been sicked on me by Tom Rivers of the International Association. Good informant, editor of *Textile* and other magazines, much interested in education in a culture where the tax base is in the cities and at that only touches a few top people, while nothing comes from the mass of people who live in the villages. Nor do newspapers or magazines seep into the villages. I agreed to meet him and his group tomorrow evening to lecture as I had in Holland, Japan and other cultures that were ignorant about the great revolution going on in our republic—the use of leisure, hobbies, do-it-yourself, all of which is shifting our people from an audience to a participating culture.

After visiting Foreign University went to President's Palace and talked on the lawn with several officials and Aly. The President, Mohammed Ayub Khan, is a big and decisive man. Lots of charm and the picture of strength without cruelty. Discussion, of course, went in direction of mass media for literacy, and he was interested enough in my kerosene-run movie machine to set up a date with his new commission on education. One tidbit: I referred to three memorable quotes—F. D. R.'s "Nothing to fear but fear itself"; Churchill's "Blood, sweat, and tears"; and Ayub Khan's "Democracy without literacy is hypocrisy and an illusion." He quietly and promptly said, "My predecessor said that," indicating his agreement with it. Talk went to India, U.S. policy in general, Dulles, diplomacy; and finally he showed his interest in aerial surveys cooperatively financed by prospective franchise holders.

Thursday, February 12

This has been one of those days full of satisfactions, without a single letdown. Busy, exciting and pleasantly rushed. But still able to enjoy the camels sticking out their greedy long necks as they cheerfully tug their carts, the burros with their constant rhythmic trot, a snake charmer or two and his weird musical flute. I was reminded of the first time I saw a camel culture. It was in Egypt, where camels and Cadillacs vied for their places in the stream of traffic over the bridge over the Nile near the Semiramis Hotel.

Received letter from Maggie. She caught connection on Monday at Rome, but jet not running in Paris—so stayed overnight at Georges V. Life can be worse than being stuck in Paris overnight—or overday, if that's a word.

Sandwiches on SAS well-serviced plane, and then to sleep, off to Beirut, ten hours' flying time. Hurrah: hooks on sides of planes for pocketbooks, coats, etc. At last one company has satisfied my little demand.

Friday, February 13

Relaxed on SAS plane. Blond people are a good sight, particularly with my passion for Scandinavian women and even men.

Beirut airport cluttered with U.S. planes, and the airport crowd a conglomerate of peoples of all nations. Those airports with which I have a familiarity must be the counterpart of the old stagecoach taverns in New England where the traveler enjoyed the sense of recognition and recollection, ingredients of feeling "at home."

And later there below us were the Aegean Isles, probably as good sailing as Maine. Years ago we spoke to Mr. Benaki, owner of the Byzantine Museum in Athens; he was commodore of the yacht club, and we inquired about chartering a sailboat to cruise the waters. Maggie laughed at my inquiry, I asked why and she said, "It's like asking Mr. Morgan at the Morgan Library, 'Can you tell me where to rent a rowboat?' "

Saturday, February 14

Rome, Paris, the Azores and home by eight fifteen A.M.—one of those long, confused days with three breakfasts on three different continents. The Goldsteins away, Mike and Connie to apartment, spoke to Roger and Jean, dinner with Alan and Paula, went over bunches of office notes, a few naps, big rehash with Maggie of the days when we were separated. After dinner to the Bessies', where Rosten,[*] Lael[†] and Gollancz[‡]

[*] *Leo Rosten, author.*
[†] *Lael Wertenbaker, writer.*
[‡] *Victor Gollancz, British publisher.*

from England were solving the world's problems.

Thus ended the month away. In a way, the start seems like yesterday. In another way it seems as if we had been away longer than a month. I got much education and some amount of sheer gaiety. My return was saddened by learning of Lucy's* death. My mind turns to what I can do for Russell.

Sunday, February 15

It's easy to get back to home grounds—when a home is so beautiful and looks over Washington Square, and the kids and their kids can stroll in as they did. And then there is my Wooden Pirate from Nantucket and the carved fish with gay Jonah riding on its back, and the Dufy which takes a long time to make inroads. To be sure, I missed twelve hours of sun time or had twelve hours extra—whichever way, my internal alarm clock needed slow reacclimatization. So between snoozes and worrying about Russell I got back into New York City stride.

Lunch with Alan and one of my Cuban Castro informants, discussing Cuba, and the complete absence of any administrative ability to run a nation. It looks as if Castro will be president and then dictator, and then the people will develop cynicism, with the dollar already down to fifty cents.

Dinner at home, with Maggie fixing snacks and my promise to take on the slave function at breakfast.

* Mrs. Russell Leffingwell.

Tuesday, February 17

I enjoy working under pressure, a kind of satisfaction in taking a stack of papers and working them down until my desk is clear. Paula slaved all day yesterday, and between us I'll be in the clear by Wednesday or Thursday.

Breakfast uptown with clients, partners' luncheon meeting, home for dinner, up to Barry Gray's program for a half hour on radio. This is the skeleton of my new life—new after the trip. It's funny how my life fits into separate pigeonholes and how easily I mold myself into different ways. I don't know whether it's a virtue or a sign of lack of depth in each thing I do. For thirty-five years I've had a basically different way of life for three months during every summer while in Nantucket. Now I have dictated memos on my Pakistan conference for Aly, and on Israel for Syd. And then that chapter will subside into the crevices of the past.

Wednesday, February 18

Got Alvah's* book on Catholic position on birth control. It's good and will be so important that even the organized groups will have to spread it and even read it.

Lunch for all the girls in the office. This is a tradition by now. I talked on Pakistan and Israel. There were about twenty-five present, and I got some good questions. Not to my surprise, the Jewish-conscious

* *Alvah Sulloway.*

"We can't adjust, we will be the first to be driven out if trouble comes here" questions bobbed up. I did not persuade too successfully when I said Jews have no *right* to be liked. No more than Catholics or Negroes or Protestants. All we have is a right not to have a rule laid down against us. The best comments came from the non-Jewish girls.

Next Tuesday I cover approximately the same ground with the lawyers in the shop. I'll be interested to see the difference in type of questions, if any.

A few comments on my new British suits—but only because I'm back to wearing vests after twenty-five years. The lure is in additional pockets, although Lord knows man has plenty compared to the ill-designed women's clothes that necessitate valises instead of pocketbooks for most women.

Thursday, February 19

This was another mop-up day—dictating to three stenographers for no less than five hours. I never have accommodated to the dictaphone, even though many of my friends have done so—even Jerry Frank, the most footnoting writer I ever knew. Maybe I need the personal touch of a receiving human being, just as I react best when engaged in mental badminton, in tripping ideas back and forth across the net. Penelope tells me of a new device that can print a single copy of a book for about five pounds—less than fifteen dollars. What a grand idea, and what a kind present under proper circumstances!

To my one and only public dinner—I detest them all. If a speaker has anything worth saying, he will probably write it and then I can read it with shoes off at home. But to the Astor for a dinner that Syd wanted me to attend, a dinner to honor Carmine De Sapio, who deserves more than honor from the people of this city. Barristers Morty Hayes and Herb Lazarus were there, and de Falco and others whom I seldom see but enjoy. Syd was a delightful and cultured master of ceremonies.

Alan home to Two Fifth for the night.

Friday, February 20

Off to Washington with Maggie to work and spend the night at Roger and Jean's spacious and elegant new home. Maybe the perfect society will give the peak of income and free time to those in the prime of life—aged thirty to fifty. Then they can best use money and leisure—for lush living in spacious homes, children, and thoughtful effort. A good culture will fittingly arrange that men and women as they get older contract their abodes, slow down the pace of life so as to want fewer possessions and require less income.

For lunch with Hubert Humphrey in the Senate dining room, where I chatted with many friends—Wayne Morse, Russell Long, Ernest Gruening, Mike Monroney and others. Our nation is in a mess. Dulles insists that evil will give way to good and hence Russia will fail of its own evil weight. George Humphrey and his school then say, "Since good will prevail anyway, don't spend much money on foreign affairs"; and a third group at the White House says, "Spend only enough to 'deter' "—which derives from the same root as "terrify." So our nation has no basic philosophy for a basic strategy. H. H. is provocative and should be a leading president for our people.

After lunch to State Department to report to Assistant Secretary Donald Kennedy, Harry Spielman and William Spengler on my observations in Pakistan and the two projects—mass-media education and aerial surveys. Though I represented no one except my own excitements, I did as I always have done, check in with my government. I think they were interested, and now that Dulles is sick we may reinstate our State Department as a working entity, just as our ambassadors may soon be raised from their present status of messenger boys.

Stopped in at Lud and Dorothy Denney's for a drink. What a joy that couple is! Late in life the miracle came to D. D. They are in love and live sane, unrushed lives with themselves, their books, and a few close friends and still let their excitements constantly grow. How rarely I find couples like this, who have excitements on many levels.

For dinner at my favorite Washington restaurant, the Genghis Khan, where the Fermans met us for coffee. Good food of all the Eastern lands, and those beautiful high-slit, tight-fitting dresses on—to me—beautiful oriental waitresses.

Saturday, February 21

Played with David and Debbie, who came into our beds a trifle on the early side and with a vitality that we met, although through purposeful effort, with calm and seeming pleasure. Big breakfast by Jean, who seems to enjoy housework and cooking for the family in a big, many-roomed house.

To lunch with Robb, attorney for Fulton Lewis, Irv Ferman, and Fulton to discuss the problem of multiple-libel actions. Fulton is sued, as Drew was in the Sweeney

cases, in many cities where the plaintiff can with ease
hire lawyers on a contingency-fee basis while the radio
stations or newspapers must pay for legal services case
by case. This raises some tough problems on freedom of
press.

Home with Maggie by plane, and this is the first airplane trip I remember that both left and arrived on
time. Joan brings Steffie over for the night, Bessies come
in after dinner, Alan comes in. And so to bed, after reading a miscellany of magazines collected since January
16, when we left for England.

Sunday, February 22

To Pakistan House to see Aly, who works any and
every day. Went over my talks in Washington with him
and now we will wait to get reports from Karachi. To
Cornelia Otis Skinner and Alden Blodget's for breakfast party. Fun as usual.

In the evening started Edwin Gilbert's *The Hourglass*. Don't know the author, but he wrote me a flattering letter saying that I had affected the novel and that I
was in it. Somehow it deals with a censorship trial.

Monday, February 23

In the afternoon to Elysée Hotel to see Allen.* I
think I helped him make important decisions. And still
he fails to realize that his Penguin is the only world-wide
paper-back book company. He has started a whole group
of U.S. publishers who now compete with Penguin in

* *Sir Allen Lane.*

U.S.A. But Penguin is the only publisher who in U.S as elsewhere can offer authors and publishers of hard cover books world distribution in paper back. No U.S. house can offer a world market as can Penguin. I think I got him excited on this level.

Back home and finished *Hourglass,* and promptly called up the author to say I was flattered by his references to me. I'll see him before he goes away next week. I could not read *The Hourglass* as a book because I was told I was in it. The scene is in sight of my living room window, the lawyer studied law at night as I did, and so it went—so I never knew where, if at all, an intended identification with my practice of the law existed. I enjoyed it in less than objective fashion and of course always like a book that, in fiction or nonfiction form, pleads against the frightened and the censorious.

Thursday, February 26

Delightful hour in the morning with Syd Baron in connection with his representation of a foreign nation. We then discussed the need of shifting the image of Israel in the United States from one of religion or even racial sanctuary to the more valid image of the one nation in the Near East that is least likely to go communist.

In the late afternoon I picked up Joyce Morrow for a drink. Of the valentines I received there was only one that still has me baffled. It read, "Re-joyce to see this gay design and I will be your Valentine." My tip-off was that "re-joice" was spelled with a Y and Joyce Morrow is the only one I can think of—other than Peggy Joyce, whom I have not seen in years—who may have sent the card. I am quite sure that Joyce Morrow did not fool me in the examination I put her through. So I must look elsewhere.

Saturday, February 28

Slept a little late and then started great fun of reading Curtis Bok's new book, *Star Wormwood*. He is a delicious writer and the kind of lawyer I love—not only because he is a good sailor.

A friend representing non-Communist elements around non-Communist Castro came in to see me at the office later in the morning and he brought me up to date on the Cuban situation; I may decide to act in behalf of an agency of the Cuban government. My concern at the moment is the instability of that government. It wants to look like a democracy but acts like a dictatorship.

At a luncheon with Jim Bruce* and his bride, discussing in nostalgic terms the Truman campaign. He is really a gentle man.

We fixed dinner at home, walked down to see Mike for a few minutes, then went to the University Place bowling alleys to watch a championship match. For a decade or more we bowled at Teutonia Hall every Sunday in what McAlister Coleman called the John Roach Stratton Bowling and Breakfast Club. We chatted about those days and that group and how many of our then friends died long ago: Gil Gabriel, Henry Souvaine, McAlister Coleman, *et al.*

Before going to sleep listened to Ann Ronell's music on an FM radio station. She is an odd combination of mysticism and mousiness.

* *Former ambassador to Argentina.*

MARCH

Monday, March 2

Excited about rights of prisoners to read. The issue came to me through Oregon friends interested in half a dozen convicts who have been denied the right to read, of all things, law books. To be allowed to read such might even be considered cruel and inhuman punishment! What an old-fashioned penology we practice—related only to man's need to punish man, and unrelated to re-educating the antisocial.

Not surprised that our Embassy in Bolivia was picketed because of an article in *Time* magazine. Some years ago I wrote Harry Luce about the danger of his reporting in India and the East. At lunch with Harry I tried to tell him the frightening complaints I gathered in the East about *Time*'s making tasteless references to heads of foreign states, pointing out the magazine's seeming ignorance of the fact that our folkway attitude toward elected officials does not necessarily conform to that of other nations, and is not necessarily the only correct attitude, which all the people of the world must adopt. *Time* does not appreciate its great responsibility as the leading reporting agency of our culture around the world. *Reader's Digest*—not a news gazette—has some appreciation of the distinction in habits and mores. How do we get this across to Luce and Larson? Voice of America cannot succeed on any level in face of the Luce empire.

Tuesday, March 3

Tough working on such a lush, gay day. It feels like our best season of the year—October. Chat with Victor Lasky about the mess in Cuba, lunch with Sklar at Columbia University Club on book publishing matters, long conference on monopoly of cigarette distribution in the New York City metropolitan area, long dictation about the mess of the bar in respect to conflict of interests. For example, a report comes out on limitation of liability in airplane accidents. Some of the lawyers so reporting represent air lines, without divulging to the bar and the public their honorable responsibility to stand by their clients who want to limit liability; others represent claimants, and we must guess the extent of their lack of objectivity. Why are they disinclined to disclose their conflicts? Why should they serve on such committees? Their great knowledge might be better utilized in the capacity of witnesses rather than reporting members of a committee.

Went to Phoenix Theater to see *The Beaux' Stratagem* and then the Hambletons* came to Two Fifth. I think the theater needs above all an economic report— on featherbedding, building restrictions, box office thefts, closed unions, etc., all of which add up to ticket

* T. *Edward Hambleton, producer and co-founder of Phoenix Theatre.*

prices that prevent much of our public from ever going to theater. Outside of New York few of our people ever see a live actor. The Shuberts with their permitted monopoly destroyed theater on the road and prevented advanced thinking in our city—the inevitable effect of giants who rely on power rather than on ingenuity.

Wednesday, March 4

An interesting idea from Congressman Abe Multer: a four-nation joint airport at the point on the Red Sea where Egypt, Israel, Jordan and Saudi Arabia border on the Red Sea. The project would cost less than ten million dollars. Its value would lie in the opportunity of getting some symbol of cooperation in that neck of the woods. This might be better than the idea I offered when in the Near East—joint research on rain making and taking the salt out of water.

Mentioned to Penelope that there were only a few important inventions of man and that the best dealt with travel—the wheel and the centerboard. Without the former man was limited in his capacity to roam the earth; without the latter, vessels on the sea could go only in the direction of the tide, current or wind. But now both are becoming passé. The wheel was a cutie—unlike the lever or the hinge which existed in man's own body. The wheel is slipping into an unimportant status—in the plane and the rocket the mere demand for speed destroys wheel values because of friction. Penelope gives the sled even on roads or rails high preference for the future.

Cold out, but walked around our beloved district.

Thursday, March 5

The high spot of the day was lunch with Burt Aginsky. As a professor at City College, he carves out enough time to be chairman of a committee for the ACLU on the problems of the American Indian. I know of his wife, who is an anthropologist, and I had heard that they were deeply involved in the study of the cultural patterns of Puerto Rico. After chatting with him, I once more concluded that if I had a little more ruthlessness I would take a sabbatical year and study anthropology and the social sciences. We talked at length about the hundred pages of notes I made on the subject of the advance of our economy for the last 350 years. How did we happen to release the ambition of all our people when in the rest of the world only the very rich, royalty and the clergy had the opportunity to dream of their own advancement? If we only knew the secret of this pattern, we could export it to the underprivileged on the planet. Why did we abolish primogeniture and thus create ambition for all sons, rather than just the eldest son? Why did we give women the right to inherit and the right to divorce, thus providing them with a status so that they could have personal ambitions beyond tending the home? Why did we never admire wealth and only admire the ability to *make* wealth? Why were we the first nation on earth where the people had a right to succeed and the right to fail, and, more important than everything, the right to try again? I found Aginsky sympathetic to my approach and forgiving of the fact that I had no knowledge or discipline in his field of skills. He came back to the office and I turned over my notes on "the just society" and my memorandum on the social forces at work in Israel. I must see more of him.

I wrote a letter to Hiram Haydn of Random House suggesting that that firm might well organize some kind of a ceremony to celebrate the twenty-fifth anniversary of the decision in the *Ulysses* case. I am sure that neither Bennett Cerf nor Joyce foresaw the great advance resulting from the decision to allow free circulation of *Ulysses*. I, least of all, had enough imagination to realize its impact. As a matter of fact, I still don't understand the mighty example for freedom set in that case compared to the results I fought to abtain in a case such as Mary Ware Dennett's involving the right of wide latitude for sexual education of children.

Disturbing news about Cuba. The Communists are creeping into every force in the government. But the most disturbing trick involves the taking over of American-controlled telephone company without the payment of a nickel and without the public condemnation which would follow from nationalization. The government of Cuba rightly should control the rates to the consumer as it has in the past, and rates should be based upon valid and necessary expenses. But now comes Castro who, without nationalization, makes the securities of the investors valueless by taking over the management. As a result, in time there will be no dividends for stockholders and the stockholders will hold worthless pieces of paper, so that in the end they will be forced to beg the government to redeem the paper.

Friday, March 6

Went uptown with Maggie last night to see the movie *Gigi*. It was a great delight. It made each of us recall beautiful, pleasant memories of visiting Paris. It is wonderful how Maurice Chevalier has an individuality unique on the screen. It is more than his lifetime of training and discipline; maybe his personality comes through as it does because his own ego is not involved —he does not even ask cooperation from the audience: he gives, and in return the audience gives through taking. Leslie Caron is another example of great charm without beauty. She denies the concept of the beautiful feminine form from the Gibson girl down, and makes a laughingstock of the symbols of beauty used by advertising agencies to sell products. One by one her features add up to little, but something shines through that is really beautiful.

This is a great and gay country in its use of capital. I just received word that a new business has gotten three people within a period of about a month to put up a minimum of $250,000 apiece without voting control of the enterprise, which is in the hands of management which puts up no money. There won't even be the need for long-term contracts of management, and management will get more than half the profits above reasonable salaries. Once more it has proven to me that J. P. Morgan was right in his basic thesis that the only thing worth betting on is character, integrity and ability.

Steffie came for dinner and then we went to the Goldsteins' to baby-sit so as to let them have a night out.

Thursday, March 12

The great slush is inconvenient, but as every emotion arouses a counter-emotion, to paraphrase Newton, every universal complaint creates a speck of warmth. At street corners I found strangers directing me how to cross and get less wet, strangers who ordinarily wouldn't even say "Sorry" if they brushed against an old lady and knocked her down. Another plus was the speed-up of taxi traffic because of fewer private cars.

Worked with Eddie a bit on Farmers Union Supreme Court argument, discussed with Alan his great concern for injecting a bit of unorthodoxy into the Bar Association, had a drink with Joyce Morrow, my horse-loving friend, and all told had a most pleasant day, because Drake Sparkman sent me details on a Concordia yawl which he might get for me for charter in Maine this summer. I can't wait, which means I can wait but don't want to. But on and off all day long I looked at the picture and read the description over and over. It should have made work more pleasant, but it didn't. Wow—Nantucket is near, only about eighty days away.

Saturday, March 14

To office to listen to a weird tale of a man who was seeking legal advice. A story unfolded such as occurs every day in our big cities. A group of entrepreneurs latch on to a man with money but with little business experience outside of his own craft. The pattern is always close to the plot of the sunken treasure, and the gradual infiltration of the confidence men into the bank account of the innocent victim is funny as well as sad. He always thinks he is so smart, and his subconscious, correct desire to stick to his last is subverted by the possibility of easy quick money. As is often the case, the name of a respectable lawyer is used to certify and attest to decency and legality. Often, as in this case, the lawyer himself is duped to the point where he is trapped and becomes a party to the venture. The tale I heard was too dramatic to be put into the movies—no one would believe it.

For lunch to the Aginskys' with Prof. Knes.* Four hours of digging into needs of business for the services of anthropology.

At seventy, I'm "entitled" (funny word) to a year off for further education—but I'll never get it because I'm boxed by loyalties to partners, a firm: my G. W. & E. But I would love to take a year off to study social science.

To dinner at Bessies'—a gay, great party: Lael Wertenbaker; Ungerer, a delicious artist; Lady Cohen†, Wayne Andrews‡ and Mrs.; the Maiers§; Alan; and later Deighton, of Oxford University, just returned from talks with Faubus and the Nasser leaders. What an evening: the new House of Books is public—*The New York Sunday Times* broke it on first page. Hiram, Pat and Mike—a trio of culture and thoughtfulness, with Dickie Ernst‖ as the business guide. I would have welcomed this evidence of growth in book publishing anyway, but surely with Mike involved I am emotionally involved; and so was Nicky, who lifted a glass of wine to toast the

* *Professor at Hunter College.*
† *Wife of Sir Andrew Cohen of U. N. Trusteeship Council.*
‡ *Historian.*
§ *Howard Maier, of Voice of America.*
‖ *Richard Ernst, second cousin.*

new publishing venture. It's great whenever any birth is announced of a baby dealing with what goes to the mind of man, and books are our most precious commodity.

Home late, exalted—couldn't sleep. Mike and Connie and the new adventure stormed around inside of me. Hiram and Pat became part of my family. Woke up many times, and around six dropped into the bathtub and snoozed there with my head on my new tub pillow. It's a good thing for me to get embroiled in extensions of the lives of Maggie and myself—the Goldsteins, the Bessies and the little Ernies. Concern is a neat and sweet and lovely behavior for all mankind. I don't happen to care about humanity in the abstract, but I enjoy being vitally involved in the dreams and battles of those I love dearly. It ends all too often, I suspect, in dilution, because my capacities can't match my desires.

Sunday, March 15

Mike came in early for coffee. Put in a conference call for Mike to talk to Pat and Hiram at same time, a trifle that always surprises the unsophisticated. The *Times* compares the partners in the new unnamed publishing house to the vice-presidents of Ford, General Motors and Chrysler leaving to start a new auto firm. It's a rich figure, but I suppose in a week someone will say to me, "I hear that your son-in-law has left books to go into the auto business."

Saw Bob Moses at Plaza last week; he's as young and attractive as ever, and let no one tell you he has really mellowed. His love for the battle, his admiration for action, and his respect for the politician, rather than the reformer, are good—very good. But he has no faith in groups of people or knowledge of the need to develop responsible government by gradually exchanging efficient autocracy for less efficient democracy. It's a costly investment, but man without responsibility can contribute little to the civic life of a city.

To hockey at Garden. A heartbreaking game. We may just get into the playoffs. It did me in—my loyalties are acuter than I thought. Home and saw Harry Golden on David Susskind's television program. Susskind is a relief because he is a thinking man.

Tuesday, March 17

Zeisel of the Chicago Law School dropped in for breakfast. The Chicago Law School and its too-grand new building plans to run exhibits on matters of law. They don't want ideas; they want money, money without ideas. These great experts in the law, with more adventure than exists at most law schools, honestly believe that they, as lawyers, can popularize legal knowledge for the American people. It is funny how each profession decries the gobbledegook of every other profession. I tried to point out that no book on the law, other than of the Mr. Tutt school of fiction, has ever met with wide popular favor. But they think they can get charts that will be meaningful to the American people. I have long been excited about the use of exhibits. I told how twenty-five years ago the Junior League put on its magnificent exhibit of books banned through history, with a special table for books suppressed by dictators Hitler and Stalin. The charts as shown are entrancing and might be meaningful to the top, top portions of our culture. The Law School is really not concerned with the flow of this knowledge to the American people, at least Profesor Zeisel rather resented the idea that on each subject there is a national organization with local branches which could underwrite the transit of the exhibit after it has been put on in Chicago. I suggested suppressed books and the American Civil Liberties Union branches; bigotry and the law vis-à-vis the Church groups; integration vis-à-vis the deep interest of the YMCA's; tariffs vis-à-vis organized labor and the automobile industry, since the latter cannot sell abroad unless tariffs are lowered enough so that other nations can pay for our cars in goods shipped to us.

Someone told me that a study has been made of attitudes of delinquent children toward parents. These kids with energy and drive do not regard their parents highly. They think better of themselves than they do of their parents. The nondelinquents think more of their parents than they do of themselves. If this research is true in fact, then big new vistas open up for our society's coming to grips with delinquency.

Wednesday, March 18

Home for dinner. Agile-minded Dickie Ernst dropped down for several hours. After discussing books we took half an hour to exchange memories of our ancestors. I have no ancestors. This has always been a lack in my life. I once saw, for an hour, my father's mother. I have never learned whether his ancestors were farmers or shopkeepers, or anything about where they lived or what they did. I did know my mother's father and mother, who lived in the United States, but as to their parents I have never heard a blessed word except that they came from Neunkirchen and my father's heritage was somewhere in the neighborhood of Pilsen, Bohemia. I am not much for *ipso facto* relatives. The way to get close to relatives is by the movements of living, so now there is a firm and developing bond between Dickie and myself without any strand of artificiality or blood compulsion.

Thursday, March 19

Off to Washington for the day. Lunch at the University Club with some of the staff of the Draper Committee. They have keen minds and are deeply concerned with the image of our republic presently existing throughout the world. I think they were interested in the possibility of a change in the image from shooting guns to shooting ideas to the mind of man. The trouble, however, is that if there is no adventure at the top, that is, at the White House, all people lower down become less than dynamic. So our republic ends up with a mass of meager, unimaginative projects.

Saw some Democratic senators, who evidenced more despair than I enjoyed sensing. One scholarly senator said, "There is nothing we can do. Eisenhower should resign. The people are getting what they voted for and they are stuck for the next two years." This is not good for our country, and maybe this mood exists in part because the opposition party has not dramatized to the people its own dramatic over-all programs.

Talked to Hubert Humphrey's staff, finding them exciting.

At dinner at the Cosmos Club I had a very good time

because I was with people who have good will toward me and with whom I am in basic disagreement. This was a party given by Irving Ferman, a sober and wise lobbyist for the ACLU. The gathering he had of what is known as right-wing senators and commentators would, unfortunately, be looked upon with suspicion by many liberal and worthy defenders of freedom. Is it implicit in liberalism to be unwilling to sit with the opponents and open a bottle of wine? Why do so many worthy liberal people feel that if you sit with an opponent you have sold out? Is this because a few liberals have switched their stance and joined the people more concerned with security than with individual rights? It is more likely that this attitude is held by those very people who are so insecure that they doubt whether they could withstand the arguments of the opposition. Maybe in part this defensive insecurity derives from the old socialist doctrine of class struggle, a doctrine of hate, a gospel of bitterness and a pattern that only divides a culture. I know that many look with distrust on my forty years of battle for birth control because I have dined with the Cardinal and constantly have eminent members of the Roman Catholic Church at my home for dinner. For my part, I know of no way to deal with an opponent other than to pick his brain in friendly fashion. My image of an opponent is often substantially altered by such meetings.

I came back on the late plane with Jack Jessup, who had also been at the dinner. He related the thesis that in the discovery of desalination of water the so-called exploding population problem may evaporate. The theory goes that with rain making and conversion of salt water the resulting tillable soil could support many more billion men and women.

I wonder if it is true that all the people on the planet

today could be put on the island of Bermuda. Woke up Maggie, had a snack and a chat. It is fun touching home plate, even after only a day's absence.

Saturday, March 21

Stayed home to see our Washington Square parade. The Goldsteins came, and Connie and Richard Llewellyn Davies of England stayed for a phoned-for lunch with a bottle of wine. R. L. D. spreads graciously and knowledgeably from his field of architecture into pastures of anthropology, labor unions and many other cultural areas.

The parade was small-town and gay and could not have taken place anywhere else in this too-big city. Block festivals take place, most often in Italian segregated neighborhoods, but Washington Square has its prides— some exaggerated, some artificial. But any pride (other than false pride) is better than none.

Monday, March 23

At Pakistan House, watching Aly slide from one telephone message to another. In five years or so he will hold one of the important posts in international affairs. Then to lunch with Dave Sarnoff. We had lunch alone, jointly deploring the sorry state of our nation. I asked him to explain why so many of our leaders in Washington seem surprised when it is suggested that our propaganda is not excelling that of the Communists. I never appreciated so fully how easily Russia and China could isolate us by cutting cables, etc. Russia, he said, spends more on jamming radio than we do on all our radio propaganda.

With Maggie to a party for the Edwin Gilberts at the Lynn Carricks', full of publishing people, many of whom I like much and don't see too often—Virginia Kirkus, Tay Hohoff, Irita Van Doren and cheery Belle Rosenbaum. The right-size cocktail party—not crowded and no overdrinking, and all in publishing excited about Hiram, Pat and Mike. It seems as if everyone connected with books stood a couple of inches taller because these three had turned their backs on security, jobs for life, distinction and safety—for what? For their own adventure and the joy of their very own imprints.

Then to a party at Aly Khan's: just the opposite—a function of probably a thousand people. Left after a few minutes, then for a bite at Voisin's, where I didn't eat too much, then we walked a mile or so, took the bus home, read, dawdled—gentle living, good living. Watched the television showing of *Green Pastures,* the Bradford-Connelly opus, so good that Maggie will go out and buy a Hallmark card, the sponsor.

P. S. Forgot: brother of Lama of Tibet dropped in to chat. I had seen him in Tokyo after his escape from the Communists.

Tuesday, March 24

The high spot of the day was lunch with Peter Straus and Leon Goldstein of WMCA and Alan. They seemed to be excited about an idea I first explored more than fifteen years ago. I still believe that there are several hundred significant, thoughful people of influence in our society who two or three times a year are burning to speak their minds to a mass audience. I remember years ago I had in mind people like Edna Ferber, who made our community aware of its untidiness and dirt in the streets; of Cornelia Otis Skinner, who dared speak out against cellophane and the waste of wrappings in our economy; of Oscar Hammerstein, who is always thoughtful and has a deep concern over the market place of music in our culture. It is easy to get up a list of people who have no easy access to microphones, syndicated columns or print in national circulation magazines. I suggested that WMCA set aside fifteen minutes a day and invite speakers to what might be a new kind of academy, composed of people who will stick their chins out to say what is on their minds. They should not get paid and the program should not be sponsored. The main difficulty lies in the need of excluding hundreds who will form a waiting line to get hold of the mike. The organization would cost little, and I suggested that Nathan Straus might invite people to share his ownership of his microphone or allow three people who will deny themselves the opportunity of using the mike to make up the list and send out the invitations. I think such a group could provide ideas that would be picked up throughout our nation. I remember that years ago, when I talked to Toscanini about the plan, he mentioned that while he had nothing to say he would like to introduce under his name some new musicians who should be permitted to seek favor from our public.

I went to an interesting exhibit at Joyce Morrow's American Institute of Graphic Arts. These designers are a distinct class in our society and quite different from the designers of homes, who apparently do not live in the homes they create, otherwise they would be aware of the functional purposes and uses of gadgets and equip-

ment stupidly placed or missing from most of our
homes.

Wednesday, March 25

I have always been an enthusiast of FM broad-
casting, which gives a good tone and far better precision
than AM. I never did understand why it was virtually
killed by the producers of the receiving sets. My prejudices lead me to believe that the decisions were not
made by the listening public or by the government, but
arose from private motives of the dominant manufacturers. This kind of result is typical of many situations
that give economic dictators the advantage over a free
economy. But now I learn that man will get advance
warnings of heart trouble because sound inaudible to the
human ear can be transmitted by FM. It is possible that
tape recordings can be made as a result of special microphones placed over the human ear and interpreting the
activities and power of the ear muscles.

To lunch with Eddie and Herb at the Williams Club.
It is seldom that we snatch an hour to meet each other
all alone. Why did we let our lives get enmeshed so
deeply with other people's troubles that we had to sacrifice the essential pleasure that goes with the concept of a
partnership? I wonder if it is too late to scrap half of our
office and get back to civilized counseling as lawyers.

To the theater with Maggie after dinner to see revival
of *Our Town*. This was a lovely experience. The delicate writing of Thornton Wilder, the superb casting and
acting, the joy of seeing Johnny Beal on the stage again,
the surprising youth of the audience—all made for an
exceptional evening at the theater. The matrix of

Wilder's art lies in his knowing that life in its sweetest and bitterest terms consists not of any giant event but in the galaxy of minutiae that bring tears or smiles. In fact, Thornton can with a single line produce a tear or a slight lift of the ends of one's lip. This is more important than a belly laugh or a gush of weeping. In a perfect world there will be no humor or moans based on man's missteps. To touch the heart with a fingertip is important and far more difficult than a body blow of pronounced dramatic violence. Every couple left the theater a little more in love than when they entered.

Sunday, March 29

Easter Sunday. Goldsteins drop in with new hats and a gift of a lily plant. Their constant wish to show gratitude and love is touching because it flows in tiny, undramatic morsels—as casual as saying what most people dare not utter: "I love you."

Although, or maybe because, I am of no religion or religious faith I find myself, on days of formal religion, turning in my mind to matters of spirit. And today several times I reconsider which is more painful—or what is the difference in the quality: suffering for which I can feel a personal responsibility or what is called fault or guilt, or, on the other hand, the pain toward which I made no conceivable contribution and about which I am impotent. The latter is beyond the bounds of relief by self-criticism or self-confession or relief in outer confession in any religious dogma. Comfort yes, but not relief—and comfort can come from sitting with a good person, touching a tender hand, hearing a tuneful voice, seeing a cloudless sky, beholding a child's curiosity—or a trillion other manifestations of goodness all around me most of every day.

My favorite holiday lunch: Baked potato covered by a half-cooked, runny egg, Bovril enough to make me want to hurdle the nearest fence, and a dish of mixed ice cream and water ice.

Monday, March 30

Today is a dreary day but it was brightened by the fact that last night on the way home for dinner we found buds on some bushes. So life comes back to our part of the planet. Maggie has taught me to get excitement out of the first buds even though she failed utterly in teaching me the Latin and English names of every bush and flower. She knows them all and has a magic thumb. My ignorance in part is due to the fact that I was brought up in the city and she was brought up in a civilized small town. Moreover, she knew so much that I was frightened by the standards she created for me. Because I never could match her knowledge, I was afraid to make even a meager attempt and my unconscious dictated that I should stay ignorant.

A bit of sorry news. In the lovely lobby of our apartment house, beautifully decorated with old prints of New York, there stood a bust of George Washington on a pedestal. It was about two feet high and made of plaster. Now it has disappeared. What is wrong with our society that vandalism is on the increase? In my dream life I rather hope that the bust was stolen by some young lad who did not want to sell it but had fallen in love with George, and that the bust now stands in a pleasant thief's bedroom. If this were so, there would be an additional bit of irony if the thief believed the cherry-tree story.

Tuesday, March 31

Off to Washington to smoke a peace pipe with FBI. It's been an odd and at times trying period, when Edgar and the agency were forbidden by Brownell to confer with me or even visit me to get my files on the Galindez mystery. It must come out some day that even though G. was employed by our government he was not destroyed by the Dominican Republic; that our government has always been aware if not more than aware of the million dollars G. used in his double agentry. With Cuba going into Communist hands, with Castro's announcement of neutrality in the next war, with Communist advances in Paraguay, Bolivia, Panama, etc., maybe the only way to stem the tide is to tell the full story of G., his relation to Communist and related areas, transactions, etc.

APRIL

Wednesday, April 1

In the morning I talked on the telephone to Representative Cella, a member of the Massachusetts Legislature. He asked me if I would appear tomorrow to give testimony on his bill which asks the government to give a pardon to Sacco and Vanzetti. He said he understood that I was the only person alive who examined Joe Morelli at length, and he would like me to appear in Boston. Miss Gross went through the files and a miracle happened: we found the files in the warehouse. This is not bad, because the files in this matter go back about thirty years. I spent a good bit of the day going over them.

In the evening Julie and Sandy* and his bride came down to the house and we traveled sitting still. We talked about India, the Philippines, Pakistan and Israel. I put up to Sandy the project of organizing a group of political and social scientists who would service the big American corporations and educate their staffs as to the folkways and mores of countries where they operate.

---

* *Julie d'Estournelles, Director of the Woodrow Wilson Foundation, and her son, Alexander Trowbridge.*

Sandy thought it would be of great value but that the difficulty of such a program might lie in the fact that the high officials of a company ordering such reports would have no system for educating and training the men who were going out as operators into the field.

Thursday, April 2

Planes not running. Dismal weather. Took a train, that antediluvian instrument for travel, to Boston. Service was terrible and it looks to me as if the presidents of the railroad companies have lost their courage and their nerve.

Went over to the Gardner Auditorium in the State House. Seven or eight members of the Judiciary Committees of the House and Senate had been sitting since ten o'clock taking testimony. Except for a few five-minute intervals and an hour for lunch and an hour and a quarter for dinner, they sat with unbelievable patience, listening in the main to serious accusations leveled against Judge Thayer, District Attorney Katzman, Governor Fuller, President Lowell and others, at least until ten o'clock in the evening, when I left for my plane. The auditorium was crowded and the hearing was interrupted by applause and at times by a few hisses. It was an indecent hearing in terms of a search for truth. Two of the senators were utterly cruel, and I thought that most of the speakers were self-defeating.

Massachusetts is no different from the rest of the union. Errors are made in the judicial process. I doubt that there are more or fewer of them than are made in the other two branches of government. It is good to have even neurotic, intemperate picket-line group action in our culture. This, in a way, is our built-in machinery for correction and change; picket lines prevent complacency no matter how irritating one-track fanatics can be. But at this hearing the mood was one of hope that the Legislature might be persuaded to admit that an error had been made in convicting innocent people, and the argument toward persuasion was solely one of attack. I gave testimony for about an hour and a half; told about my examination of Morelli and my attempt to see Mancini. I had letters of Morelli's in my hands and of course referred to the book he had written and wanted to sell. I may have interested the legislators in the need for a new search and told them that I was thoroughly persuaded that I had talked to the head of the gang that had committed the murder for which S. and V. went to the chair.

Two interesting footnotes. Members of the committee asked my advice as to how to proceed. Should a commission be appointed? If so, could I name some members? I took my traditional position that I would rather have one man write a book than a committee make a report, and then indicated that the many pressures in Massachusetts were so great that possibly they should follow the strategy of Governor Earle of Pennsylvania who, in the bootleg anthracite coal days, appointed a commission of which some members lived outside the state. I further indicated that whatever was done should be done so as to create a new image of the United States in the minds of the free world; and I told my pet story of how only the brave can admit that they were wrong.

Tuesday, April 7

This was a day with many high spots. Alan and I went up to the Lotos Club for lunch, where we had a couple of hours with Harold Gardiner, Philip Scharper* and Bernard Berelson.† B.B. is the closest thing to Mitzi‡ I have met in the social-science field. He is soft-spoken and undogmatic and in part gives me the impression that he is looking down from the stratosphere on the human race. I rather felt that he had less red blood than Mitzi, but I like him much. We all made one point: that we wanted to tap whatever knowledge lies in the halls of science on the subject of censorship. The exploration should be made if for no other reason than to direct discussions at the top of our culture into more thoughtful and fruitful grooves. We said we did not care how small the area of inquiry might be. We went over our need for some more knowledge on subjects such as the following: the difference of impacts of obscenity on women and on men, on children and adults; the difference in impact of fiction and of non-fiction. I think Berelson agreed that our group was more or less blocked until we had some more factual knowledge to chew up or to bite into. I shall send to Berelson the Gardiner-Scharper work papers. In any event I rather gathered that the study we propose on radio and television will be forthcoming. This would comprise, in the main, these questions: Do the networks give the public what it wants? How do they know what the pub-

* Editor, Sheed & Ward.
† Social scientist.
‡ Marie Jahoda.

lic wants? And is this the function of the owners of the networks?

Thursday, April 9

The Gargoyle* meeting was the best in fifty years. Phinney Baxter, the Williams College prexie, got sick and sent a professor to speak and answer questions about the College. Just because the image of the faculty member is less forbidding than that of the president, the questions were braver and more penetrating. How should a private college be financed? What is the optimum size for our alma mater? Should sons of graduates get preferred treatment on admission? Must not sons of old Williams grads be admitted though more stupid than others in order to get financial support from the alumni? And then I asked one of my favorites: "What is the trend of reading books for pleasure?" I found there is no trend—there is no such reading habit. Reading, yes, lots—but all under curriculum compulsions. I suggested that a course be given with points toward graduation, a course of voluntary reading of books, with discussion papers filed on each book. Why not try it out, with a minimum of x books per term and a possible exclusion of some types of books, such as those appearing in magazine condensations, whodunits, and other material of lesser cultural value. The undergraduates were intellectually more curious and more articulate than the alumni on the average. But what a burden these lads carry with segregation from dames, hence an unreasonable accent on female bodies at week ends. The

* Senior Honorary Society at Williams College.

abnormalities that are reflected in divorce statistics may reflect this segregation in our college population sector.

Friday, April 10

It takes a jolt followed by a period of relaxed thought to comprehend the real initial basis of a human relationship. If my client likes me—or, to put it more honestly, if the client appreciates me—I think well of the client. In other words, a favorable base for a relationship exists if a person feels that the other party appreciates his abilities and potentialities. My happily married clients can't conceal, even if they want to, the fact that a man feels that his wife has a high opinion of him. In fact it can't be too high. The man says to himself, "She's a wise and smart person—she appreciates all my great traits of character." Whether such appraisals are true in fact is quite irrelevant, since the only reality is what is in the man's mind about his wife's appreciation of his "sterling" virtues.

Monday, April 13

Usual work at the office, with good zippy weather, which made everybody a bit more pleasant. For lunch to the ACLU where we discussed what are euphemistically called "policy statements": Does the owner of a two-family house have a civil right to discriminate on the ground of race, creed or color? Is there a maximum number of apartments where the individual right of selection must give way to the constitutional concept of nonbigotry? If radio and television stations have the right to editorialize, should there be a duty to make time available to opposing points of view? What about the hundreds of areas where there is only one radio station to present news of a locality, as distinguished from national or international news? What if the only radio station is owned by the only newspaper? How then do we get diversity of opinion out of which truth might evolve?

I am always fearful of statements of principle. If, like the U.S. Constitution, they are accepted only as an ideal, that is one thing. If, on the other hand, they are accepted by a director as a guide for legislation, it is quite a different affair and the Union is in trouble. For my part I wish the ACLU would act more like the U.S. Supreme Court, which develops policies on a case-by-case basis and not in the abstract.

Great news of the day: Roger will be given the William A. Jump Award for distinguished service to the government. It is only the second time since the award was inaugurated that a member of the Defense Department has been so honored. Since nominations are made of men under thirty-six years of age in all branches of the government, this is truly a great distinction, coupled with the fact that he was sent to the War College when he was below the age limit—a fact that required an amendment to the rules. He has certainly made his mark as a public servant.

To Dinty Moore's with Maggie for dinner. I have not been there since we had dinner upstairs with Groucho Marx twenty years ago. Then to see *Raisin in the Sun,* a play that carries on in the mind of the audience even during the following day. I must write Harold Stern* to congratulate him on his part in the production. It has

* *Attorney, former partner.*

an integrity and objectivity lacking in the plays of the Theater Guild, Odets group or Arthur Miller. Maggie and I agreed that even though this play could not have been written by a non-Negro, all of the compounded confusions of life which happened to this Negro family could have happened to a white family. This is proof of its basic value.

Thursday, April 16

Last night after dinner, went to see a delightful English detective picture. Scotland Yard is composed of gentlemen, suave and quiet-spoken. This symbol of quiet decency and persistence is a better image than the flatfooted cop and the big-necked "dick" of our culture.

Went through the Mews. Saw a light in the Armsey house and dropped in to report on our trip. Jim is going to lose out if he takes on every assignment offered to him. It is a nasty failing of our culture that if a top person is spotted in any organization everything piles on to his desk. He doesn't want to reject those who ask his aid, and eventually becomes overburdened without time to contemplate.

Read a mighty volume, though small—*The Image Industries,* by Father Lynch. I am taking it to Baltimore with me on the two-thirty train and will try to get the Maryland barristers to read it. I know of no writing from any dignified source that indicates more sober fear of the "present commercial masters" of the mass media. I agree with the thesis that our republic needs powerful pressure, not of the censor but of the national intelligence, to be brought to bear against the handful of people who control our culture.

Train with Maggie to Baltimore. What a sorry decline of the great Penn. Railroad. Now the company wants to discourage passenger travel. The profit lies in transporting the goods humans require.

To Eli and Amy Frank's* for dinner and the night. Good company—Judge Oppenheim and his artist wife, the Paroissiens of Penguin, the Guttmachers (Johns Hopkins people) and others. To bed late.

Saturday, April 18

To Washington—hot, dirty and sticky. Spoke to Karl Mundt, de Loach and others in Washington concerned with my Berlin diversionary theory. Picked up Kay Halle for lunch and in turn was picked up by Broadbent of London *Daily Mail*. It's always a pleasure to sample the brain of a sober British correspondent. I guess those in Washington are the best of the British crop—just as ours in London are the best of ours. And still there is a subtle but large difference, like that existing between our attitudes toward responsible government. Our cabinet consists of political amateurs, and our civil servants have little prestige—attitudes the British can't understand.

Sunday, April 19

Good weather. Jean fixed pancakes for breakfast. David slept coiled up in the back seat of the car for two hours. Why do we lose this delectable art of sleep at any time, at any place? Only recently Maggie has

* *Baltimore lawyer and wife.*

learned to nap with her clothes on—but of course she must lie on a bed. I'm a lucky one: I can sleep anywhere, any time and in any posture—in a chair, on the floor, dressed or undressed. As I grew older I found that shoes were antisleep, but otherwise I can go off for ten minutes and be refreshed for hours.

Home by plane and stopped off at annual party at *The New York Times* for the AP officials and other bigwigs of the press. On the plane read *U.S. News and World Report* and found the first forthright report on the Communist inroads in Cuba. I must write Lawrence* to thank him and at the same time find out if he had more luck than I did in getting a publisher for Sister Barbara's† book on U.S. Supreme Court.

Monday, April 20

To an overloaded desk, and too many dates and what are called conferences. Calls from Washington; at last I think many officials are reviewing the 1948 Berlin crisis and realizing its great power as a diversion. It misled Truman, Acheson and the Pentagon—in fact, all of Washington—and now the press is looking only at Berlin and not at Latin America or the Near East or Formosa.

* *David Lawrence, editor and columnist.*
† *Catholic nun, teacher of law at Nazareth College.*

Wednesday, April 22

Last night Mal Hoffman* and his wife came in for dinner. She and Margaret had much in common, since both have been actively and deeply involved in the education of children.

We spent an hour or so discussing the ideal system that should exist in our nation for the production, distribution and exhibition of motion pictures. Originally, production and distribution were in a combine. This resulted in excessive power in the hands of a few people who controlled the celluloid diet of the people of our nation. In behalf of Pickford, Goldman, Selznick and others, I participated in the breakup of this power. I suggest that we are now shifting to the point where creative people—writers, directors and actors—control their product and hire money, studios and distribution facilities from the business ends of the industry. At the moment, however, there is no capacity for the owner of an individual theater to use his mind and judgment to determine which picture is suitable for his audience. The real problem of the market place is to set up a machinery by which each community shall be serviced through the manager or owner of its motion-picture theater for a product selected after reasonable thought by the manager or owner.

The big event of the day was that Maggie and I set up our own egg incubator. I have always been more interested in birth than in death, in sex than in sadism. I hope now to have the opportunity to see a chicken hatched, a miracle known to all people who live near

* *Attorney.*

the soil. As usual, the written instructions that accompanied the incubator are stupid, faulty and inaccurate. They were written by a man who knew how to do it and hence could not communicate to the mind of an ignorant person like me. The chances of success are, of course, not a hundred per cent, because not even when under a hen does every egg hatch. In this big city we are so remote from life that Maggie had to scout for days to find a fertile egg. We bought our egg from one of those interesting food shops that deal in what are called health products. There is one such on Eighth Street, as there is one of everything on the most interesting street in New York. Miss Gross asked what will we do with the chicken, and Mal wants me to try my incubator with a duck's egg.

Thursday, April 23

To the Astor to get a glimpse of Castro at the Overseas Press Club lunch. He has "It"—and is full of danger. He is a Latin Dulles—he hates government administration and hence runs away on the meagerest invitation from other countries. The Commies can steal Cuba right from under his beard.

In late afternoon to sit with Charles Denny at RCA, at Dave's* suggestion. He is tops—and may set his company on the right track for millions of profits well deserved in the setting up of mass media for educational purposes. I'll be hearing more from him.

Read in the *Journal of the History of Ideas* an engaging piece by Keith Thomas on the double standard. It is the first thoughtful discussion in historic terms I've

* *David Sarnoff.*

read of the societal pressures that led to the double
sexual standard which is now in a process of radical
change. Man's desire for treating women as *property*
changes, not only because of glandular attitudes, but
also because of economic shifts in a society. Also a nice
piece of Dewey Anderson's on our natural resources. I
must send him a copy of my aerial-survey projects. Also
read a review of Lynn Thorndike's *History of Magic
and Experimental Science*. So few histories of science
point to errors, and I don't know how to appraise history
if I learn only of successes. Ditto as to my appraisal of
men and women.

Friday, April 24

Andrew Loebl dropped in at nine o'clock in the
morning for a few minutes. I kept him for over an hour
because he is the wisest and best-informed small businessman I know of.

I have sold a piece to *American Weekly* derived from
my attitudes about divorce. I hold that the main function of a lawyer is to make the clients face up to the
situation *after* divorce. It is not for me to judge whether
people are wounded more by living together with dislike or by getting a divorce. The main function of a
lawyer is not the ten minutes spent in a courtroom pre-
senting irrational but legal evidence, but rather in opening the eyes of clients so they can approach divorce on a
risk-for-risk basis. Few of us mortals can have much of
a judgment on problems we have not lived through. I
am immodest enough to believe that I pose valuable
questions to clients as a result of living through maybe

a thousand broken homes as a lawyer for the children, the husband or the wife.

Saturday, April 25

This was perfect weather, and so I can't explain why it was my lowest day in years. I felt as woeful as during the period of gout—or so-called gout—in Nantucket, when even the Stetten theory of joining genius and gout gave me little comfort. Today I was just low, with the feeling that provides the only valid justification for a stranger as a concealed confessor. The modern couch of the analyst is not comparable at all. Its uses are deeper and quite different from the need for a person to talk *at*. How can a usually secure, self-sufficient person pour out his worries to a loved one, or to anyone other than a stranger? There is a limit to sharing with the person one loves.

So I plough along all day by myself and come up with at least two bits of ore. I'm lonely for men or women of the mind. I've not felt any impact of my aging before—Oh yes, I remember that on my forty-third birthday I started to go up two instead of three steps at a time. (I still go up two.) But as I have reached my elder years, I've lost my intellectual stimulators— L. D. B., Heywood, Jerry* and others. Then again, I dare not bother R. L. as much as I need him (and I need him sorely). So I keep up an eager, greedy search. I want a player—not on the tennis court, to bat a ball to, but in the opposite chair, to bat an idea back and forth. At the office the partners are madly busy—too busy to experience or even recall the idea of duets in

* *Brandeis, Broun, Judge Frank.*

mental whittling. To be sure, I relish the erudite and selfless conversations at Ford, Carnegie and a few other foundations. The big table at Morgan's will not likely be the same after the merger with Guaranty and Henry's moving his desk from Twenty-three Wall to One Forty Broadway. Although I traveled to Twenty-three Wall only once a fortnight for the past twenty-five years, these trips have been my greatest source of nourishment. So I'm lonely. I fetch and fish and cast my best bait for companionship for my crazy, odd mind. I never hear of a social scientist or read an anthropologist that I don't think of hiring him by the hour, as the patrons of olden times put musicians on their payrolls. But in our profit-motivated society the use of coin would spoil the relationship and tarnish the talk.

So I lower my pride to hunt up the next generation. They have fewer facts or less experience and in a way less wisdom, but their substitute is priceless and balances out their other shortcomings: they have not yet compromised their lives away, as we older people have done, day by day and year by year. So I go to the colleges—next week Dartmouth—pursuing a will-o'-the-wisp, in a search contented too often at a cheap price with a swatch of an idea, one clear-eyed question—but it's never more than a passing flirtation instead of the mental love affairs I want so desperately.

It makes me reject all the more the unchanged continuations of my life that still exist. I have received *The New Yorker* from its very first issue. It's the same perfect, but now old hash as that produced by the old people under the Ross traditions of the mind and style. I don't have to go to theater opening nights as we did years ago. I can wait—if it's a good show, it's likely to be running six months from now. I have never felt a lift when alone;

I'm not really a self-starter—except on a sailboat; so the intake from a top novel is pale compared to the effect of the lives that are stretched out in all their human clarity and misery on my office desk each day.

I must learn that the third generation from mine, the boys and girls of eighteen to thirty, are to be my dish. I was not wise enough to collect a large enough circle of my age to survive in life and in good health. Most people my age are tired and have started to wither up. So I end with little hope, but with some faith and a clear objective. But how do I change the eyes of my young friends so that they do not meet me with respect —that destroyer of equality, that tool of convenience only where normal attitudes are so specious that the older requires artificial advantages? My gap from the young is full of obstacles. I can afford Voisin's and elegance and may not want to pay the price of self-service at cafeterias; and they may not be able emotionally to accept my grabbing the checks at bistros. They look to me for advice, unwilling to believe that I seek to learn much from them. They haven't the time to spare for men like me; they are on the lower rungs of the economic ladders and on all sectors of living in our culture are on the busy upgrade. They can't rest much for me.

So do I at this age have to learn what L. D. B. with his talks on rereading of books—or R. L. in his lifetime of self-sufficiency—have told me for more than three decades? I don't yet want to live on my own fat alone.

Sunday, April 26

I wrote on this sunless Sunday my feelings of a glowing Saturday—a day when I would ordinarily have taken wing. So why this sudden low spot? The cause is still hidden—it can't be anything of giant proportions, because only the little tidbits have ever been significant in my life. Shall I search for the cause? I guess not—it won't be worth the while or the effort. I'll go to my Double-Crostic; it's probably more satisfying to lick than my riddle, and I can find its answers.

Loafed all morning. Tried to read further in Sybille Bedford's *The Trial of Doctor Adams*. The fluent, graceful writing could not hold me. We went to see the Gauguin show. I must lick my desolation. Thousands at the Met. This is heartwarming, but I felt further dejected. I have long known the great passion of our people for art and music and all the goodly graces of our luxurious leisure. But the people of our land feel inferior and ashamed. We are held up as materialists and we are led to believe the accusation to be true. This is what the mass media do to us. So I'll write again to the *Times* and beg that the attendance at the galleries be recorded for all to read. More people at the Met today than at all the baseball games in the nation. Why not run it on the sports page and not just in an art note? Millions attended amateur and professional symphony concerts last week in hundreds of cities. Why isn't this news as fit to print as the fact that twelve thousand attended the hockey game at Madison Square Garden? We make our press, but our press also makes us.

At the Met saw Ellie and Leonard Bernheim, waited

for them for coffee. They didn't show up but I was cheered a little by the Millis sculptures—all gay and hopeful, with arms and lips turned up and not down, full of joy as are his animals in Helsinki.

Thought of the two approaches to sensory joy: look at Gauguin and feel, or look at Gauguin with feeling infected with things of the mind such as "See, he's starting to use pinks, see he is now influenced by Van Gogh" —all those additions that reflect from the mind to the belly. I'm not saying which is better or which is worse, only that it's two different cuts out of life and I prefer the glands first always, and pity the people who can think before they feel about a picture or a piece of music. It's like my love for the law—the first impression is the best in many ways. First, what ought the rule to be; and only then, what did the past say about the present?

Monday, April 27

Last night I met a remarkable lad—Buck and Anna's* eleven-year-old. A mind full of *whys* and in many fields—biology, chemistry, history, government. He was a greater pleasure than most adults. We brought along an ant farm, and the slightly younger sister hugged it with a tender devotion.

I write to Elizabeth Barber—here's the letter:

MY DEAR ELIZABETH:

Several years ago while in England I dropped the idea that enough Americans go to your shores, but that we suffer from the absence of visitors from England to the United States. I spoke to government of-

---

* Mr. & Mrs. Russell Crouse, playwright, authors.

ficials and was told shortly thereafter that travel allowances were increased. We still get too few visitors and those who come include primarily people who have friends or relatives in the United States who can supply the shortage in dollars, often with repayment in sterling in England. Will you take up with your Board to see whether the following experiment would have value?

What if I rented a small furnished apartment for a year and made it available to the Authors Society so that you could designate British authors who would like to use it while in the United States. I would not want to be nuisanced by the project. The apartment I have in mind would be furnished, could accommodate two people in the same room which—despite the present British sex rampage discussed in Parliament—would be no recurrent obstacle. The user would have to buy his own provisions and put them in the ice box. He would have to arrange to tidy up the place for the next occupant. He would have to leave the key with the superintendent or somebody else in the building although, if necessary, my office could handle that chore.

In brief, has this idea any value? Would it be used? Would it create competitive problems for your organizations as the Dispenser of the Bed? How is that for a new title—more modern than Master of the Rod although possibly akin to Master of the Revels. If you think there would be value in having this minor benefaction flow to England, you might take the matter up with Nuffield as a kind of practical Fulbright Travel Fellowship for other than students, plumbers, etc.

The peace of the world depends on the bond be-

tween our two nations and the bond, in part, is
tightened by exchanges at the tops of our culture.
Best.

Yours,
MORRIS L. ERNST

I spewed letters, one to Charlie Merz of the *Times*
about the distorted image that paper—our best—gives
of our nation. Let's see if I can get the *Times* to install
a scoreboard of attendance and scores of Things of the
Mind—music, television concerts, art exhibits, etc.

Rainy day. Long talk with Dick,* the tops of all the
cultured young lawyers I have met, and then talked
with blue-eyed cheerful Paul B.†—he must be near
ninety, old, wise and gracious.

Wednesday, April 29

Mike and Pat—and what a team they are!—
picked me up at Two Fifth to go up to the office. I'm
happy that we could provide space for Atheneum until
they locate in their own modest quarters. Mike told me
about the dinner Harper's gave him last night, and to
which Pat and Hiram were invited. My affection for
Cass Canfield increases because I like secure people, of
whom there are very few, and only a secure person gives
a dinner to an ex-employee who must look like a peril
to Harper's.

I see that the President is having trouble organizing a
committee on national goals—a group of utopians. I
think the difficulty lies not in the absence of skill, but
because only old people near the end of their lives write

---

* *Dick Ader.*
† *Paul Baerwald, banker.*

utopias. This is true from Plato on. Young men are so
busy living and climbing up their own confused, separate ladders that they have no energy left over to dream
about man in the future. They neither know nor believe that dreams are the most potent makers of history.
In a real sense, our Bill of Rights was only a dream—
but "only" is a word not to be used as implying deroga-
tion. No utopia has been written by a woman. Women
are consumed by their basic biologic function of child-
bearing and the ensuing function of educating the children. I wonder if in the Kibbutzim, where babies are
taken away from mothers for communal upbringing, the
women are released to become utopians.

Connie of the office secretariat, called up the Audu-
bon Society and I think has the solution to the problem
that has long been plaguing my mind. Nonmigratory
birds living in the north do not sleep continually during six months of darkness. In our isotherm, birds grow
quiet in their nests when it is dark, and wake up to
chirp with the advent of light. Connie tells me that the
answer lies in the fact that darkness is not absolute, and
that the birds, like the insects, sense gradations in light
that we do not sense. In addition, I suggest, they need
to be less active when the insect life is less active.

Went to see the new picture from India which won
the St. Marks award. I suffered throughout the picture,
with its true but sadistic clash between the lad's drive
for affection from his mother and his zeal for education.
I have had my fill of India, when four hundred million
people prefer the fetish of a cow and the sacredness of
a murderous snake to a high standard of living, good
roof and full stomach. I'd like someone to do a book
on the twenty or thirty phony myths that, without a
bigot's retarding influence, batten on man's pursuit of
health, wealth and comfort.

MAY

Friday, May 1

I was called a paraclete and could not tell whether it was complimentary or derogatory, such was my ignorance. I found it meant only comforter, not even advocate. I must look up the religious connotation.

I've located twins in the Bible—Jacob and Esau— but not a pair that I know of in any royal family in western Europe or at our White House. Mean something? Does twinning occur in nature to increase the species? Or is twinning difficult, like the bearing of a male fetus in the alien body of a female? The chances of male or female ova occurring must be fifty-fifty, but male deaths in embryo or at birth are greater than those of the female—no wonder we must adjust to the alien female womb.

The New Jersey birth-control case went to argument. I wish I'd been there, because the Catholic and Protestant churches both appeared. This is a long stretch from the time when religious groups as such refused to take positions in court actions.

Saturday, May 2

Two big thrills during this year, and one sad-
dener. To get the latter down first—Alan had a relapse.
I was hoping to see him, with his collapsed lung and
his self-healing perforation (like a self-sealing tire, I
picture it). Again he is in pain. Man probably could
not survive if the memory of pain endured. But does
the memory of joy—in such different form? It's difficult
to recall *in detail* the joy of a picture of love or the pain
of a cut finger or a broken toe. And, still going down
the animal scale, I assume that joys and pains diminish
in fact in retrospect.

At lunch with Msgr. Salcedo, UN Delegate from Colombia, and Dr. José Chaves, with whom I have worked
for some time on spread of literacy. The priest is a
youngster of about thirty-six and has done much in his
country. The hours at lunch with liquor, food and
coffee were sorely needed by me. Although my sorry
ignorance of language again made me ashamed, we got
along far enough to discuss motivation for becoming
literate. We who have it assume its value, and just because we have it we are unable often to tell others of its
value. How then develop friends of literacy? In Colombia, that Catholic land where a few Protestants and Jews
have been allowed to survive, the award for the teacher
who gave literacy to the oldest pupil is a medal and a
trip to Rome and a visit with the Pope. I wonder if this
is the best prestige symbol?

Sunday, May 3

The fountain in Washington Square is full all day—not with water but with people, all ages, playing all kinds of instruments, variously dressed. Loafed over papers, mainly *New York Times* book section. Will buy Vance Packard's book on castes in our culture—even though reviewed by smarty-pants Spectorsky. I wonder if, outside of Siegfried or Brogan types, any recent anthropologist has written about the U.S. folkways?

The advertisement of Sulloway's book on population is good, and I wonder if it will be reviewed. Would it be wise for Beacon, the publisher, to bring out a brochure containing the letters of fright from eminent publishing houses which said, "It's wonderful, get a publisher, but please lay off us"? So stupid, this indecent fear of Catholic reprisals. I'll suggest to my Catholic prelate friends that they could reduce this fear, which adds to concealed bigotry since bigotry is often rooted in fears of power of reprisal.

Lael, Albert and Nell* for breakfast at noon. Maggie served a delicious repast—all precooked or preprepared in her own fashion. Nell has the brevity of wisdom that goes with age.

Called Ethel A.† to find an anthropologist expert on Republic of Colombia for me to hire by the hour to ask questions of. I can't get a document from the expert— I don't know what I want. That will emerge only from tit and tat. I'd like to hire such information by the hour,

---

* *Mr. and Mrs. Albert Boni of Readex Microprint.*
† *Ethel Aginsky.*

for talk. Has that been done before, like piano or Spanish lessons?

Stuart Novins may have helped save our republic. For three months I have been writing and talking to *The New York Times,* Harry Luce, Fulbright, Mundt and dozens of other leaders. I have known and said and written that Cuba had gone Communist. Novins gave the documentation. It took guts.

Monday, May 4

A beauty, but so busy I scarcely looked at my bit of East River. Busy writing and dictating. Kept two girls hammering away for seven or eight hours. Long letters re Colombia literacy—what a field: 45% of population has no schooling, 35% less than one year, only 5% literate. Wrote Paley about the Novins show and asked why he should not reinstate a weekly show dealing with important items omitted by the dailies.

Heard from Ed Williams* about the changing function of ACLU directors; good talk with Spengler of Pakistan desk at State Department to clear way for talk with Colombian desk man (State Department is being reborn); correspondence with Harold H.† from London about an idea for Prince Philip; wrote outline for Lizzie Marton for Music Prestige show; interviewed half a dozen clients—and on this level concluded that a profound difference was obvious. Some have an idea to make wealth; others think of making wealth and use an idea as an aid. The distinction is one of emphasis, but of great importance to an advisor.

---

* *Edward Bennett Williams, Washington attorney.*
† *Sir Harold Hartley.*

Read parts of the *New International Journal of Parapsychology*. I'd love to live long enough to attend the discovery of the technique of thought transference. This will be more significant than the exploits of Galileo, Einstein and the Wright Brothers combined, since it will be just among us—man to man, and not man to stars, air, or galaxies.

After dinner a nostalgic surprise. Leo Mayer* telephoned about nine o'clock. He had been reading Newman Levy's *Double Life,* saw the reference to me and called up and came down on my urgent suggestion. He's been alert and active about life, and carries his seventy-five years without any infirmity. In 1900 I lived at his home when my mother was hounded around the land for a possible t.b. cure. It was Leo who tutored me without success for my Harvard entrance exams. He gave a real belly laugh when I told him about the Harvard 1904 rejection slip on my office desk—I had flunked each and every examination. I had forgotten his devotion to Henry Wallace when Henry ran for president. I had not known, since I have seen him only about three times in a decade, about his Zionist activities, his many trips to Israel. It was a good evening, with memories of my substitute mother, Aunt Rachel; my mothers' parents, immigrants of dignity and some simple beauty; Leo's devotion to the violin; his 1905 classmates at Harvard, Ballard and Roy Wallace, who became my vicarious heroes while at high school and camp. I liked him this evening and each of us was tender with the other's dogmas. He is my only worshiping cousin, and he reminded me how close he came to going into the rabbinate. He had a great influence in my life—an older-boy relationship.

* *Orthopedic surgeon, cousin.*

Tuesday, May 5

Partners' lunch—too much ducking of the constant problem: how inspire and increase the partner concept as distinguished from separate entrepreneurs. I hope Mike and Hiram will share one office. I'll try it any day if I get up the nerve.

The big part of the day was Eileen Garrett* at dinner with the Bessies. I love her much—not only because her psychic abilities are so striking but also because she is gay and free-flowing and unpretentious. We must get her life recorded—from Ireland to the gangsters to Hauptman-Lindbergh case, to oil in Israel, and to Francis' contributions and Babs and all.

Wednesday, May 6

Lunch with Herb and Eddie, which is always an enthusiastic pleasure. It must be no fun to be a partner with people all of whose eyes look in the same direction. No partners could have differed more than Laurie, Eddie, Herb and myself. Our ability to adjust and overcome at times irksome gaps in our attitudes added to the value of the relationship. None of us are yes men or no men. So we always had to fight through to agreements without voting. It is an odd and valuable kind of soviet operation, whereas in most law offices one personality becomes the boss.

I had a wonderful hour with Sidney Kingsley. His is an imaginative mind, rounded by his craft as writer of

* _Head of Parapsychology Foundation, author._

plays and television shows. To be a dramatist is some-what like being a lawyer in that it is a profession that touches a variety of intriguing problems. The major difference is that the dramatist is entirely free—as free as a man can be—to select his material and his area of operation. Lawyers must sit back and wait to have their minds invited by the problems of clients.

I am worried because the press has not yet reviewed the Sulloway and Zimmerman books on population. So I write and give book editors a bit of information: the important Zimmerman book bears the imprimatur of the Catholic Church.

Good old-fashioned, wonderful evening at dinner, and then for five hours Margaret and I were educated by Msgr. Salcedo and Dr. Chaves in regard to the basic social problems of the Republic of Colombia. Msgr. Salcedo is in a way more important than his govern-ment. He is bringing education to the peasants—educa-tion that in the universities is a producer of communism. Wherever the top levels of a society are educated beyond their social use in the community, they go for the dog-mas and certainties of the religion of communism. It is the unemployed educated who cannot make decisions and need a church or communism to ease the tensions of indecision. Jessie Canning and Charles Foster, also at dinner, were helpful with their wisdom, the one in public-relations terms and the other as an expert on education through mass media.

I have agreed to go down to Bogotá, Colombia, for a week. I don't know as yet how I can be of help to the government or the literacy program, and I discussed in detail my opposition to the Roman Catholic Church on birth control, divorce, etc.

Thursday, May 7

At lunch with Judge Fuld, his eager barrister son-in-law, Milton Pollak, and Roy Cohn. Roy had been told by NBC that I did not care to debate with him; I think it was difficult for him to understand my position. I enjoy, and in fact particularly enjoy, talking with people with whom I disagree. The amount of good will needed in such conversations is slight compared to the minimum of good will required for a public discussion. I rather liked meeting Sokolsky or even Earl Browder, but I would never debate with them again because that minimum quantity of respect needed for public discussion would not exist and the program—whether radio or television—would take on more heat than light.

Friday, May 8

Off to Dartmouth to take over some lectures today and Saturday. I only hope they keep me busy. I have constant trouble because people do not know the difference between chronological age and spirit age. Good Prof. Smead, who was so helpful to us in our Farmers Union case, indicated that he did not want to burden me, little knowing that it is a relief rather than a burden for me to meet many adventurous minds who can offer challenging questions. This is particularly true if I don't know the answers to the questions.

I find that I wound many young people in a kind of individual evangelical mood. I want to get them jobs and help them in many ways. Deep down, of course,

this is a matter of some vanity and personal ego satisfaction. But the young are unable to take benefactions
without feeling in debt and therefore awkward. In our
culture the hurts to young people, people in the prime
of life and aged people have very different qualities. I
suggest that in Japan, where the most cautious period
is the prime of life, feelings are scarred least in youth
or old age because in both those periods the people are
excited and adventurous and are less affected than we
are.

Sunday, May 10

Sometimes day and night merge, when I stay up
around the clock, but at times even a couple of days
merge. So the past three days merged in the mood of
lovely college-town Hanover. I love college towns—the
best aggregates of our culture. The buildings, the main
streets, the stores, the clothes—the informalities—all
look and smell different.

I was in Hanover in 1907 debating for Williams (no
doubt we lost since I do not remember the outcome).
It's all quite different. Girls in 1907 wore their fineries
—now in slacks and shorts and that odd coverall, a
ragged raincoat. But then as now the girls were on the
beauty side—few smart, tender, intelligent ones are usually invited. This beauty prestige is not too good for our
nation. Maybe the General Electric TV Goucher and
Barnard College Bowl winners will change this pattern.
By and large the beauties have no real virtues, are often
spoiled and do not have to nurse the affections of the
beaux—and affections are best when tended.

Met with the Smeads and arranged for my lectures—

which weren't lectures but paragraphs to elicit questions. And it was swell for me; I learned several attitudes
good for me. We talked law in its relation to life—the
right to an attorney, the curse of monopoly and bigness,
Sacco and Vanzetti case, monopoly of the press and radio,
and then censorship, with obvious excitement in the
questions on what is obscenity, etc. The second day, on
my return, even house party girls joined in my education.

Lunch with John Dickey, who wiped out reservations
I had held against him. We discussed financing of colleges, status of teachers, status of faculties and raising
of monies. On the latter, he accepted money raising as
part of his function and he resented the college presidents who complain about their need to speak for their
programs to people who give the cash. Amen!

Dinner with Dorothy Thompson, dinner the next
night with Olive and Bob Carr, lunch with Pen Haile.

Amused by the boat races, the fly casting, the wood-
chopping contests, the sadistic whipping of underclass-
men, the library in use.

Corey Ford delightful on trip down. Noted sign:
"This is not Route 4" in Vermont.

Tuesday, May 12

Exciting news: the birth-control case in New
Jersey has been won by those who are concerned with
the U.S. population problem and those who believe
the state should not try to control men and women in
their decision of size of family. The judge decided
handsomely—he declared the statute invalid since it
said in effect contraceptives could be lawfully dispensed

if "for just cause." Too vague, said the judge; must men and women of New Jersey guess themselves into jails by guessing what cause—religious, economic health, etc., —is "just"? I called Stamler & Targon, the New Jersey barristers who carried the main load of the battle.

Dinner at home with Dan and Virginia.* These are refined thinkers in the best sense of the word, and I forgive Dan for shifting from sail to power since he has now sold his big stinkpot vessel. Then to Barry Gray's radio mike to chatter—to talk about the New Jersey birth-control case and other less important matters. I guess I'll get a score of intemperate, anonymous postals from people who usually write, "You dirty kike" or "You Commie" or, "Go home where you came from." Incidentally, the latter is wise advice—some day I want to see my birth town, Uniontown, Alabama, which I left sixty-nine years ago—without a trace of memory of the trees, the streets, the stores or anything. Is there a trace of memory of that environ tucked away in my brain? A return visit might resurrect a tidbit or two.

Wednesday, May 13

All predictions were for rain in the afternoon. So of course it rained in the morning. I should think we will get to the power of making the weather before we will get to the point where we will correctly predict it.

I guess we were fooled by our fertile-egg dealer on Eighth Street. For the last two days, in the evenings and in early morning, I have put my ear close to the egg in my incubator to see if I could hear the baby chick

---

* Dan Fuller, of Fuller Fabrics and his wife Virginia, of the New School.

pecking at the shell. Not a bit of sound. So we will take out the egg, open it near the garbage pail because of stench, and discover if we were sold a nonfertile egg. In any event, I will take my incubator to Nantucket, where I am sure I can get a fertile egg from a farmer. It is not likely that this particular egg needed more than twenty-one days, which seems to be the proven period for conversion from egg to chick.

Went up in evening with Maggie to see Bob Fowler, my favorite Canadian. He is knowledgeable on newsprint, informed on matters of government and interested in nearly everything. I tried to tell him again that the newsprint industry of Canada—the best of the Canadian industrial economy—should keep an eye on the increase of literacy through mass media. It is hard to imagine what would happen to the newsprint plants and to the need for more forests if there should be a two-per-cent increase in literacy in our world. My guess is that we cannot rely on trees for the newsprint of the future. We will be compelled to discover synthetic alternates.

Friday, May 15

Birth-control situation quite exciting. Eminent Catholics, including one upstanding judge, earnestly want to explore legalization except for minors. This seems reasonable—and increasingly, with the decline of the family as a unit, society must create sanctions of public market-place behavior by drawing lines between adults and children—sale of liquor, cigarettes, etc. Why not contraceptives, they ask me?

Read an entire stack of pamphlets on literacy—world-wide, Communist national experiment and South America. To City & Country School Fair—which we've attended profitably every year for thirty-five years. Few old-timers there—except for many of the Van Doren tribe: Maggie, Ann, Dot, Charles, etc.

Home and read more on visual education.

Monday, May 18

Busy on law matters all day. The best item: quiet small movie projectors are proven better for literacy, etc., than closed-circuit television; color on TV adds an additional objection. The operation of the movie projector must be silent for movies to beat out TV. And above all, the reflex identification in our culture from entertainment to education seems to be a hindrance. Movies connote fiction rather than education. What of Colombia and other cultures, where there has been no television ever?

Wrote a review for Williams *Alumni Review* of Max Eastman's *Great Companions,* in which I put a few caustic words about Williams College, from which Eastman graduated, and which has looked on him for fifty years as an anathema. The only important chapters are about Edna Millay and his mother. He's tops when he is in love, and illuminating on those whom he swore by long ago and now abjures. Max is a suppressed poet, and I like poets because they can't help always being in love. Even Emily Dickinson, who may or may not have had a real, honest-to-bed lover, was always in love in all of the potencies of the mind.

Wednesday, May 20

This was one of those hectic days, with many random tugs of the mind and few at the heart. No wonder the expression, "cold logic." In a sense, intuitional leaps might be called "hot logic," and in a race between the two, I suggest that for most people hot intuition will win out as against cold logic. But most people are afraid to trust their intuitions.

The only restful moment I had was while waiting for Aly Khan to show up at his apartment for lunch. I am cursed with the need of being on time. I will never really confess that there is such a thing as "Aly Khan time" and "John L. Lewis time." At Aly's beautiful apartment I treasured the river view and wandered around, increasingly falling in love with his three Dufys.

In the evening I was taken up to Stamford and made a speech before a goodly audience of Democrats on matters political. In this I have only one qualification—I never ran for office and, as I told them, I deeply regret not having had such an experience.

Thursday, May 21

Writing a diary for the first time after one gets to be seventy should in itself evoke some observations, pure or impure. As a matter of fact, I rather enjoy it, in part because there are no compulsions and I really don't know why I am doing it. It certainly is not for my kids, because they will probably never even look at seventy-five bound volumes of indexed correspondence and documents that Miss Gross had kept over the years. For my part, I wish that I had an ancestor who had left me a diary or even some letters. I remember when I first had this notion. It was when Lewis Gannett showed me letters from his great-grandfather, who had been president of Yale University. My volumes may have value, what with letters from F. D. R., Henry Wallace, Ickes, Edna Ferber, Hugh Walpole, Trotsky, Rockefeller and, above all, Leffingwell, the last of the great gracious letter writers. I certainly will never reread the diary, but I sense that it has followed no pattern as to length, format or material. I guess this is consistent with my own life which, as far as I know, has no pattern other than the absence of a pattern. Maybe in part this is related to the fact that, as far as I can remember, my parental controls had no resemblance to the controls under which my friends suffered. In the main parents say: don't drink coffee; wear rubbers; wear a hat, etc. I have no recollection of any mandates along those lines, nor have I ever cared to associate with those women who too obviously take command of situations.

Busy all day with a myriad miscellaneous law matters, none of which can ever go into a diary.

Saturday, May 23

A thirteen-hour plane trip to Bogotá, then woke up in a modern room in a modern hotel refreshed after the trip, which was twice as long as my last journey to London. I realized I had been quite awkward with the reception committee of four estimable Colombians and two women translators who met me at the airport. With the latter I chatted until after midnight, digging for the most obvious of the folkway items: sports at such an altitude, relation of cancer, smoking, increasing forbearance of dominant culture (Catholic in this case) toward other religious groups, difference of church from that of our northeastern (Irish) or French, or even gayer Puerto Rican.

On the sixth of June, I am told, there will be trouble —a kind of hunger demonstration "filtered" by the Commies. They are not ready here to show their hands and teeth as in Cuba.

This morning papaya for breakfast, and then picked up by guide-translator-nurse, an intelligent woman, with daughter at school for journalism, and son at college; she has lived in France and U.S. for years. She will be most helpful.

Spent morning at ACPO the literacy-radio enterprise of Msgr. Salcedo, who set up arrangements for me to meet the President, Secretary of Mines, Ministers of Education, etc. For lunch with guide Beatriz Comacho, who with her daughter and a law student as chauffeur took me through the mountains to Sutetanza. On the way we stopped at one-radio schoolroom, radio and all donated by the one farmer. Why he did it is the question. He had no image in sight of the better life of a "literate" educated farmer on earth. When he started, he had not been propagandized with pictures or stories of the easy (chrome-plated) life with quick-growing seeds or fertilizer magic. He led the way because it was an act that would get him into a better heaven, or nearer to God or whatever equivalent image was set forth by the priest. This was the primary urge, while the pursuits of the mind were secondary.

Three-hour drive much like the one in Puerto Rico that made Roger car sick thirty years ago. Beautiful when viewed as scenery—tough soil for the decent life. At Sutetanza again welcomed by a group; after dinner we heard a band composed of the young lads in the neighborhood (practice once a week all year round); to social club with Beatriz, her daughter Mary, and Priest Velasquez, a good belly-laughing priest, quiet, thoughtful and an argufier of the type I enjoy. Drank coffee and discussed all sorts of matters, even the evils of marriage of Church and State, with an audience of young lads that pitched in every once in a while. I'm all for the Radio School with its 38,000 radio sets, its 200,000 graduates per annum, etc. The advertising of insurance, fertilizers, etc., reminded me of my talk about commercials in Pakistan.

To sleep after being serenaded. Maggie should be here. It's the first time that I've been completely on my own in a foreign culture for years, except once in Morocco. I'd get much more out of it with Maggie, even though she seems to be the silent partner—i.e., one can't hear her mind and she talks so little.

Sunday, May 24

Up early. The entire vicinage at mass in the church next to my bedroom. Breakfast—no new foods but oddities like soup for breakfast. Then to see transmitter station down the hill. Beautiful G. E. machinery —which the people now adore and which may some day lose its magic and enslave these peasants, in a town with two priests and one doctor and no dentist. Then to Square; a thousand people out in my honor; I'm embarrassed and feel I'm a fraud. Singing, dancing, speeches; I had to reply; "Star Spangled Banner" was sung while I hoisted our flag—which was later put at half mast for Dulles. Then to girls' institute—again singing and speeches. Then to boys' school for lunch with faculty. Too much food, good round cornbread. An Indian Chief from lowlands was there and I cross-examined him—why he came, was there resistance, was there envy? This is a four-month course in agriculture and these lads go back to teach the villagers. The dedication is so great that no discipline is necessary. Ages sixteen to seventy—but all serious.

Today saw a radio school in action—twelve women from very old to six or seven years old. One room of house given over to the school. I asked why they work, who inspired them, do their husbands go to male radio schools, why should a seventy-year-old woman start to learn to read and write? Is there an example of literacy to be envied? Was it enough that the priest said to do it? Then to see boys' farm, to which the boys walk at five-thirty A.M. every day—with lights out at eight P.M. every night.

Monday, May 25

Getting used to the altitude, which at first knocked me out, for I slept ten hours and woke up a little fatigued—not like my usual pattern. To the ACPO printing press; rows of grand polished machinery run by two hundred men and women, doubly effective because after they get their jobs they are sent in small groups to Sutetanza to see the end result of their part in the operation. Only too seldom in our economy of bits and pieces are the working people helped to see the end result of their creations. Even this joy of partial creativity is denied man on the assembly belt.

Then to ACPO office to meet with heads of divisions —accounting, electronics, etc. I argued that with fifty thousand more sets the graduates will run to four hundred thousand a year. Then these literate, educated farmers will look for earthly rewards. The concept of education will require implementation of capital to lend to the farmer to buy a cow, seed, fertilizer, etc. If there is no loan capital available, cynicism may develop. Why should not ACPO borrow a million dollars—good sound loan—for rediscount to its graduates. Surely the graduates are better risks for small loans than are the *"ignorantes"* next door. A woman of forty in a class, when I asked her why she went to school, said, "I don't want to be an *ignorante* like my mother and father." Must not the government or ACPO supply the "food" —small loans—to satisfy the hunger ACPO is creating every day?

To lunch with Betancour, whom I had met in New York for breakfast with Chaves a year ago. He is head of ICETEX, an organization financed half by government and half by employers to send skilled young people abroad to return as leaders in industry. The students in effect borrow the money and repay with interest after they come back and get employment. Roberto de Zubiria, Vice Chancellor of the University of the Andes, was there also. We explored means of acceleration of educational movements by loans with interest.

I suggested the University of Andes give an honorary degree to an exceptional teacher in one of the ACPO radio schools. He told me with pride that last year for the first time a professor—unknown outside of Colombia, not an author, just a great teacher—got an honorary degree.

Brief moment at U.S. Embassy with Manning of Point Four, and Walls, Chargé d'Affaires. Back to hotel, then to dinner with Mary Comacho and few of her friends at a good, small French restaurant. The young folks talked about the Spanish Revolution as we did twenty years ago and as if it were last year, talked about the CP as we did ten years ago, and of whorehouses such as existed in our big cities fifty years ago. On the go sixteen hours a day or more, and each day is fun. Learned a little from each person—but conflicts of testimony increase.

Tuesday, May 26

Today the plans were changed. Went back to ACPO with Salcedo and his cabinet. Worked over the need of financing for ACPO graduates—in fact, for all literate farmers who read and learn about their crafts. If ACPO takes on the operation, it will get too big and may become a threat to the government soon when there are a million radio listeners—a kind of Pay-As-You-Hear radio (sets built to receive only ACPO), since peasants pay for their own receiving sets. If the state had the money, which it hasn't, the loans would be political in many areas. So I am trying to design a division of the State Agrarian Bank for such loans—but in cooperation with ACPO, using ACPO's experience of the borrowers and its testing of validity of purposes of the loans.

Then to Embassy. With the feeling once more that our Foreign Office will be run as a department, the staff is heartened and quite excited.

Then for lunch with Martin del Corral, Gerente General of the Banco de Bogotá. Many suggestions as to techniques for handling farmers' small-loan setup—with decentralization as per my Polish setup of 1921. Jockey Club good fun and surely elegant and good food.

Then to Minister of Mines, Mr. Gran, who went over my proposal for cooperatively financed aerial surveys. At night to the circus. Quite empty, but always a good feel of part of a people. Maggie and I have seen them all over the world. This was a three-ringer—I like the one-ring ones better.

Just before bed, letter from Maggie. Beautiful as always, and it was amusing to learn after all these years that "fond" came from foolish. I wonder if that will spoil one of my favorite words.

Wednesday, May 27

To prison by eight A.M. Forty prisoners in an ACPO radio class. Quite unbelievable, the interest of the boys and men, the neatness of their copybooks, the simplicity with which one literate can guide the radio course for forty *ignorantes,* all concentrated and dedicated. ACPO is in 111 prisons out of 159, with four thousand pupils daily. A few write letters to a literate relative. Although a factor is earlier release, the prisoners are not told so when they enter a prison—so ACPO has failed to capitalize on rewards and stimuli. They still don't realize that the effect of the Catholic Church is to hold up only one reward—Heaven, or proximity to God. And still they know that man produces most if his prizes are nearer to hand, smaller in dimension and attainable with effort. I keep asking, "Does anyone give a window to a church only for reward in Heaven? Does anyone make such a gift anonymously? Surely he wants his neighbors on earth to thank him or praise him."

The retarded Spanish people are low in productive ability, not because the Church took much wealth for church decorations or for support of clergy, but primarily because nearly all churches with an accent on Heavenly rewards reduce the prestige values of earthly rewards—the real creator of higher standards of living.

At lunch at the Gun Club with Minister of Education, Abel Villegas; to president of agricultural small-loan bank; then to Salcedo's home to clear minds before I leave. I think he is coming around to my first proposal: no government financing, either U.S. or Colombian, but setting up a separate cooperating bank for small loans for ACPO and other literate, educated farmers.

Thursday, May 28

Beatriz and Theresa and my chauffeur insisted on taking me to airport. A last cup of Colombian coffee, which I like. It's been an unusual week—the climate was tough. I saw no seductive women, was aware of high degree of homosexuality and, above all, once more had the chance to watch the priest mind at work. I have seen a great feat of a great man—Salcedo.

Friday, May 29

Spent most of the day reporting my Colombian adventure. Caught up on mail.

Home for dinner with Goldsteins. Steffie examines us as to death. The United States died? No, it was a man. What was a Dulles? Does he spread his arms out when he "death"? (Possibly a carry-over from church sights with Jo and Delia.*) Will you die? Yes, old people die. All of them? Yes. (We avoided saying that the young die also—although I treat death lightly and gaily, since I look on it as the end of a good game.) Great fun watching a young, open mind at work on the "eternal verities," which to me mean everlasting ignorance of man.

Read the U.S. Steel-financed printing of report on the *Problems of Scholarly Publications* by American Council of Learned Societies. It's a disgusting job to treat the problem of diffusion of scholarly books without a word on the technique of popularization, value judgments as to what the scholars did write, the inadequacies of alerting our public by book reviews, etc., and, above all, to leave the impression that scholars are willing to reach results by an assembly of statistics irrespective of any thought process. I'll write Mahoney and others to see if they will allow this report to stand unanswered.

Read back issues of many publications. Much of the honorable material that the Committee on Economic Development utters is so written and organized that the eye of anyone but the head of a big business rejects it. Bosses seem to feel that they can issue pronouncements that require no popularization techniques. We lowly people should accept their words without the powers of persuasion! I wonder if anyone on the staff or Board of CED ever disagreed in basic folkway terms. The material reads as if it had not been subjected to basic dissents.

Hot—and great to be home.

* *Our Irish Catholic maids of many years.*

J U N E

Monday, June 1

Not much time to contemplate—too rushed a day, too many people in what they think is trouble, too many wanting comfort of my guess as to what they should do with decisions in their lives.

A few relief periods. The stenographers and office boys came to lunch in my office to talk about Colombia. Quite a few have deep anti-Catholic prejudices—and I mean literally pre-judgments. Wrote fan letters to John L. Lewis on his TV appearance—must see that stout symbol of humorless but mighty arrogance soon. Long talk with driving personality, Jack Kaplan.* Brief talk with Thayer Hobson—publisher with one of the most distinguished lists of titles for the past decade. Visit from Chaves to get report on ACPO.

Connie and Mike for dinner. Mike just flew in from Vienna. A fast-moving and restless family we are this past week or so.

* *Industrialist, philanthropist.*

Tuesday, June 2

Lunch with seven or eight bigshots of RCA. I was terribly disappointed because they kept on saying that I had stimulated them greatly. This is not what I wanted at all. I had hoped that this group might include one person who would stick his chin out enough to prepare a memorandum for David Sarnoff—indicating the hope for the decent profits that will be made in the future if RCA gets really excited about the demands that are in sight for the equipment of communication (radio or television) for literacy and education. I am quite sure that no one there understood me at all. Their minds were blacked out because of suspicion. If I only had a client and could say that I could make money out of something, then my argument might have been persuasive. I failed even to create an analogy between my efforts in this field in the Dominican Republic, Pakistan and Colombia to the work any one of the gentlemen was doing on the board of a hospital or school. I could not get over the one hurdle. In our culture it is normal to be on a hospital board for free—which means for social prestige and inner satisfaction. But we are a long way from accepting as rational the idea of anyone who would spend money, energy and time to help the battle against Communists by creation of education so that democracy is not an illusion.

No use kidding. Much has happened to me that would have raised hairs of joy right through the derbies of most men—but for me I'll give away all else today for one brief visit from Hiram Haydn. Alan Collins, my agent, sent my diary to Hiram on condition that only

Hiram would read it for Atheneum. Today Hiram visits to say it excited him more than anything he had read in a long time and he wanted to publish it. So my jury gives me its vote. And this for me and not just a client or a cause. A bit of joy dispels lots of desolation.

Called Maggie, wrote Joan and Roger, called Connie —rang the bell, to let them know I'm happy, to hope they will be happier, and no doubt just to show off to my Maggie and my kids; as if I needed to show off to folks who love me all they can already. I'd like to tell Heywood Broun.

Thursday, June 4

Rented a car and drove up to Williamstown with Ralph, Frank and Harvey* With Harvey and Frank I debated while in college more than fifty years ago. All three were members of snooty fraternities and I was an awkward, embarrassed, shy and phlegmatic lad. I was diffident and felt inferior in comparison to members of swank fraternities, or those who were good with brawn, or went to North Adams to get drunk. I did not understand those who went to Albany whoring. I had terrific breaks in college—fraternity, senior society, college paper, college yearbook—more than ever entered into any dream of mine; but I still feel inferior with the men who were popular and sophisticated while I was at Williams. Although my mind realizes that some of the athletes are men with little decency or men of no intellectual excitements I revert to my college attitudes.

* *Ralph Perkins, Frank Sayre, Harvey Pike.*

Saturday, June 6

Real quixotic fun. At the Gargoyle meeting, it was discovered that $600 was left over in the treasury. They were about to vote it for a scoreboard at the hockey rink. I suggested that Williams students could remember hockey scores, which usually do not run over ten, since most students can count on their fingers. So why not let the students give awards to one or more professors? This would be man bites dog. I outlined at lunch to some of the students a letter to the head of the faculty:

We are wiser than you. We are wise enough to hold marks in great disdain. Learning should be for itself and not for marks. Moreover, we doubt if you are really so stupid as to think you know the difference between C plus and B minus. So we will give awards —maybe one, maybe six, how can we tell in advance? We may find three of you to be worthy of *maxima cum laude* for teaching us work habits, opening up our minds, giving us security—in fact, doing something of importance other than being good fellows or being popular or running cinch courses.

Gargoyle sidetracked the hockey score board. I think they will agree to have students honor teachers.

Sunday, June 7

After the reunion trip to Williams, flew over and got to Nantucket before Maggie. Unpacked all the packages that had accumulated over the winter. Great fun—sort of like Christmas day. Can't wait to open every one even if only a new can opener. Almost forgot—got Maggie a surprise present, an apron with lighthouses on it, with a little tinkling bell on each lighthouse.

All looks wonderful. The flickers have picked holes in Joan and Connie's side walls.

There's my town—the windmill, the shipyard, the lighthouse. On the wall my anemometer, on my desk my barograph, over my desk my inside-outside thermometer —all over the house is us, the things we made, or scarred, or polished, things that are us by osmosis from us alive to treasures long dead but living in wooden shapes we love.

To bed at nine after dropping in to see Charlie and Donna Dreifus, Joan's tenants. Weary and tired. Those of consistent weight lose my joy of putting on weight in the winter and the great fun of work and sweat that takes off pounds in the summer. Going either on or off, it's fun. I'm sorry for those who keep their weight without ups and downs. Do they never enjoy sweets or sweats?

Monday, June 8

A day of muscle uses and little intake from the minds of others. Only *Yachting, Boats, Publishers' Weekly, The Scientist* and Nantucket papers. Stepped mast in *Nicholie* and rigged her; now she's ready to go into the water on tomorrow's high tides. Put up owl on pier to keep off gulls. I'll try the owl although I'll also put up a dead gull as soon as I can get one, then compare results in terms of gulls dropping shells on the pier. Went to meeting of School Board. Quite frightening. The new chairman trained under McCarthy, suffers from a failure to realize that democracy is a delicate operation that requires above all else good will and lots of it. Moreover, he shocked me, since he wants the Board to act as the Superintendent of Schools.

Left at about eleven P.M., the session to run until eleven thirty and the executive session, I hear, ran until one thirty A.M. Is this stupidity, fear, power grabbing, or maybe a strategy of attrition? I wonder that any teacher, principal or superintendent will stay on the island, which suffers anyway from lack of winter cultural advantages.

This scene is only a small but significant symptom of a dent in democracy caused by our innate fears, which led to driving the Communist Party underground instead of aboveground as Edgar Hoover urged. I'm glad I supported him from the beginning in the debate against the Mundt-Nixon Bill. I've seen much of Dick and Karl since those days, and I rather think if they had it to do over again they might act otherwise.

Wednesday, June 10

Have sailed a bit and pottered around the shop, the house, the garden for two days. Messed around the waterfront, and surely Kenneth Grahame was exact when he said nothing—but nothing—is as much fun as messing around the waterfront.

Cut the grass, fixed the swimming ladder, made a latch for the walnut desk I built for Maggie ten years ago—now in New York. Fun working at the lathe once more. Rigged the outhaul for the kids' rowboat, put up the kids' swing, moved a half cord of kindling, picked up Jo Houlihan and Winnie (who replaced Ellen) at the airport. Started reading Thurber's book on Harold Ross. I'll enjoy it, though Ross was in so many ways inept at life, awkward with women, cruel to all whom he could push around, so that I always asked during the years I advised him on his messy life, how much does man forgive of a personality so long as he is a contributor to literature or art? It's a compliment to the arts that the same degree of forgiveness seldom flows to the cruel and inept creatures who top big business.

Warm—swim again before breakfast, and a couple of times during the day. What a grand unimportant existence, important only to me and Maggie, diving back into memories that in a few hours or no more than a day or so ambush both of us—just as if there had been no other existence for either of us. A great intimacy—a kind of annual honeymoon.

Friday, June 12

Life is divided between real and make-believe
—but often I can't distinguish between the two. For
example: after two days of shop and waterfront, a call
comes from Ed Murrow. Is Ed and his call the real or
the make-believe? He wanted to talk about the Worthy
passport case—a clash between two desires of the people
of our land. On the one hand, the executive runs the
foreign policy and to that end claims the right to deny
passports to any portion of the globe. To be sure, during
a shooting war the secretary of state might deny all departures from our shores and make us all prisoners in a
sense. On the other hand, we claim the right to travel
the earth at our own hazard. It's only in recent times
that a law of *"ne exeat"* was enacted—a crime to depart
without a passport save only to a few areas approved by
the State Department. So the right to travel and the
right of the executive to "do" a foreign policy are in conflict. Risk for risk is the problem. But its only a starter.
The real question is: may the secretary of state deny the
right to travel to China or Timbuktu without *any* judicial review at all? Here is the rub. I should hold that any
power without review in times of peace—or rather of
nonshooting war—is highly dangerous.

To date, the State Department and the CIA are in a
sense separate governments, the latter reporting to no
one except the President. Even AEC reports to chairmen
of the House and Senate Committees. The Supreme
Court has held that the State Department may not deny,
by whim alone, a passport to a person deemed objectionable to the Department. Now the issue is, must we

learn of China through the eyes and ears of British, French and other reporters and never through our own? The unreviewed power of the State Department must, if I read history, only increase the fears of the Department and make its officials more capricious, no matter which political party is in power. If my memory is correct, Dean Acheson saw eye to eye with Dulles on this denial of right to travel. I must look at my brief in the Judge Clark case and see if I can be of further aid to Bill Kunstler and Bill Worthy.

So is all this the real part of life or the make-believe? No answer, except to shift graciously from one pigeonhole of life to the other and forget definitions and tables.

Saturday, June 13

Varied joys—Gil,* that wise engineer who refuses to double his income by living in a big city, but prefers having his home ten minutes from his boat and his ski run, telephones that he has found me a sloop for Maine this summer. *Hoi Ying*—Hong Kong built: probably all teak, just as I saw them in the Hong Kong shipyard.

Built a wooden walk for the kids to keep them off the road, with Maggie applying cuprinol and helping with the hammer. Stopped to hear town band on the Atheneum steps—chairs fifty cents for part or all of the concert. Read homosexual Gide on homosexual Oscar Wilde —a tidy, honorable and most perceptive report on meetings after Wilde got out of jail, where he first learned pity. Wrote at some length at Professor Silverman's request my Joyce episodes. Silverman, professor at Uni-

* *Gilbert Forrester, Maine engineer.*

versity of Buffalo, is visiting the Dreifuses. Heard from him a possible explanation of the oddity that Adam and Eve are promised a life of Riley provided they don't go after knowledge. Eve—a woman in a culture where women were chattels—goes for the Tree of Knowledge. It's not the male that has the curiosity that overwhelms a deal for ease and comfort. How come? Possible answer: Eve was unsatisfied sexually, hence restless and had to find an outlet for her unused gonads. Must look up Milton, who I'm told develops this theory at end of Part IV in *Paradise Lost*.

Sunday, June 14

Comforting blanket of fog engulfed our harbor last night, but the wind shifted to the north and all is clear and clean. Kept on pottering—as man can never do on a rented house or on another man's property. The price of ownership is deep in our culture and I have long felt that property and freedom are ineluctably wedded. Any time a sovereign takes away a bit of property without the consent of the owner, a hunk of liberty and freedom goes with it. Put on shoes—first time in a week. Freedom in Nantucket is symbolized by barefootedness—with legs scarred, heels calloused and splinters taken out daily by Dr. Maggie.

Plane to New York to enter another world for three or four days. Rhoda St. James came down to talk about her novel, its importance, its novelty and its need— according to my favorite reading person, Maggie—of a goodly bit of editing.

Tuesday, June 16

Yesterday afternoon flew down to Washington with Alan and went to Roger and Jean's, where Jean, with her quiet energy, was throwing a party for seventy people—drinks and buffet supper. I enjoyed it particularly because Roger and I have done a good job in preventing my relations with people in Washington from interfering—for good or bad—with the development of his own career. I was very happy that so many people knew me as Roger Ernst's father, just as in England, during and after the war, I was known in many bistros of London and Paris as Connie's father.

Spent the night at the University Club, which is sober, inelegant and gracious.

From the Senate office building I went to the Carlton for lunch, hoping to see John L. Lewis. He was not there, but ran into Tom Kennedy, United Mine Workers treasurer for as long as I can remember. Tom is unique as a union official. I wonder if he ever displays a temper or pounds on a desk. I rather think he has that kind of strength that needs little outward manifestation.

Back in New York, to the apartment to chat with Elizabeth Barber. Later to the Joyce Society, where I had an engaging brief talk with Ben Huebsch*; then to the Blue Angel. This is the first time, I think, that I have been to a night club in the United States since the days of Heywood Broun, when I used to go to Texas Guinan's *ad nauseam!*

* *Editor, The Viking Press, Inc.*

Thursday, June 18

Picked up Stef at Joan's—for once played the role of a grandpop. To LaGuardia, much plane trouble, delay and confusion—but got to Nantucket by two o'clock. Stef was no trouble at all. No running through the aisle, just consumed with observations: the man with the cowboy hat; going into and over and then under clouds. All too busy even to miss having any lunch.

A few little chores—brought in kerosene for parlor stove, cleared up new mail on desk, tightened hooks on screens in Steffie's room—and so back into a routine of pleasant nothings taken one by one, but in total as near perfect as I can reach in continued stretches. Rosens'* after dinner. Tomorrow the clan starts to gather; the Bessies arrive around noon. I did not intend to copy the Chinese family compound, but that's what we have—no mixture of three generations living in the same house, a real opportunity for privacy and still availability and proximity.

Tomorrow will start a new building project: a toy, towel and life-preserver beach house for five grandchildren.

* *Leo Rosen, one of my law partners, and his wife.*

Friday, June 19

On and off all day sorry for Lewis Strauss. I re-call some years ago L. S. said publicly, or was so quoted, that he was not fit for Washington and that never before in his career had he had any enemies. This is part of the key. In business he had power that could crush or silence opposition. In Washington he, as George Humphrey once told me, thought that a cabinet position was like the presidency of a big corporation—the Senate equivalent of a Board of Directors, with the stockholders resembling the voters. Nothing could have been further from the truth, and I suspect Lewis never understood political democracy, which is the antithesis of big business. If Lewis had asked me, I would have suggested he pose the real issue; and he would have made a valuable contribution by stating with acuteness his basic positions.

The liberal senators of both parties in the main sensed his political and economic standpattism and were suspicious that he was able and smart enough to retard what they deem to be needed changes. In a way it's what I have been told so often. The respectable average director in our corporations and foundations is reluctant to vote for an additional director who would urge reappraisals of the status quo. On this level I have even received apologies from enterprises managed by friends and clients for not being included in such select circles of power. I guess in their terms and their functions for their purposes they are right. Although many will be my fast friends and call on me in flattering fashion to counsel them in their programs, they would not care to have it known that I was sitting with them as a peer. The symbol would be disturbing to them. So Lewis should write his autobiography; for the way many conservatives want our nation to travel could be set forth by him better than by any other man with distinguished career in business, wealth, and public service. P.S. I'll bet Ike offers him a job for which Senate confirmation is not a condition.

Saturday, June 20

Signed charter for *Hoi Ying*. Examined plans and charter agreement, and am consumed by dozens of details, in rigging, construction, gadgets and gilhickies.

Sunday, June 21

Last night, after a day of pleasures, we dropped in on Sidney and Sarah Fay while waiting for the night boat. As we entered Sidney said, "Hello, good friends" —a salutation rarely heard in big cities.

Sun out. Sailed with Nick, worked on toy beach house. But always trouble on the waterfront. Waves and wind can bend iron and break steel, as man cannot do with ordinary tools. Now one pontoon of float seems to suffer a leak. I'll try pumping her dry and then swim under to see if the leak is not where pipe for pumping is attached. That's my guess, and the fun of licking troubles comes in the first instance from the diagnosis—like that of the garage mechanic who listens and knows what's wrong with an engine.

Barometer rising—all's well in the compound. Maybe

too well, as Winnie loves to cook rich and Jo enjoys beg-
ging everyone to take second helpings. I have a theory
that children who don't eat "well" can be put on the
right fork or spoon if their plates are never filled—have
always less of everything than what they want to eat.
Then they will ask for more rather than feel reproached
for leaving food on the plate—food that represents parental beggings or that is taken out to the kitchen with an
aura of shame.

Monday, June 22

Last evening to the auditorium for the forty-
piece Boston Symphony Orchestra. The first time ever in
Nantucket, and over a thousand people paid five dollars
a seat to hear Mozart, Haydn, de Falla—and to celebrate
the three-hundredth year of Nantucket.

Music treats me in odd ways. I don't feel much of it
any more, but what I do feel is important at the time
with no memory hangover. Piano and cello came to my
way out of parental desires—at least piano study was
part of my father's typical immigrant desire to give his
children whatever he didn't have as a youth—plus my
mother's performance on the zither; cello was still more
admirable and less rational—to surprise my mother on
her return to New York from one of her desperate
coughing trips to the West in the hope of curing her t.b.
I was to play *"Träumerei"* in the dining room of my
grandparents' home when my mother came downstairs.
I recall little of the moment except tears of joy from
many. It still makes me wet-eyed to recall the memory
of the episode. Of course I played cello and piano as if
I had gone to military school. I have little ear for pitch,

but I played in high-school and college orchestras—faintly and badly.

Received word from *Boats* magazine that they want a short article on my battle against "pier gulls"—I think I shall call it "Gulls, Owls and the Memory of the Dead." I suspect that, since birds have no sense of smell, my retarders may be memory of the sight of the dead. I must look this up if it is look-upable. Not remote from the mystery of salmon beating out their genital organs going up the rivers to go back to spawn and die at the place they were born.

Just looked at holes of flickers near ridge poles of Joan's and Connie's houses. None on Roger's. Why? Only hunch that comes to me is that Roger's trim is painted red, the others are blue or gray. Otherwise houses are same size, same weldtex exterior—fairly identical on the outside. Are these birds shy of red?

Tuesday, June 23

Remembered a dream in color—at least the big, bearish dog was very black. Woke up in peril—the dog obviously derived from that sheep that I watched blue-eyed Bartlett, the farmer, hold sitting up to shear yesterday. Then read a bit of *Naked Villainy* by smooth, amused Davey, one of those authors who surely has fun writing. Something I read made me think of the luck I have because I'm "adecisive"—not un- or non- but a- —as with amoral. I recall only twice in my life having faced choices with conscious concern, not exactly worry —nothing like sleepless hours—rather with a feeling that the exercise of the elective was to be significant and important. Once was when I had given up the idea of

affording a job at the law and then one wintry day in
1914 Laurie called up to tell me that he and Eddie and
Herb, all having had top legal education and clerkships,
which I still envy them, were starting a firm and wanted
me to leave my furniture job and join them. The other
was when I protested to Maggie that I wasn't the marry-
ing type—this before I realized that in our culture men
don't propose, but rather women set their caps and let
the males think they do the pursuing. But being adecisive has no discernible relationship to percentage of
error throughout my life. There is no way to prove that
my batting average would have been different if I had,
as do most people, suffered with observing choices and
then weighed with aches and pains the pros and cons.

Hot little wind. Sailing, two or three dips, helped
Nick learn to row. I can't wait for him to learn to swim.
I sorely need a crew: an unpaid hand and a lad who will
be fun watching as he remarks the mysteries of nature
and leaves nothing—but absolutely nothing—unques-
tioned.

Wednesday, June 24

Bright, clear weather. Off to head of the harbor,
Wauwinet, for lunch. It's an ideal harbor for kids like
Steffie, Nicholas and me—even though the wind will be
gently in our teeth both ways with a light northerly
going up and a shift, I suspect, to the south this afternoon. But with a light breeze we will be favored with
a fair tide both ways.

First expedition of the season, so must assemble the
grill, charcoal, tools and all that is needed for the steak.
Aside from steak it's all simple—only fruit, tomatoes

and hot and cold drinks. Picnic with all the clan; I guess some will drive up and others will drive back.

Hundreds of gulls off our shore (lots of small fish showing their silver at the surface) and a few brave ones seem to be disdainful of our owl.

Every time I sail up-harbor my mind goes back a few centuries to when the Coatue Sand Spit was quite different. Thirty years ago Bassett Jones—an improbable, lovable expert with little knack at communication—told me he had found a dug-up cedar stump from what is now the middle of the harbor. I take it this means there was more land right in the middle of the present water. This is easy to believe, since every year we see large hunks of land taken off one shore and put on another. In recent years I've lost as much as twenty feet of land sand, but to the south it's shoring up fast. So I've always refrained from giving a supercilious smile at the maps of the fifteenth century or earlier. Part ignorance but also part changes.

Here we are close to July and the oil burner still in the living room in front of the fireplace. Good after a morning dip, and today Steff joined us in our trek to the end of the pier before breakfast, although she didn't go in. Even the anti-Dewey educators would agree that on that level of life children do better what they enjoy doing.

To Bob Backus' good hostelry for the annual dinner of Rotary. Once more Maggie and I sat at the head table as the only "off-island" guests. It made us proud. The reason lies in part in a story the benign ninety-year-old Dr. Will Gardner told. Eighty years ago a high-school class wrote history essays in Nantucket every Friday. Subject one week: Napoleon. One piece spoke well of Napoleon, but the last sentence read, "But he was an off-islander." Dr. Will told of Peter Folger, the significant ancestor of Ben Franklin. Folger had been here as the first white man—more than three hundred years ago. He left for Rhode Island. Later the settlers, all twenty-five of them, wrote him to return—they needed the spiritual leadership of this early American gadgeteer, and they would give him a piece of land. This led me to suggest to Dr. Will and Brad Johnson, a gracious and invaluable minister of the island, that Nantucket each year might give a piece of land to some distinguished citizen of our republic who wanted to retire to our island. The symbol of such an award would give some slight demurrer to the present fashion of towns offering tax exemptions to corporations planning to establish a factory. Maybe a gamble on a Peter Folger human selection would add more wealth to Nantucket than the seduction of brick and mortar.

Thursday, June 25

Slept a little late—morning dip as usual, breakfast, to shop, and there Nickie wanted to make a duck walk for the start of the path from his house to the beach. We had some old lumber on hand, two-by-threes and planking. He drove in every last nail, squared up the boards, watched for parallel spacing and then creosoted the bottom of the rails. I wish someone had taught me—or rather led me toward—simple skills of the hand in my youth. Not until I was thirty-five did I use tools, and then I had to buy a book from Sears to read up on the simple knacks that can so much better be transferred from one human to another by example—through the eye—than by print.

Visited with Alan and Paula in Roger's house. They were getting up around noon. Built a fire in their grate, then visited at Charlie's—just neighborly town-crier service—during a little drizzle.

Good mail from office. Many thoughtful letters. Harold Gardiner writes that there is a process for review of R. C. Index items and that he will translate it from the Latin of the Canon Law if I want. I must see if it was ever used, what the pleadings are, whether the trial is public, who can appear for a book banned centuries ago which now, in the light of the Catholic new attitudes and areas of increased theological security, still sits on the Index as a meaningless symbol of prior fears.

Saturday, June 27

This is a sturdy place. It can be cold and foggy—but there is something that makes all the less-than-favorable diminish. Mike came up from Essex, Connecticut, yesterday—by train to Providence and bus to Woods Hole; and then, if you please, the ferry wouldn't leave the dock because of the fog. So Mike slept on board in some makeshift setup, and arrived here at eight thirty after a ten-and-a-half-hour trip. Tough commuting. But all forgotten as soon as the sun comes out.

The young theater folk over for dinner, and we went over the economics of the theater, from the self-protective boondoggling of the unions to the easily reducible ticket speculation, which drains millions out of the theater with not a penny going to actors, directors, or financing groups. Why have none of the businessmen of the theater—Dick Rodgers, Oscar Hammerstein, Leland Hayward and the like—come to grips with these problems? It's even more wasteful and stupid than the book industry. I wonder if a foundation would give a grant to report on the economics of the theater. Years ago the heads of the unions admitted that their practices were induced to spread the work and take care of unemployment. I condoned this; such moves are valid in the light of employer practices. Twenty-five years ago they were ready to sit around and discuss other and wiser techniques to achieve some degree of security for stage hands, electricians, etc., but the producers would not join in any explorations of a constructive nature. So the theater, burdened with economic inefficiency, finds it easier to go in the direction of subsidies than to look for internal reforms. I'll try to find a young Leon Henderson to prepare an outline of a book, go to Actors Equity and other unions for a blessing, and then approach a foundation for a small grant—say $25,000. Only by such a move will the estimable—even great— people of the theater become truly concerned with the millions "stolen" by the sale of $6.00 tickets for hit shows going for $30.00, with not a penny of the $24.00 differential going to those who work and invest in the show.

Sunday, June 28

Read C. P. Snow in *Encounter*. Remarkable document on divisions inside Western cultures. It's the most important document I have come across on the breakdown of communication between our men of science and our men of letters. Typical of *Encounter:* an Edmund Wilson piece on "Legend and Symbol of Pasternak," a gimmick piece by over-stylized and over-educated Wilson, given the lead in the June issue. This editorial choice points up the Snow exploration on the ignorance of literati with respect to things of nature. But Snow's documentation of the color blindness of the nonscientist culture in the U.S. and England will be quoted, I think, after Wilson's piece is long forgotten. The scientist surely can have a sense of the balance of the forces in our culture, but I'm inclined to agree that the writing, intellectual, thoughtful group can't even know what they miss—having in comparable cultural terms what color blindness is in visual terms. This all ties in to what I have for several years been shoving under the "nonscientific" noses of foundations. This is the damnable gap where communication breaks down. I don't pretend to understand even the vernacular of simple science, as Snow points out, but I can't help but think there is a crack in my own rainbow, so I suffer because I sense a bit of what I miss. In our folkway the gap between the two cultures leads the scientists increasingly toward optimisms, while the writer and artist sectors relish and wallow in despairs and hopelessness. I wonder if Snow in his next article will discuss the counterpoint and interaction between the two cultures and the subtle effect of each on the other. I suggest that each makes the other more extenuated and extreme, with few people understanding both parts of our cultures well enough to encourage a common ground.

Why should not the *Times* run a science section to stand up against the book-and-art-theater sections? The *contra* positions would point to the breach in our cultural wall—through which advertising gentry slither with neither optimism nor despair, cynically propelled only by the hunch that content and objective are irrelevant. Their God is the technique of persuasion by repetition—persuasion without thought.

Yesterday spent much time with many minds trying to define *demagogue*—long perverted from its original Greek meaning. Query: is it defined by the fraudulent motive of the speaker, by insincerity, or by techniques employed? Amused to see weakness of definition when we asked each to place the tag of demagogue on Hitler, Billy Graham, Benton, Huey Long (financially corrupt for friends, not self), Joe McCarthy (not proven to many to be insincere until after his debacle in the Senate), Adenauer, Mussolini; and then we all admitted that millions of Republicans deemed F. D. R. a demagogue. My own problem: is any character whom I favor and support ever a demagogue in my eyes?

JULY

Wednesday, July 1

Back to New York, and a busy, busy day. Breakfast with Joan. She is homesick for Steffie, as she should be, and Steffie is homesick for Joan and Irving, as she should be. Homesickness when valid is a good emotion and should never be apologized for. In basic terms it is a great compliment.

I had lunch with Russell at Twenty-three Wall Street. He is a man of great justice. Somewhere he must have tucked away a bit of temper, but I have never felt it. We discussed the export of gold in relation to living beyond our means, or, as I suggested, our competitive desire for living standards; we talked about the declining numbers of trial lawyers (he told me with amusement about the first time he appeared in front of the bench: he was in his middle age and behind the bench sat the Justices of the United States Supreme Court). We got into the power of the legislature and the necessity for the courts to make sure that discernible standards were laid down for any administrative body. To have good law we must in a vague way let the people have an inkling as to what falls this side of the law or

that side of the law. We talked about the function of
directors on foundations. My observation was that the
function was different from that of a director of an industrial or banking corporation. We talked of the value
of succession in management and the odd and valuable
concomitant that the successor wisely wants to make
changes. We discussed the St. James thesis of the insecurity of black Negroes, which causes them to seek
whiter companions as a compensation for their inferior-
ities. We talked of many things but, unlike the situation
with most of my acquaintances, neither of us was only
narrative.

Off to Nantucket on the night plane, to a world of
peaceful minor accomplishments—the use of hand skills
and the examination, in my unscientific terms, of the
mysteries of nature.

Friday, July 3

The Washington Ernsts came on the late boat
last night. David didn't wake up when carried from the
ferry to the car and then finally into his bed at Monomoy. Debbie was affectionately awake. And it was like
old times to see Roger with his towel walking down the
pier for his prebreakfast dip. The clan gathers.

Pet catbirds are back, come at our mealtimes and
feed off the ground, table and hands in rather quickly
educated steps of safety from their points of view. Mail
from office is pleasant: Senator Yarborough on *The
Ugly American,* Jack Javits on International Cooperation Administration release on the subject of the book,
a brashly flattering letter from Dean Sayre of Washington Cathedral on my Israel memorandum, and the like.

Quite sure New Jersey will lead the way to legalized contraceptives spread through clergy, clinics, doctors, druggists and all sources save those of too-easy access for minors.

To Esther Sawyer's for a drink. Good painter, particularly good, I suspect, because she started late in life. What a grand era when so many people discover that they possess skills unknown to them for their entire early life! What hope this prophesies for our people, as soon as we recognize that not many of us use even a small percentage of our talents.

Saturday, July 4

Weather settling into the delicious. Even Steffie went along for a prebreakfast dip, and the old blue wheeled table is in steady use for outdoor meals. Roses out on every roof. What better than Maggie's hidden garden built up on what, when we first saw it, was nothing but beach grass.

In and out of sailboats and water all day long. The best swimming for thirty years has been where jetty comes into the Coatue end of our island.

Ramos, the handsome Azores plumber, delivers some pipe for me to use for tree guys and adds some lettuce from his garden for each of our families.

Wrote report on use of waterproof fiber owl—not too successful in fending off gulls. All it takes is for one brave, imaginative gull, or one untrained or stupid gull, to get near to the fake owl to explode the myth. So it is with mankind. Someone in Israel travels on a Sabbath, or eats meat on a Friday in Ireland, or faces north while praying in Jordan, or—the world is full of invalid fears which explode with only a faint purr when one human questions them. Surely, however, the myths that rely for punishment on a life hereafter raise more difficult problems for the defiant.

Monday, July 6

Today my mind went to what views I have seen most in my life. Having little, if any, memories of my youth, and not remembering much even of college days without some tickler to awaken memories, I should think that I have spent most time gazing on the tree in our yard on Eleventh Street—that went on for thirty years, as has my relishing the view across Nantucket Harbor to the town and the lighthouse on Brant Point from our big window. For fewer years but for endless hours I've watched Washington Square through the Arch from our apartment window. Good views and all of the same genre—nature, rather than the works of man.

Tuesday, July 7

Monomoy is a "town," in the sense that "neighborhood" means that people enjoy doing favors for each other. It's like Connie's garden on Sullivan Street, where the way of life is hand-me-down, from velocipedes to coats, from larger children to smaller ones. Today Ann Harmon called to say that there was some lumber in their garage which Loomis would have liked me to have. Loomis, of the whimsy and smile, built the lowest of houses out here, and I always thought he wanted to do penance for the social horror known as the Empire State Building, for which I held him responsible.

Albert and Nell Boni came on plane for a couple of days. They had never been on the island before and, as I told them, I envy those who are seeing and feeling it for the first time. It must be different living on top of Mt. Everest from going there for a short visit for the first time. Much is worth sensing only for the initial impact. Few experiences, scenes or people are a continuing delight. The trick of life is to come upon those rarities that are exciting on first vision and prove to be livable for long stretches thereafter.

Bright, clear, cold—winds up to twenty-three. Sail in afternoon with Albert, and then to Roger's after dinner with the Ballingers* and a British doctor. Good talk until after midnight—latest we have been up in Nantucket, except in our beds reading.

Wednesday, July 8

Albert's Readex continues to fascinate me. I tried to put myself back in the days when someone at Gutenberg spread the gossip that ideas could be broadcast more quickly, widely, and cheaply by type and running off copies than by scribes reproducing with quill pens. That must have been some era—when many were frightened that too many would learn too much. Maybe the Library of Congress should get an appropriation of, say, twenty million dollars and then send to all the libraries of our republic all the indexed knowledge of the English language. Maybe Ford should undercut that enemy of adventure, the Foundation Committee con-

* *Walter Ballinger, Philadelphia surgeon, and his wife.*

cept, and vote a hundred million, which would be more than ample to put all the indexed knowledge of man in all languages into all the universities and city libraries of the planet. Maybe Albert should stay put and carry on his institution, which for all material with a market of more than, say, fifty libraries is not only better but cheaper than microfilm. Maybe the profit motive is needed for a decade or so, delaying the spread of this great new gift to man. The inducements for increase of experimentation which derive from a monopoly will prove to have values that will be lost if a government or foundation takes over.

Thursday, July 9

Many cruising sailboats come into the harbor. There are always one or two that look homemade, and the people on board look as if they were having a better time than those with a crew. Maybe not so, but I'm sure that the bigger the over-all length, the more conservative-Republican the owner is. Also those who cruise on big powerboats no doubt still hate F. D. R. and love Coolidge and Harding, forgetting that the New Deal saved the capitalist system and that all that awful legislation—SEC, Banking Act, TVA and the like—would get little support for repeal from any quarter. But the intriguing vessels are those that have no name on the transom. This I can't explain, not even on the theory that they are stolen. Surely the thief would want a name so as not to appear unusual. The increase of quantity-built powerboats of identical appearance and style must induce theft. And the only protection I have heard of is to take the ignition key, cut off the tip end, insert

this bit in the lock and then defy a burglar to match
the balance so as to turn the lock, never knowing how
much of the tip end is left in the lock. That's a cutie,
and so far no one has explained a way of beating it.

Ed Williams telephoned that he must go to the hospital and so cannot join us in Maine. Talked about the
horrors of our Senate in the Hoffa matter. Where are
the liberal voices? Few if any have protested the un-
lawyerlike operations of Kennedy, or the extra-legisla-
tive preachings of McClellan, coming from Arkansas
and silent on Little Rock, ducking the integration issues,
using Hoffa as a smoke screen to try to protect his image
of bravery.

Maggie feels better, and so to auction of a house and
possessions out our way. At the few public auctions I
have attended I have been happy that the prior owner
was not in evidence. Odd, but auctions spell, for me, a
sad compulsion. This one today was a desperate affair
—well-built home and *all* the belongings were for sale:
powder compact, leftover canned food, linens, and all
the intimate belongings that had surrounded the owner
were held up for public display. No heirs; the lady had
died and no one had known of her death for three or
four days. Why am I sentimental about death when
there are no close friends or heirs in the offing? Maybe
it's not death, but the aloneness preceding it—because
I'm one of those who would hate to live all alone. I'm
desperately sorry for the many widows we know who
live by themselves, even though they make believe they
like it. I could possibly stand waking up in the morning alone, for then I could hasten out, but to go home
to an alone apartment at night is uncomfortable even
for the few nights each summer when I go back to New
York and live alone. In the old big house I was lone-

some and afraid. Many a night I heard many men climbing up the water leader that ran into the yard. I'm
sorry for all those who have no hand to touch in the
morning while coming out of escaping slumber to so-
called reality.

Just heard former Senator Bender testify before
super-prosecutor Kennedy of the McClellan Committee.
Shocked beyond description. One would have thought
that the Senate of the United States had been desig-
nated by the Constitution of our nation to try to drive
out of office the head of the Teamsters Union. This
young lawyer is a new type of McCarthy with all the
disregard for due process, Congressional duties and fair-
ness that Joe displayed with similar approval of the
press.

Friday, July 10

Sir Andrew Cohen and Helen and kids are staying with Connie. He should, from his experience in
Uganda and on the UN Trustee Council, offer me helpful criticism on my mass-media programs.

Irritated at our birds—what right have they to be so
choosy and fussy? One, the catbird, will eat blueberries
but not cantaloupe, enough of them like Portuguese
bread but won't touch brown bread; another can't stand
rice pudding. I'm offended. Where do they get off with
finicky acceptances and rejections? I object even when
the grandchildren start with such timidities—like birds,
rejecting without ever having tasted. With birds, since
they have no sense of smell, it's still worse—rejection on
sight alone.

Saturday, July 11

Storm on way up the coast. It misses us by sixty miles to the east, but the ferry doesn't go off, hurricane signals are up, and everyone battens things down.

Met Doctor Quigley of Surfside. I asked, as is usual when rejoining a kindred mind after a winter, "What scientific tidbit in your profession occurred since we met?" He told me how Navy doctors had licked problem of the storage of blood, formerly storable for only a month without deterioration. This important invention came, as so often, from a fluke. This time a woman veterinarian in England was shipping animal semen for artificial insemination; there is often a little blood with the semen, and this unnamed and unsung woman noticed that the blood did not go sour and connected this with the glycerine solution that had been used to preserve the serum. That's all. Fortuity is the word for much of man's progress. So now man can store semen and blood for centuries. If we had discerned all this a few hundred years ago, a child of da Vinci or Jefferson might have met with an Emily Dickinson or a Willa Cather. After writing these names, I tried to conjure up better combinations. Can't do.

Last night the ferry carried the airline commuters, since planes were grounded. The dock was gay, as if a transatlantic crossing had been completed. Everyone friendly, close to the fine, high mood of men and women at times of real trouble—bank closings, snow storms and the like. Many welcomers had no one to welcome but had just come down as people do to railroad stations wherever there is only one train a day. What a friendly

species we are, and how desperately we try to hide our
genial warmth from one another.

Sunday, July 12

Maggie and I went to Anne's to gather our collection of goodies—wood, nails, brads, quarter- and
half-rounds—all of which Loomis saved just as I do.
The motive is not money or thrift; it's really more commendable: the dream of finding the tidbit, the gilhickey
just at the moment in the future when you really want
it in a hurry. Kind of patting on the back—"See, I was
smart enough to save it. It fits. Its just what I want without running down to the lumber yard or hardware
store." A kind of personal predesigned treasure hunt
that may never take place.

Maggie just reported something short of a miracle.
She found demanding need for a lamp-switch button,
and in the secret trove she stores in her desk she found
the exact black button, which she had hoarded for probably twenty years or more. It's related to the collection
of clothes buttons tucked into a drawer of our home-
made portable sewing box.

Monday, July 13

Fog drives me into the shop or to the printed
word. Sun seduces man into activities of wider ranges
and greater distances. The operating mind is less the
accent in the outdoors.

No planes; many took ferry. Being a loafer, I just
stayed.

My owl antigull experiment on the pier has failed. On boats it's effective. A little motion of the owl may do the trick, as Rog suggests. So I'll set my owl on a wooden platform under which I'll place a gentle heavy spring. This spring and platform must be strong enough to survive strong gale winds and still flexible enough to move in gentle winds. So I seek moderation once more as in all else that deals with animate parts of life. But so also with governments. Our 1776 Revolution survived because of Jefferson's concepts of kindly moderation, while the French Revolution failed because a guillotine was used instead of a goose quill pen. For duration, an idea introduced to the mind is better than a knife blade held to the jugular. So I play for a gull's "mind" or "instinct," a word used for something man has not yet deciphered. I'm trying a very gentle motion, for although I have had no converse with an owl I suspect it is a sedentary, quiet-moving beast except on rare occasions when it acts with unexpected violent, precise speed —a kind of action similar to the short right punch of Johannson when he really knocked down the champ Patterson. The animal—man or owl—is superior if it possesses what to others looks like an acquired knack— but with owls it may be the result of experience inherited over thousands of years. If I have licked this problem of motion, my real question will be answered when the next crop of young gulls fly to us from Muskeget Island, youngsters that had never seen or, I was going to say, "read about" an owl. Do they carry the fear from ancestors they have never known?

Tuesday, July 14

A picture sent by Monsignor Salcedo from Colombia of a classroom full of wonderful, elderly faces intoxicated by the mystery of the alphabet, made me think of the different ways in which the old gnarled fingers grasped the pencils, and wonder if instruction was given in holding this most important tool of man. And as I write I recall the increased pleasure I had when I first used a Parker 51 pen, and then the thin Remington ballpoint that Marie gave me, and the neatness requirement fulfilled when I used a Hammond script-type typewriter at college. The Double-Crostics are more fun in the *Times* than in the *Saturday Review* because no pencil I have used works with ease on the coated magazine-cover paper. There is a sensual pleasure in writing or typing, a tactile pleasure from having ideas flow from brain down the arm to the fingertips and from there reflected and appraised by the eye, returning once more to the brain. As pleasant a circuit as is known to man.

Roger off to Washington on a rush mission. He will meet us in Portland tomorrow noon. These hectic moves do not delight Maggie; she seldom enjoys the unexpected. Two different types of people can be discerned —those who enjoy the unexpected and those who need time to make new shifts in plans.

Wednesday, July 15

The Goldsteins came in last night, and Steffie went home the necessary few steps, alongside the shop. She never dressed so quickly, and so full of anticipation. What a marvelous thing love is! Here Steffie goes to a world so very different, a world where she can't communicate in the least unless Irv and Joan happen to be looking at Steffie's lips in the light. How near to impossible it is to build bunkers to block the flow of affection, once it is established!

No planes, so we took the ferry and at Woods Hole picked up a car and drove to South Freeport, Maine, with one stop where Maggie consumed a revolting peach ice-cream soda. I had only an egg sandwich while Jean tried out rum-peach or some new combination.

Arrived about sundown. Roger, coming from Washington, had been aboard and stocked up the vessel, so with hamburgers and blueberries inside of us we stowed and looked over *Hoi Ying*. It's always a surprise to note the personality of sailboats—no two really alike even if the hulls belong to one class and come from the same designer's boards. Like twins—I dare say even identical twins, who are identical only to the unsearching eyes of strangers.

It will take Maggie a day or so to get settled in—used to bed, locker, storage and stove. We have had only coal and bottled gas, now we try alcohol priming and kero cooking. *Hoi* feels sedate and secure. Shut-eye by eleven.

Thursday, July 16

Others up before six and then they woke me. Outside for a dip—good and warm water. Eggs, bacon, orange juice, hot buns and coffee.

Fog, but we chugged out. It got thicker; we turned around to find a nook to await the turn of the windy clouds. Cleared a bit and we, and probably no other sailing fools, went east to Seguin, the demon of the coast, which except for once has always been kind to us. For elevenses I fixed onion soup. Ashore at Boothbay for shopping, ice cream sodas, etc. Then on to Christmas Cove—same snug nook.

Friday, July 17

Fog when I first looked out at about five thirty, so all back to sleep until eight. With my burgee aloft I feel a little as if the boat were mine own. For my seventy-fifth birthday I must buy my dream boat—a forty-foot yawl, designed by Olin Stevens but laid out below by Phil Rhodes, who senses better than Olin the comforts of leisure cruising folk like us. My relation to my boat is far more than that of a user—it's a chance for constant gadgeteering and improving. So on this boat I look around and in my mind have rebuilt everything, and the first thing I do is to replace kerosene by a combination bottle gas-coal stove, take out the wheel for a tiller, and so on and so on, for my dreams do not get easily blocked.

On through Maine Maggie and I remember all the

nun and can buoys with far more accuracy than we do the same water marks along Nantucket Sound. It may be that this acuteness of recall is due to the greater pleasure we have cruising up here, or maybe because here rocks lurk under the water—rocks that demand more respect than the kindly sand of our home shore. I think we could make all harbors from Boothbay to Northeast without charts, and few friends do more sweetening up the recalls of memory than do the lighthouses, gull-stained fishery roof sheds, new modern houses—even rock slabs.

In late afternoon we weighed anchor and started looking for a port, depending on how visibility showed up outside the bay. Hazy but no mist so through Thread of Life—as intriguing as the name of this line of rocks and underwater ridges—and then past imposing Pemaquid and its stately lighthouse up to New Harbor. Narrow entrance, full of fishing boats—one of the few harbors west of Corea that yachtsmen seem to miss. Directed to a mooring by a friendly gent in a rowboat.

Loafy day, several swims. Not a thought of courts or laws or what might help the human race. This is the Maine Coast—the villages have the expected New England pride in white-painted trim and even white houses, but on the shore, increasingly to the east, there is no orthodoxy; all colors, good reds to awful browns, capped in rainbow fashion at towns like Jonesport on the Moosabec Reach. And it may be that the so-called orthodox are more unorthodox than the so-called odd ones— look at the orthodoxy among the Beatniks in dress and speech; ditto for the followers of Communism, or of Joe McCarthy.

Sunday, July 19

Nearly forty miles before two thirty yesterday, to Pulpit Harbor. But today peasoup fog, drizzle—not nice weather. Visited Tom and Ellie.* They have turned life into its most gracious channels—their home, garden, pictures, fireplaces all point to the best of the moderate in our culture. I never am quite sure whether I should take up the casual invitations of important citizens like Tom. Maggie, my best booster, always thinks they might like to see us. And what nonimpetuous, sober good citizens these Lamonts are.

Back to boat. Fussing around with an ample amount of suppressed fuming about the weather. But we each have memories, so that we hold our faith that the sun may come out some day. As Barrie wrote, memory is for the purpose of having roses in December. Now, of course, for those who have money, there are roses, strawberries and all kinds of foods and flowers any month of the year.

Monday, July 20

From Pulpit to Andy and Katharine White's† cove with a variety of perfect weather. Memories ranging this coast confound me. I don't remember a single grammar-school teacher by name or looks; I can't, as others do, recall a first bicycle or the furniture in the bedrooms of my youth; but here I spot a sloop and Mag-

---

* *Mr. and Mrs. Thomas Lamont.*
† *E. B. White of* New Yorker, *and his wife.*

gie and I remember where it has its anchorage in Somes
Sound, or the precise location of a pier or clump of trees
or the shape or shade of a rock. Inexplicable, except, as
Maggie suggested, the outcropping of a kind of snobbish-
ness—we are so proud that we are of the select, the elite
who cruise the Maine coast. Maybe that's the answer,
since this is my only area where I have complete recall
as in a kind of Jane Austen or more recent *New Yorker*
style of writing. Do all people, all families have such
areas of joint and mutual reliving? Maybe this is a compliment to any intimate relationship.

Today is Herb's birthday—his seventieth. I sent the
kid and his child bride a telegram of good will and
wishes. Let's see: since 1915 we have been partners, and
for maybe twenty years or more he, Laurie, Eddie and
I never had a word in writing about our division of
duties, income or death contingencies. The important
meetings of mind never need recording in writing. Except possibly to refresh memories, honorable people
should never use pen and ink. But as relations spread
widely—that is, when we took in younger partners—
agreements were, as lawyers say, "reduced" to writing;
but never because we four needed more than our original statement, "Let's try a partnership for the practice
of the law." I've always been fearful of termination dates
for client contracts. For labor management it means
little more than a tag on a calendar reading, "Let's start
trouble." Only once could I persuade management and
labor leaders to have a contract without termination—
that is, one to last as long as good faith endured.

Tuesday, July 21

With a bright sun we dropped the hook at a northern cove on Great Gott Island, built a fire between some water-polished rocks, cooked our chops, swam, ate and then back to the boat to drop anchor in Maggie's favorite harbor, Northeast. Here we know the town with some intimacy (we exchange Christmas cards with the owner of the Pine Tree grocery store), and we looked to see if there were any changes other than improvements on the new dock.

Many of these harbors can be entered by using the Champlain charts, which survive centuries after being drawn. The art of charting a shore line so that others can enjoy it is beyond my imagination. To get comparative dimensions from compass, pelorus if he had one, astralabe and a pair of eyes is something beyond the discipline of handling a sailboat. Northeast is a concealed entrance coming up the Western Way and Maggie and I love it, as we do all the small gunk holes and those harbors that do not shout an invitation. The privacy of the nearly landlocked has a value of its own, and the gunk hole that holds only a boat or two, like Lairey's or behind Orono off Swan's, or Leadbetter Reach, are near maritime divinity for dropping an anchor, particularly after a wet, hard passage. It's the difference between Ben Sonnenberg's mansion on Gramercy Park and our hidden garden in Monomoy.

Wednesday, July 22

A topsy-turvy day. After a full moon the sun-up was good and clean, so off we went through the great thousand-foot narrow water chasm called Somes Sound. Maggie and Jean departed, hoping to make Nantucket by air or somehow. At Somes chatted with Hastings, the manager of the Inn, who deplored that he used to get fifty dollars for the hay on the hotel meadow but now must pay a hundred dollars to have it taken away.

Rog and I sailed in a peasoup fog to Henry Hinckley's shipyard. H. H. was away delivering a boat, so I missed my annual chat with him. I tried to charter one of his thirty-six-foot yawls this summer but no luck, so put in an order for one for next year—in fact, said I'd commit myself to charter for three years.

Back to Northeast going from buoy to buoy by compass, seeing less than two hundred feet in any direction.

Paula and Alan arrived by car from Bangor, having been unable to use Bar Harbor airfield. Supper in town, then to boat and turned in, early for them. Stars out— here's hoping for a good sail to Ile a Haut, one of our favorite nooks, in which we have lain often without seeing another boat except the lobster men in the early morning. From our anchorage we see both Mt. Desert and the Camden Hills. On a clear day, what better?

Friday, July 24

Mixed weather yesterday, and we fooled around Bass Harbor. Thick fog did not keep our crew in harbor today. Probably we went out to test and dare ourselves, for we had neither a log that was reliable nor a speedometer that worked—and of course not a fathometer, the latest inexpensive navigation guide.

Too thick to start, so a little shopping and then, as so often in cruising, we had a bit of serendipity. At the end of a North Haven pier we saw Franklin Roosevelt and Sue, in a beautiful forty-foot Concordia yawl. After dinner Frank chatted in our ship about foreign affairs, politics and what-not. He is one of my favorites and has been ever since he was at law school. I regret he has temporarily left the law, and urged him to return. If he weren't called F. D. R., he would have gone many places where the handicap of his titular inheritance caused the public to set unreasonable comparative standards on his behavior. Must see more of him next year.

I recall that years ago I promised his Pop to arrange to have Canada retroactively cede Campobello to the United States so that young Frank, if elected governor, would not be disqualified for the presidency because of the constitutional insistence on birth in the United States. It looks as if I'll not be called on to carry out this pledge.

To bed late, but will get up early to get Roger to Camden, as he skips ship for Nantucket tomorrow. What a chance to renew and refertilize family relations cruising provides. No other leisure occupation gives such cement to a family. Unequal skills disturb this subtle factor in golf or tennis or even mountain climbing. But on a boat all take part, share and participate, and everyone can do all bits of craftsmanship except only for heavy anchor hauling, at which the very young and most women think they are disqualified. And as in all of life, what people think is the only reality.

Saturday, July 25

Let Roger off at friendly Camden gas float, filled up on gas, water, ice and a few provisions, did some telephoning to Nantucket and New York.

Then off for northern tip of Islesboro in a strong northwest wind that held so stout and gusty through the mountains that we made five knots on mainsail alone. If I were a mountain of the Camden hills, I could look down with nasty pleasure and see my power of deflection make the mortals at tillers and wheels every now and again appreciate their own insignificance. At Buck Harbor got a mooring through my dock friend, Mr. Grey. Up to town, and on the way back to Yacht Club the taxi lady, suggesting a charge of fifty cents asked, "Would that be all right?" Big City greeds and fears have not reached this neck of America, and maybe never will.

Lay next to *Desperate Lark*—a forty-eight-foot yawl —a vessel of several distinctions: built by Herreshoff in 1903, first equipped with power in 1957, and presently inhabited by one man of at least seventy-five, who handled the sails when out she drifted at eight thirty P.M. Two tots in life preservers called, "Hello" to us through a megaphone—difficult to get to infant lips because of the bulky life preservers all children who can't swim wear when sailing.

It reminded me that once I let Zack Chaffee and two of his old cronies take my boat from Nantucket to Maine, and Zack, who had ranged the Maine coast from his home in Sorrento for years in an engineless craft, took with him as food little more than dried herring and Indian pudding. A great guy—and, of course, therefore an odd guy. The most important scribbler on freedom and the law, and still he never had the courage to teach a course on censorship or the First Amendment. But he sailed this rocky coast without an engine.

Sunday, July 26

Another day of friendly warmth and hot sun and strong, favoring winds—except "down" the Reach. I'm never sure what is up and what is down save only Down East, a confusing phrase if one looks at maps where east is up. But all you have to do is to recall that the prevailing winds were and still are from the southwest, so from Nantucket to Maine was downwind. We have trouble finding a picnic shore on the lee side of some island with water shallow enough to drop the hook. Most of the shores are bold, running fifty to one hundred or even one-hundred-fifty feet, and few small-boat sailors carry enough line or chain, even though the back be willing and able to pull in from such a depth. We finally anchored in Herriman Bay opposite Andy and Katharine's, went ashore, built our fire, cooked steak and corn, and thus fully stowed went back to *Hoi Ying* and sailed in a stout southerly to Blue Hill through the tricky entrance, only to have trouble feeling sure that we were firm for the night. Deserted the Danforth for the plow anchor, which has heavy chain.

This Blue Hill harbor gives me many fond recalls, although the first time we entered we came here in a hailstorm that lasted all night, with General Patton's wife's big boat *When and If* dragging anchor, rubbing our sides so that Roger boarded her and yelled, "Ma'am, you're adrift." Each year we chatted with Ralph and Kay,* with Ralph antagonistic to boats and waves and the feel of a tiller. And we relish the decorum and modesty of the Yacht Club—as good an example of inconspicuous wealth as I know along the coast: one room, no bar, a Coke machine, a telephone—but dozens of young people developing a sense of proportion about the power of the sea, the need of cooperation with humility, with waves and tides and currents and wind.

Saw *Dovekie* and spoke to the skipper, recalling that we had met him in some harbor twenty years ago, when he had just bought this interesting double-ender. I recalled that he was a professor at some Maine college—he said Bowdoin. But why I should have tucked this tidbit into a cerebral crevice, I'll never know. The burying away is, I suppose, limitless and unavoidable, but the selectivity, logistics of recall, this is one of the mysteries, dramatized for me most acutely in moods of relaxed leisure. Not unrelated, I suppose, to the fact that man's mind, if it leaps at all, makes its greatest vaulting leaps while at peace, at rest and making no effort.

Quite thrilled that ten-year-old Michael Wing, Nick's cousin, comes for a week with Nick. I wish I had cruised when I was seven, as Nick now is doing, and I'll enjoy watching him gather experience of the ways of a little boat on a big sea.

* *Mr. and Mrs. Ralph Perkins.*

Monday, July 27

Adversity came down on *Hoi Ying:* the voltmeter failed to register plus or minus. Being afraid of engines, as man fears his unknown, I sent for Mr. Cousins at Weber Cove Ship Yard. Soon it was apparent that a thing called a generator was *kaput.* So called Col. Powell in Freeport, scoured neighborhood, loafed around my favorite yacht club, had delightful talk with Mrs. Rausch and later with Howard Fuller of *Gesture,* inspected *Bally Hoo* (which in livability does not compare to *New Horizon*), had a couple of swims, enjoyed good mocha at Miss Heywood's art gallery-tearoom (relative of Phil Heywood of Monomoy Road), finally got a generator installed before sundown. If any cruising man has to be stuck in a harbor, all I wish him is a clear, buoyant day with a view of Blue Hill and Mt. Desert.

The bill for the job was, I guessed, a little on the high side. But as I thought about it, I recalled overhearing at the Yacht Club a little haggling for a few dollars allegedly overcharged by someone. Surely the man was very wealthy—for the type of scrutiny of bills by the very rich, particularly the inherited wealthy, has a distinct refrain. The very rich not only are in doubt whether their "friends" like them or their money, but they also want to make sure that they are not taken for a ride as suckers. So they total up the bills at Voisin's or "21" before signing, just to impress the captains that they are not suckers. The twenty-dollar item in dispute has no reality. To the man with a million, his net worth is only "real" when once a year his accountant tells him he is worth nine million and two thousand or nine million and seven thousand dollars. He can't swim in more than one pool at the same time, or drink two martinis at the same time. Those of new fortuitous fortunes have an opposite oddity. They overpay, they overtip. The mink on their wives' bathing suits is a pathetic hope that their friends will think they are desirable husbands (but I doubt that they make love to their wives while these are decked in mink). The hoboes and those with the assurance of the ability to earn a living have similar money attitudes—but I like their special patterns best of all. Heywood Broun, who never balanced a check book, was a phenomenon in a world of checks and balances. Roger Baldwin, who all his life kept track of every two-cent stamp he bought, is a combination of arch capitalist and dreaming anarchist.

So in the end I conclude all folk have their oddities, but the cruising sailing men make the most sense because they have made the decision: a boat costs much, but what it costs is worth more than anything the equivalent money can buy.

Left the wheel to clean out icebox and find some stoppage in the outlet drain. That's fun because I do not *have* to do it for a living.

The care of one's own is an innate passion of man. It may be the essence of tradition and the continuity of a culture. This goes beyond offspring (note the presently admitted failure of attempted interruption of this passion in Russia, and until recently in the Kibbutzim of Israel where children were handled mainly by people other than their own parents). It concerns my fence at Monomoy and even to a greater degree a boat. To clean the icebox of a rented boat is a duty, an obligation, but to fix up my old *Episode* was an act of devotion no matter how disagreeable or uncomfortable the job might have been. Who in hell enjoys repairing his neighbor's fence or cutting even his best friend's grass! I must soon own me another boat!

Wednesday, July 29

Changed crews, usually a damn nuisance. This time Alan and Paula left aboard the plane that carried the Bessies and Mike Wing, who brought aboard the damnedest landlubber equipment imaginable—a medicine chest full of drugs and the largest book ever put aboard a 37-foot vessel: the complete, unexpurgated writings of Conan Doyle. But the kids are fine, and Nickie with his life belt is going to get an education as good as a year at school.

Everyone stowed, we tucked ourselves into bed. Since none used sheets, I could not brag too much about my second great scientific advance of the trip: I have licked the washing and drying machines; I can start them, put in soap, take garments out—gee!

Lizzie, my outboard motor, seems to like me better than any engine I have ever tried to dominate or cooperate with. In fact, she is responsive to my fingers at six A.M., whereas most engines I have met don't like to be disturbed before seven or seven thirty. So, I am a part of the modern scientific age.

Friday, July 31

Just read an item from my other world. Someone proposes that no subsidy to a magazine or a newspaper should exceed five million dollars. When I was on the Post Office Advisory Committee (I squeaked through a confirmation in the Senate by a stroke of luck—overcoming the painstaking campaign run against me by the magazine lobby), I urged a shift in policy. Why subsidize a magazine of a million or more circulation? Why not subsidize heavily the new and the small, with subsidies tapering off as circulation goes up?

Fog for two days now. Lying at anchor in the fog, people become more interesting than unseen nature. So I discover that I can shop for adults, any adult; but young boys of middle-class-income homes—they are hell on food with their violent dislikes, their timidities about trying new foods and, above all, their devotion to a special breakfast food and rejection of all others.

Nick, the only other prebreakfast Maine-water swimmer aboard, takes another dip before dinner. And all pray for a nonfog day, but speak nothing about our disappointment with the weather—a condescension to the art of gentlemanly cooperative living. One grumble is too likely to start an avalanche.

A seeming break came at noon, so off we scooted, only to find that we needed our best ears and a favoring wind to pick up bells and gongs. The deaf are often better sailors, compensating as Joan and Irving do for not hearing bells and gongs, just as the totally deaf are the best of all auto drivers. Some insurance company could make a sound and valid gesture by providing preferred rates for deaf drivers, those who do not rely on their own horns or the horns of others.

At Bass Head Light we congratulated each other when we saw the beautiful lighthouse and then, hugging the shore, we went into Bass Harbor, dropping an anchor among the boats, all of lobster men except for Alan Klotz's beautiful Concordia. I chugged over with Nickie to pay a visit, and we were invited aboard. Alan is a good sailorman and even looks it.

Mike and I were about to shift our anchor, a humbling chore because it spells less than perfection the first try, when the sun came out and off we breezed to a little nook between Orono and Garden Islands, on the northern tip of Swans. Maggie and I have lain there often, picnicking on either island. On the worst night we ever spent at sea, the anchor dragged, a gale force wind came up and we shifted in the dark to another harbor and stayed up all night watching to see if our anchor would hold. So here, with predictions of great winds, we dropped both anchors, fought mosquitoes, cooked a thick steak, and had a fitful night.

AUGUST

Sunday, August 2

Clear, cold wind from the North, so Mike and I break our backs on the anchors and off we go—cold, and cold, and cold! At Stonington we went to the gas dock, took on water but were told the folk were Christian and did not sell gas on Sunday. I suspect Stonington is jealous of its neighbor, North Haven, which has captured the cruising business, and as jealousy often spells perversity, they make believe they disfavor cruising boats, can't say it frankly and so use religion—so badly misused so often through history as the rationale for being anti-Samaritan.

One good day proves, as Connie observed, that fog is like pain. Memory is impotent to recall pain with any precision. Man has a built-in forgettery, without which he could scarcely survive. A revival of the feeling of pain, or of frustration in a stretch of fog would be beyond the power of man to withstand.

After Nickie, age seven, held the wheel for an hour (lucky Nick—I never touched a wheel or a tiller until I was thirty-five), we made for Tenants Harbor. This is one of those harbors with outstretched arms, saying,

"Come in, I invite you; I have good holding ground and plenty of water at low tide, and I'm exposed only to easterly winds." I enjoy Tenants but, as with people, I prefer the more secretive, more secluded, more reserved, even in harbors. For if the quiet, who have no great confidence in their acceptability, are really explored, they blossom, open up and are appreciative and appreciable.

Monday, August 3

A good run from Tenants to Boothbay, and I listen to the heated argument between a ten- and a seven-year-old boy: does infinity apply to anything but space and time? So what about heat and cold—in galaxies other than our own? Words like "infinity" I can't use. They are clichés of the upper reaches of man. In fact, I have never understood simpler bits of the vernacular such as "courage" or "sacrifice." To me they are elections: choices of a kind the actor makes with his eyes and heart open, but which, no matter how soberly he chose, society in effect says it would not have made. Being a coward all my life and never having "made" a sacrifice, I'm likely to be called a brave sailor, when all it may mean is that I have too little imagination to foresee dangers obvious to the more sagacious.

I have been on sand bars, and rocks, I have lost my way, I have been in doubt as to what steps to take to get into a port (and this goes for all of life as well as sailing), and so I use another word without real content: "luck" —meaning that in the end life has a way of turning its kindly side to me, without credit or explanation.

Years ago Laurie came to Nantucket in a twenty-five-foot undistinguished powerboat, little more than a putt-

putt. He was a scientific inventor of gadgets. As he was leaving, he asked if he could go home via Muskeget Channel. I said, "Show me your chart," and he brought out a road map. I showed my amazement, and he said, "But all the blue is water, isn't it?" I was reminded of this episode because two outboarders asked us, "Is this the way to Boothbay?" I was inclined to say, "You can't get there from here," but instead gave directions as if I were on Park Avenue.

Wednesday, August 5

At South Freeport, tidied up *Hoi Ying,* had a fine end-all party with Gil and Bobby, then today took the crew to shore, waved to our three-week, red-hull acquaintance, and planed to New York. Then to one of my other worlds—the office, the telephone, the life of communication not face to face but by the intermediaries of stenographer, typewriter, postman and all the intervenors of organized life.

I'm disturbed about the confusion Nixon's trip will bring to the American people. It will not be easy to carry on with good will to the Russian people and outward pleasant amenities to the Russian dictators, and at the same time hold up our guard. Soon this trip may make us soft to the cry, "Why does the United States have to have bases in Europe, six thousand miles from Chicago? Why do you want troops in Berlin, so far from New York?" We are a people so eager for peace that we may give away our greatest advantage—the awareness of the danger of Communist dictatorship. It's not easy to drink wine and jest with an ambitious enemy. Our great protection lies in the fact that Mr. Khrushchev will believe, not without some validity, that he can elect or at least defeat a candidate for president in our nation. By election time things may be tough and strained between Russia and the U.S., and Mr. K. could then put the kiss of death on a candidate by seeming to favor him; and certainly before election the image of Nixon, the pacifist toward Russia, will become cloudy, as inconsistent with the violence of his Hiss record.

To the office, nothing to say or write or feel. Just a mountain-high mass (or mess) of letters. I'll adjust, but at the moment no diary entry would make sense.

Thursday, August 6

How can there be two such different worlds? There is a vast difference between intimacy and selected friends, partners or associates. In close quarters, in a small town, there is no constant chance for selection. Here in New York, people work, cast warm smiles and friendly words, but—I don't understand it. As Maggie said, I should have come to Nantucket for a few days, a kind of transition period.

Off to Nantucket on late plane, thanks to Miss Waite of commuter service of Northeast Airlines. To Maggie, our lawn, our view. It's a long absence, and now, as always when separated, a new honeymoon—each one with a quality different from the last—not better or worse, just not the same.

Friday, August 7

The entire stream has changed, not only the tides and currents. What I see, think and feel is little goodies. Why does the need for eyeglasses practically vanish? Why does man's vision improve with old age while his hearing so often starts to fail? Why didn't I discover the outboard earlier in life so that Maggie could not say, "You and the Russians invented the outboard, I assume." What a job she did painting the front door—but, as with all refurbishing, there is the corruption of comparison, so we will now have to paint the screen door. In a month all the trees in the garden have grown as never before—the crab apple has branches twenty feet long, the self-planted maple will, of course, outdistance the bought and transplanted other trees, and will show off its pride by a superlative shape and contour. A big loon or a Canadian goose is on the beach—twice as tall as any gull, which eyes it with fear or envy.

Fuddled around all day, toted firewood, took out my telescope to look at the many boats across the harbor, fixed up the shop, took out some broken windowpanes, visited the Dusenberys on their Nighthawk moored off our pier, swapping with him ideas for new boat gadgets. On a boat it's easy for me to travel sitting still—I can go further in less time than by any jet ever to be made.

Picked up correspondence with Walter Yust of Encyclopaedia Britannica—he requests me to do a revision of the Sacco-Vanzetti piece. Can't get near to actually doing it, even though it's for fun, as shown by the Britannica pay scale—five dollars a printed page for revision or two and a half cents a word for new material. Incidentally, years ago when I was approached to do the sections on censorship or some kindred subjects and queried the justice of a twenty-five-dollar fee, W. Y. wrote, "That's what G. B. Shaw, and Kaiser Wilhelm get—no discrimination."

So the days fly by, with island produce for eats: corn and steamed clams and blueberries. Barometer comes alive—I've looked at it a dozen times, but the barograph line is steady, so no hope of change to a stretch of clean summer. But Maggie is always Maggie. Not everything needs variations to become livable.

Sunday, August 9

Joe directs me to a dead tern on the beach near a big piece of driftwood. I'll put it up on the pier—it's a tiny animal and mingles in friendly fashion with gulls, but hanging dead it may be a taboo for our pier pests. At least it is an event for speculation and observation. What better?

The moon and sun have really put their minds to their tidal jobs today. Very low and very high water when these two powers really have a summit operation and pull together—that is, pull the water, of course, with the full cooperation of our planet's speedy twirling. But the barograph card still shows a straight steady line, damn it. Some day I want one instrument to record wind speed, direction of wind, temperature, humidity, status of moon and a few other factors. I'm confident that by just looking at such a chart correlations may become apparent—sufficient to predict weather in advance, based on prior cause-and-effect patterns.

While lolling in bed before our prebreakfast dip, we

got into making a list of peculiarly Southern U.S. expressions—unique to that formerly slow-paced gentle living: "kissin' cousins," "barefoot time," "kin see and cain't see." These phrases, each with a meaning of pleasant precision, couldn't be created in stone-fenced Connecticut.

Monday, August 10

Joan remarked, "How time did fly today." I agree. We laid foundation and a floor, and measured and cut the uprights for a shed running off the northern end of her house. Lots of measuring and thinking, and then sawing and nailing. Tomorrow will finish all but the door.

The other great event was that Maggie and I, in the fashion of Brushwood boy and girl, recall concomitant interlaced dreams and not a result of predesign. We had not made up our minds before going to sleep that we would have a unison dream, so it was doubly impressive and enjoyable. I doubt if any two people—and certainly not Maggie and I—could plan a frightening dream, one of those chasing-and-being-chased ones. Since I seldom have dreamed in color as Maggie does at times, and as the deaf so often do, we can't try the trick of seeing if we perchance would have coinciding colors.

Tuesday, August 11

All houses in the compound run so smoothly because, from Margaret, the women of the families have learned by social osmosis that maids and cooks and helpers are essential parts of a home. Rose at Connie's and Allaner at Joan's are not only considerate and affectionate but are noble in their looks and gracious in their movements. Jo Houlihan, our fixture, runs the house as she has for about thirty years. Winnie, new this summer, is a quiet delight.

These four are surely more significant in our lives than are any relatives outside of the immediate circle. And for reasons easily explained by all who know her, Maggie always has a waiting list of house helpers who will come to us in New York or Nantucket. I'm always surprised when I hear housewives crying that they can't get adequate help. I'm sure it's not the fault of the help or the market place but of the bosses. From the days of Delia and Kitty and Jo when we first set up house-shop, we have had affection and concern for women who help us, and I'm sure they also love us dearly in return.

There's a myth about domestic work. Never did more than two per cent of all the families in our nation have living-in help, and now a social revolution has quietly taken place. The word "menial" is lost, and in fact vacations of many people depend on thousands of college boys and girls who wait on tables, make beds and mix salads or what you will. Many are from upper income houses; they all seem to enjoy the work, get a rich experience and earn much cash toward an education. An entire shift in social attitudes.

Nick picked me up just before eight, in a thick fog, and down we traipsed for a dip. I guess he is committed to the early cold-water-rubdown way of life. Some like it, some don't—but the "don'ts" give the wrong excuses and the "dos" puff up their reasons: all as usual.

To the Fête on upper Main Street and on the off-streets. All done with great appreciation of the costumes, "cent" schools, baby carriages, etc. of three hundred years ago. We have no permanent Beef Eaters—no continuous reminders of the past—so it is rare and appreciated when a community makes the effort to take a passing glance at its past. Just as youth grows up wiser when it has the adult male and female images in close view, so a collective group of people—a town—is enriched if it has its predecessor culture in view, enough to admire, appraise and respect but not enough to feel unthinkingly bound to it. There can be societal apron strings—just like maternal ones—but our culture is in no danger of doing anything with its past but distorting it to conform to current conveniences and needs.

Wednesday, August 12

In our garden an inch-long baby frog jumps out of the sun umbrella into the hedge, leaping thirty times its height; a partridge eats seeds in peace with a scrappy sparrow who fights with a peaceful robin; and our catbird has given us up in these rainy days when we did not eat in the garden. Jo reports that the catbird has found nests of ants—as good as our blueberries or bread, and no fads for different diets, I suppose.

This summer I've experienced few frustrations. One took place in Blue Hill harbor when I thought the cruise would end if no generator could be found to fit the British engine; it worked out with surprising ease. The other is today when I'm having a devil of a time squaring and leveling the concrete blocks I'm using as roots for the shed at Joan's house. This took not only lots of strength to shift the blocks but constant "in-and-out" operations until my old level allowed the bubble to find its proper resting place.

I get peeved when most of the women around the place tell me to "take it easy." This is one of the killers among slogans and shibboleths. So I worked with saw and hammer for about six hours, came in for iced coffee, listened to some chatter and then went for grass cutter. So I should take it easy—why? Do folk think they appreciate the limit of my muscles better than I do? Desire and zeal reduce the strain on muscles. Are my would-be mentors expressing their own regrets? If so they might better express themselves, "I wish I could keep going ten hours a day as you do." To which I add sotto voce: "All about nothing of value, just physical double-crostics, just eating up some fat that I just enjoyed eating at lunch." I quit only with the sun and maybe I'm slowing down. Some years ago, I put light in the shop for night addiction. Any hobby knows no time and has no limits in energy. The trick of a society, and it was ours a century ago, was that nearly every worker was plying his hobby. The best compulsions must come from inside rather than outside and/or above.

To Bob and Mary Parker's for dinner with the Fays. Good food, elegance, good badinage. The Parkers make a good marriage, I'm sure—but one of those partnerships that builds and thrives on differences rather than similarities, comparable to quarter-tone accords in modern art or modern music. He is the only man of decency

I have met who, when asked his occupation, says, "I'm
a speculator." He is, but does not talk or look it—which
may be effects of Groton.

Thursday, August 13

A white dory sailboat and dinghy were up on
Joan's beach this morning. Someone was in trouble last
night. So Nick and Maggie and I, while walking for our
early swim, let our minds do a fast crawl stroke—we
each selected the kind of big boat we daydream of having washed up. We agreed it should be a big cabin
cruiser or a fishing boat, to be set up on even keel, used
for guests and for all us kids who in such a setting
would travel the seven seas while holding an impotent
wheel (impotent for everything except the most significant—our vagrant minds).

Off to Martha's Vineyard where the uncourageous
stop off. It's a beautiful island, but without the feel of
an island. Too big in all directions and no neat harbor
for small day sailing. It has high trees, which many
friends cannot vacation without—the rolling moors are
not enough for some. To the Kaplans, and the Pilpels
who were visiting them. Ben is a distinguished teacher
of the law. Somehow I imagine that, although to be a
teacher of history or geography is a great end in itself,
a teacher of law should carry an additional joy—ref-
ormation of the process and not just increase of the
vision of the neophytes.

Just received a copy of the symposium that Alan and
I instigated at Pittsburgh Law School. As planned, the
needlers were chosen because of potential disagreement.
The most telling contribution came from a law student,

Jack Olender. He and a Professor Silverstein conducted a survey among some Pittsburgh Law students, showing that, although there is a slight variation between first- or third-year students, the responders agreed in feeling that a Communist is entitled to counsel, but, by an overwhelming tally, they felt that an overwhelming majority of the general public would suspect such lawyer of being a Communist sympathizer. Ditto if he represents a tax defrauder? homosexual? nudist?

What if the president of the Bar Association of New York City had added his name as counsel to the defense of an alleged murderer, as requested—so the gossip goes—by the chief judge of our Court of Appeals? Why won't the bigshots participate for clients unpopular within their own social circle? Can it be money? Or loss of clients? I doubt it. Rather, might it not be fear of being kidded at their social clubs? I'd like to do a questionnaire to the wives of the hundred so-called leaders of the bar—the titular heads. I'll bet a good demurrer that the wives have fewer social fears than the leaders; but would they have the nerve to answer the questionnaires without telling their husbands?

Vineyard still is like Sconset—cocktail parties and chitchat and gossip, as a kind of side circus for worthy mental types of men and women. I did snag a few minutes to pick Ben's brain—one of the best I have sidled up to in my life.

Events pour in. Loaned $10 a while ago to an unknown youth, caught short at airport; after waiting in vain for reimbursement, wrote him, got a neat letter and money—and I'll never know if he really lost my address or was still broke. Sarah Fay explains how she uses strands of her gray hair to patch Sidney's clothing where there are pipe burns. Dream last night proved for me the separate personality of my unconscious. I was swimming off *Hoi Ying*, ladder not down, no one on the vessel, stumped as to getting back on board; thought of Genoa halliard on deck, grabbed it, made a loop for my foot, put other end in jam cleat, got safely aboard. Woke up —my conscious knew I had solved the dilemma and my steps were rational, workable and sound. Back to sleep and my unconscious persisted in putting me in the same predicament. I argued that what I had done before was the answer; but good old subconscious, with a will of its own and not easily beaten, made me go through the entire episode, from the water back on to the boat.

Friday, August 14

This morning swam, sailed, cut grass, shingled shed. Didn't want to eat lunch—would rather work— but gave in to social pressure, since most people are slaves to regular eating hours (zoolike) even when riding a hobby that satisfies the stomach nerves, that is, any *real* hobby—often a book.

Marie and Austen arrive from Vineyard on the ferry. Too much time has intervened—don't know where to start. Not like visits with Dr. Felix Adler years ago, when he or I on a next meeting took up the conversation at the precise point where I had been interrupted by folk who think vigorous people need sleep.

Saturday, August 15

For dinner, Howard and Dorothy,* who are in town for Dorothy's Edna Millay performance. They are more than good citizens—they live much of their philosophies. Also Representative Mooney and his photographer and photogenic bride. It's good for Austen to meet Bob, who is more typical of our elected officials than are the top-echelon creatures whom Austen would be likely to get to know as a British M. P. Also Mort Goldberg, who is vacationing in town and will intrigue Austen on the flow of thought over the ditch with respect to copyright laws.

Gracious, delectable meal, and not too much food, as so often at buffets in our circle. Winnie's too-rich desserts did destroy many guests. They had to make stomach choices—always disturbing—so many took some of each.

Tidbits. Saw mother and son play pelota at Surfside. Read magnificent, sober high-court opinion of Norway on Henry Miller's *Sextus*; delighted at letter from Trygve Hirsch, whom I counseled on the case. Learn that chimps detest water in jungles but zoo-born chimps like it. Irv, a real craftsman, corrects my carpentry work on the shed. Connie and Mike make the big decision to build a new wing. Steffie, after telling a fib, gets out of it by asking, "Would it be all right if I made a mistake?" We try to invent a name for Dorothy's one-woman show based on Millay poems and letters—monodrama, vitashow, life drama (after Maggie sees it she will come up with something nondeceptive, clear and

* *Howard Lindsay, playwright and producer and Dorothy Stickney, his actress wife.*

based on historic etymology). Heard that Lafayette, Indiana, boasts that it's the first city with all one-way streets and an auditorium that holds more seats than Radio Ciy Music Hall—horrors!

Sunday, August 16

To Efrons* for lunch. Good talk about the infirmities of our governmental structure—the division of legislative and executive. Out of this comes rather complete amateurism of cabinet—few have been engaged in the arts of leadership of people in a democracy; our press conferences are meant, not for knowledge, but for headlines and embarrassment of president; the lack of cabinet action. I wish Taft in 1910 had pressed further his argument that we can never have good secretaries of departments until these men sit, but without vote, in the Senate; then they will face up, as in England, to constant questioning by the Congress, rather than by newspapers looking for scandal and dirt.

Monday, August 17

Albus left and Dorothy Parker arrived. It will be interesting to learn what this experienced editor will want to cut out of the diary, which Atheneum will publish next year. I guess it averages eight hundred words a day—or nearly three hundred thousand words for a year. This is too much without overstuffing a prospective audience and pricing the book out of the market. I have often thought that increased retail prices of hard-

* Sam Efron, Washington lawyer, and his wife.

cover books would bring authors to compact and tighten their writing so as to get to a three-dollar price instead of four dollars or four fifty. Maggie will have to do the scissor work. After I have written, I'm bored by more than one rereading, have little skill at organization or rearrangement and, above all, hate to kill what I have created. I'm always too inclined to think that any thought of mine does not deserve being murdered, but I have so little literary ego that I don't care what Maggie and Dorothy will do to my child. In fact, I'll not even care enough to spend the time to reread—if I reread, will probably not recall the original with precise enough memory to remember the eliminated material. I do wish I dared write a real diary—free of professional-confidence limitations, and free of fear of hurting those I love most by touching on my own hurts. I firmly believe, as do most people in appraising pain and incurable scars, that my miseries are the deepest and worst carried by any of God's children. I don't even dare touch collaterally on this area of life by mentioning, for example, that German lieder, if gently voiced without overmodern orchestration, automatically produce moist eyes. To show my utter timidity, I know that between Marie's departure at noon and Dorothy's arrival at seven, I felt much closer to Margaret—an "all alone but us" feeling, nothing to do with the horrors of "togetherness," which carries the odium of excessive "team" spirit. What I refer to uses no words and scarcely the angle of the eye. It's so acute that fingertips, man's best communication medium, are not needed for the mood.

Tuesday, August 18

After working to put the manuscript to bed, we went to sleep early. Off fast enough, both exhilarated, and Maggie's ear seems to be on the mend. But we woke up simultaneously at about eleven thirty. How come? What happened at that same instant? Maggie suggests it was because Connie had returned at that moment from the Vineyard, where she was visiting the Haydns, Knopfs and Roths—all involved in the Big A, as some call it. Arose, looked out and saw Connie's room lit up. Could it be that her presence back in her house stirred us out of sleep? Was it the noise of her plane? There are just too many of the *whys* of life that are never answered with certainty—and I'm not referring to the queries of galaxy proportions or what the earth looked like before it held any water (although I'm still on a search for a globe showing our planet with ocean depths, etc.).

Eileen Garrett should start with collections of moderate and reasonable bits of pre- and post-cognition before getting on to the fabulous. Maybe thus man will arrive at the theory of telepathy. Often man has the *fact* before he has the *cause*. We are on the doorstep of touching this cause. This will be fought, as were the theories of Galileo, Newton and Freud. The Romans had cement, used it, didn't know what it was, and cement was lost to man for centuries.

A slack this morning. In the file of pamphlets that represents a small section of the printed material that is received daily and thrown out instanter, I came across a U.S. Chamber of Commerce brochure on *The Com-*

munist Offensive—and to my surprise noted that Erwin
Canham, publisher of the *Christian Science Monitor* is
the president of that organization. What a people! Erwin as I know him has as liberal a mind as any editor
of our land. Not only does he head up the group that
usually speaks for Stabilized Non-Action, but also as-
sembles for the anti-Communist documents such men
as Milton Katz of Harvard, Stace May of New Deal days,
etc. I like this pattern.

Special Announcement: just learned Connie did *not*
get back last night. Was my seeing a light in her room
a dream? Now we will never feel that we know why we
woke up at the same second last night.

Just heard on radio—sandwiched between murders,
earthquakes and drownings—that the President has
asked Secretary of Labor to give out steel industry figures. Telegraphed Jim Mitchell as follows:

My Dear Jim, In connection with proposed release
of steel statistics might it help people of our republic
if we had your figures for last decade for example on
rise of steel prices compared to other items more
particularly services, perfumes, soap, etc. My recollection is inflation more pronounced in services and
consumer items as above compared to raw materials.
Don't hesitate to telephone me Nantucket if you want
further elaboration provided this makes sense to you.

I'll be interested to get his reaction and see how he
handles the inflation issue, which Blough of U.S. Steel
never popularized to the public.

Wednesday, August 19

For cocktails yesterday on Phil Handelman's *Chee Chee V*, which sailed in here from Maine after Halifax race, then to theater to see Dorothy do her Edna Millay vitadrama. Dorothy has done an unbelievable job—with sympathy and understanding. It will do well in New York City if directed toward the young, the Thornton Wilder audience. This is a happy format when based on writings of a poet. Escape audiences prefer love even to death, so the life of a poet, who is always in love, starts with a great advantage. The protagonists are usually built into the heroine—so I hope Dorothy will look at Emily Dickinson. Easy to research by reading the Taggard and other biographies, each searching for Emily's active or imagined lover. Emily exposed unwittingly so much of her frustration that the mosaic continued after her death. She would not dare send her poems out for publication but she kept them all—nearly eight hundred—preserved for her real motivation: a speck of immortality. How many creative people ever destroy their brain children? They may hide them, refuse them a public, but not destroy; for creativity is not only a thrust from within but also an ineluctable dart for public favor. Hiding of product has little to do with standards of the creator, but rather the result of the thickness of skin—and fear of rejection.

Ran into Norma Millay, whom I had not seen for thirty years. Remote shots like this start many streams of recall: Elinor Wiley, Barney Gallant's saloon, where that circle hung out at times, gentle Bill Benét—all recalled without a single rough-edged memory.

Wind in the northern sector—a rare event this summer. This is the breeze that opens all eyes. With this clean breeze and the recent memory of Dorothy reading from Millay, all emotional relationships between man and woman are a little warmer. Chosen tender words and clean air open up all kinds of pores.

Never laid canvas down before, so was clumsy on my try at removal of old porch canvas, some of which has not been changed for thirty years.

Thursday, August 20

To our list of games of identification we have added a new one. It's to identify subject matter of radio and telephone by voice of speaker. The weathercasts are all the same nasal, dead-level pitch; the clergy go down somewhere deep to get their pontifical sounds, except for those evangelists who go from soft to shriek, high to low; recipe dames have another pitch, not sonorous and quite high. This is an important game because at the very first sound, without listening to a single word, one can decide whether to turn off the radio.

Letter from Captain Watts, my favorite ship chandler, in Albermarle Street, London. He can't get anyone to make me a coracle. I had ordered one of these boats, which are built to width of shoulders and height of owner, used on rocky coasts, suggesting dinghy possibilities beyond Fiberglas. Birthday presents are coming, and I'm a good boy—for Maggie's sake, I put them away unopened. She enjoys the festive aspects of life.

The Cuban-Dominican Republic affairs are getting to the point where a summit meeting is needed. The D.R. economy is the highest in the Caribbean, the increase in health and literacy is quite remarkable for the area—in fact, this economy shows the efficiency in terms of wealth of a dictatorship. Puerto Rico is the greatest experiment I have ever worked with in terms of economic growth, integrity of government and faith in the expansion of the democratic process. A successful dictator must always be a peril to all other dictators, and the comparison shows that Muñoz, one of the great democratic leaders of our generation, must be slowed up by the valuable delays of the democratic process. But these islands must meet soon—probably on a ministerial level or even through local UNESCO. D.R. needs people and has a policy of being a mechanized agricultural economy. P.R., with its explosive population and scant meager acres, is wisely committed to a small-plant industrial economy. D.R. is one of the few nations on earth with dollar parity, and P.R. operates under a budgetary system supported by the U.S. These nations complement each other. D.R. can grow cattle, which the land of P.R. will not support. P.R. should have the abattoir, for example. Once when I left D.R. I spent the evening at Muñoz' summer White House, and the next time I saw General Trujillo I suggested these two heads of state should meet on some island. I'd love to watch M. educate T. on his approach to the participation of people at the bottom of the economy, and the introduction of political freedom and democracy. I'll bet Muñoz can do the job.

Friday, August 21

I like my small-town doctors, barbers and me-
chanics. Today I went to Dr. Harvey to get what most
patients and clients desire, confirmation of my own diagnosis. Most visits to professional people is to get confirmation of the patient's interpretation of his troubles
or desires. In my case, I'm not using my glasses except
for certain close reading or for cocktail-party distance
inspections. I can see buoys far away, I see food on
table. My shortcoming is apparent when I enter a salon-
sized room. I can't spot the blondes across the room
unless I wear glasses.

I must get me some knowledge of the eyesight of man.
How much further back than Ben Franklin with his
two-pane (now called executive bifocal) glasses does history show near- or far-sightedness? Is there anything to
the legend that eyes far apart bespeak generosity? (I
once met a man who voted against F. D. R. because his
eyes were too near together.) Why are most people in
our culture born near-sighted? Is this true in other cultures? Does the high incidence of near-sightedness
among the Chinese have any relationship to their long
history of printing and reading? What of Japanese with
their passion for minutiae and detail? In Africa, where
man is nearer to his original—whatever that means—
way of life, good sight is crucial, as it is with the American Indian for work involving distance; so does far-
sightedness preponderate? I can imagine that survival
of the fittest would have entailed fitness to see and hear
dangers—mainly enemies, including animals.

I'm sorry for the fourteenth-century inventor of eyeglasses. The market was nil until the seventeenth century, when literacy began to take root. Incidentally, the opticians should join newsprint producers in a subsidy for increase of literacy by mass media.

Saturday, August 22

It's just a year since I started keeping a diary. It's been a real pleasure. It made me reappraise and reassess views that came to mind. I have talked to myself, just as do so many people in big cities in subways or buses or on the streets, moving their lips with often pleasant or obviously mean expressions. But I have talked on paper.

I'll never read it over. Maggie and Dorothy Parker did that chore and cut down the total, after Hiram Haydn's observation that some of our public may find it of interest.

If any professional man were a real thief, he would find a treasure trove, belonging to his clients, entrusted to him—a trove of gay, ambitious and tearful miseries; of horrible admissions of errors in choice of partners or wives; of destruction—seldom wittingly—of children; of avarice for a fourth or fifth million. In fact, little in novels or on the stage can match life in a law office. What I own alone, not in joint control with clients, is sober and pedestrian compared with the tales of my law shop. And what I have is only partly in my conscious, and of that part only a little sector do I dare make public. Of the secret area Maggie guesses much, but only after midnight and with wine does the adage *"in vino veritas"* become veritable.

So the family and friends have a field day tomorrow. I have never been able to feel the import of anniversaries. On the fortieth anniversary of Greenbaum, Wolff & Ernst, Eddie, a concealed sentimentalist, arranged to have Johnny Van Doren write a history of the firm; Mag loves to send birthday, wedding and any anniversary presents. So I'll let them have their way, and I'll play the role of good sport as far as possible. I want no things, no possessions—and certainly have no capacity to review my seventy-one years, for good or evil. The pain I can't recall, and I will be troubled if I ever leave my house without expecting the unexpected. Why is it not considered normal to live intimately with serendipity?

Resolutions have no real values for me. I approach them as auto-fraudulence. Sure I have dreams—based on the past. I'd like to write more for *Reader's Digest,* for my piece on Louis D. Brandeis was a satisfaction. A fiction story in *Harper's* blew up my ego. I'll not shy off when my diary is published *à la* the concepts of Maggie and Hiram and Dorothy Parker. I'll enjoy the acceptance or rejection.

I have known for about thirty-five years that my life is cut across with luck—and luck in others cannot be lightly accepted by friends or strangers. Only the most intimate of relationships can admit to accept good fortune. Isn't it odd: man shows his best sides in times of trouble—bank holiday, hurricane, snowstorm or war. Then the capacity of affection for fellow man rises to surfaces. But in times of peaceful living we act awkwardly toward people who get the breaks—responding with envy, jealousy—or is it just the absence of being needed? And who doesn't like being necessary and wanted, provided no unwelcome demands are made on one, and the feeling exists of voluntarily proffered acts of grace and help?

So I cruised through another year, visiting innumerable harbors of the heart.

MORRIS L ERNST

was born in 1888 in Uniontown, Alabama. He is a graduate of Williams College and New York Law School and has been since 1915 a partner in the law firm of Greenbaum, Wolff & Ernst. He has been very active in governmental affairs, both domestic and international, and he has tried—and won—many major cases involving censorship and civil liberties. Of his list of published books three are still in print at the time of this book's publication: UTOPIA 1976 (Rinehart), THE FIRST FREEDOM (Macmillan), and THE BEST IS YET (Penguin). Still available, too, are WORDS and MORE ABOUT WORDS (Knopf), books by Mr. Ernst's wife, Margaret Ernst.